PHIL EDMONDS'
100
GREATEST
BOWLERS

PHIL EDMONDS'
100 GREATEST BOWLERS

WITH SCYLD BERRY

Macdonald
Queen Anne Press

A *Queen Anne Press* BOOK

© Phil Edmonds 1989

First published in Great Britain in 1989 by
Queen Anne Press, a division of
Macdonald & Co (Publishers) Ltd
6th Floor
Headway House
66–73 Shoe Lane
London EC4P 4AB

A member of Maxwell Pergamon Publishing Corporation plc

British Library Cataloguing in Publication Data
Edmonds, Phil, *1951–*
    Phil Edmonds' 100 greatest bowlers.
    1. Cricket. Bowlers, history
    I. Title   II. Berry, Scyld
    796.35′822′0922

    ISBN 0–356–15701–6

Printed and bound in Great Britain by
Butler & Tanner Ltd, Frome and London

Picture Credits

All Sport back flap, 17, 28, 53, 86, 92, 151, 215, 226, 234, 239, 242, 255; George
Beldam, 39; Colorsport 61, 81, 124; Patrick Eagar left and right cover, 157, 159, 164,
172, 174, 177, 179, 182, 185, 187, 190, 192, 195, 198, 201, 204, 207, 209, 211, 221,
229, 232, 237, 244, 249, 252; David Frith 37, 46, 93; Hulton Deutsch centre cover,
12, 15, 19, 20, 23, 31, 35, 43, 51, 66, 69, 106, 120, 127, 140; Illustrated London News
55, 62, 65, 84, 94, 95 (both); Roger Mann 63, 70; Marylebone Cricket Club 9; Mansell
Collection 14, 26, 30, 33, 50; Press Association 40, 44, 49, 58, 59, 68, 73, 74, 77, 84,
91; Sport and General 97, 99, 101, 104, 109, 111, 122, 132, 143, 146, 148, 163;
Syndication International 60, 88, 118, 170; Bob Thomas 150, 169, 223, 224; Topham
79, 113, 115, 116, 119, 130, 135, 138, 154, 160, 166, 167, 178, 246

All colour photographs by Patrick Eagar except Richard Hadlee (All Sport), Abdul
Qadir and Wayne Daniel (Bob Thomas)

Statistics compiled by David Kennedy

CONTENTS

INTRODUCTION

Choosing the hundred greatest bowlers has been a less awkward task than the selection of the one hundred greatest batsmen must have been for John Arlott. There are fewer bowlers in a team, and therefore in history; the riches are less embarrassing. The first 90 or so put forward an irrefutable case and picked themselves. Only the remainder had to be subjected to the filter of personal choice.

Who has been left out? Alec Kennedy of Hampshire took more first-class wickets than anybody else who has been excluded. His total of 2874 has been exceeded by only half-a-dozen men. But Kennedy was more of a county stalwart than a regular candidate for the England side, and we hope that the inclusion of George Geary will be taken as a form of acknowledgement to the likes of Kennedy and Jack Newman, Ewart Astill and Jack Mercer. These old pros played for unfashionable counties and kept going at medium-pace or thereabouts until close of play, or the declaration of an innings, or of a world war.

Perhaps the most talented omission is Arthur Mailey. Few if any have spun the ball more than the Australian who set an Ashes record for his country that lasted until 1979. But as we may judge from his own writing, Mailey was as interested in the intricacies of wrist-spin as in taking wickets; since his Test average is almost 34, we went for another of his type in Intikhab, whose average is only marginally higher and who had to bowl in a period increasingly hostile to any kind of spin.

Of recent bowlers, the Australians Rodney Hogg and Geoff Lawson were as close as could be to being selected. One or two England contemporaries have not been included because the list of a hundred had to be limited to those who had reached their peak before the time of writing. If, by the second edition, Graham Dilley has forced his way in, and Neil Foster has replaced his old namesake F. R. Foster, it will have been to the good of English cricket. Likewise, Curtly Ambrose of West Indies should be pressing for inclusion, and maybe the first Sri Lankan.

The bowlers here are arranged in chronological not alphabetical order, so that the reader may gain an impression of the way bowling has evolved through the ages. To be precise, the bowlers are listed in the order that they flourished. Thus, although Brian Statham and Fred Trueman made earlier débuts in first-class and Test cricket, Frank Tyson comes before them both as he was the first to hit his peak.

I learnt my bowling at school in Zambia. At lunchtime it was too far to go back home as most of the other boys did, so I stayed in the nets and bowled at my older brothers until the match began in the afternoon. At 14 I was in the school First XI, and we played in the men's local league. I had to grow up quickly when bowling to well-built men who all tended to hit the ball like Brian 'Crash-ball' Davison.

In retrospect I wish I had used more frequently the classical method of slow left-arm bowling, spreading out the fielders and tempting the batsman to drive. But I became stereotyped, as one often does in county cricket, and pushed the ball through. Increasingly heavy bats were one reason for this, and the apprehension of being hit – or even mis-hit – by one of these bludgeons. My Middlesex and England captain, Mike Brearley, also liked to pressurise the batsman with close-in fielders, which was the source of the occasional altercation. So there I was pushing the ball in flat for long hours, with fielders at short-leg and silly point: the ball would pop up now and again so that one lived in hope, but all too seldom would carry for a catch.

I wish, too, that I had used the 'chinaman' more. At school, and at Cambridge, I would spin the odd ball into the right-hander. But I needed to practise it, and latterly bowled it no more than half-a-dozen times a season. It was therefore amazing in the course of this book to discover the versatility of Johnny Wardle, who could produce the chinaman without any preparation.

Where I like to think I did score was in bowling against left-handers. In the two Ashes series of 1985 and 1986/7 I dismissed the Australian captain Allan Border eight times. When bowling well I had a short delivery stride and pivoted a lot on my front foot. To me, balance and physical strength are the most important factors in slow bowling.

Bowling will continue to change and develop: that much at least should be apparent from the pageant unfolded in the following pages. But no doubt bowlers, in the future as in the past, will be applauded and rewarded far less than batsmen. May this book go some way towards redressing the balance.

Notes

Only the regional first-class teams which each bowler represented are given alongside his name i.e. it is not mentioned that Grace played for MCC or the Gentlemen, or that Trueman played for Derbyshire in the Sunday League

In the statistics, overs are of six balls unless otherwise stated

DAVID HARRIS

No archive film exists of the first great bowler, no photograph nor even a daguerreotype. The only pictorial representation of David Harris of Hambledon is the sketch made by George Shepheard of Surrey in a notebook. Yet we can see Harris a-bowling on Broadhalfpenny Down if we but read John Nyren's description of him in *The Cricketers of My Time*, then close our eyes and imagine we have returned to the late eighteenth century when cricket was, if not in its innocence (for the game was never like that!), then in the enthusiasm of youth.

Harris was a Hampshire man by birth, a potter by trade, muscular, bony, 'about five feet nine and a half inches' according to Nyren, and 'the very best bowler'. And although he bowled under-arm, right-handed, the fundamental principles which Harris observed were those which were mainly to guide Spofforth and Rhodes, Larwood and Lillee. The bowler 'should commence at a gentle pace, and increase his speed till the ball is delivered', wrote Nyren. 'The best method of holding the ball to bowl is between the thumb and fingers, firmly enough to steady it, yet that it may leave the hand with ease. . . . In a match, when running to bowl, he should fix his eye upon a certain spot where he is desirous the ball should pitch. . . . He should also habituate himself to bowl with equal ease on either side of the wicket. All these things will turn to the young bowler's account, if he play with *his head* as well as his hands.'

Nyren goes on to mention Harris's rare qualities of character – 'I can call to mind no worthier, or, in the active sense of the word, not a more "*good* man" than David Harris' – before modestly claiming that no accurate picture of his bowling can be given in words. Nyren, however, proceeds to do so, and brilliantly: 'First of all, he stood erect like a soldier at drill; then, with a graceful curve of the arm, he raised the ball to his forehead, and drawing back his right foot, started off with his left. . . . His mode of delivering the ball was very singular. He would bring it from under the arm by a twist, and nearly as high as his arm-pit, and with this action *push* it, as it were, from him. How it was that the balls acquired the velocity they did by this mode of delivery I never could comprehend.'

Nonetheless, Harris's bowling was fast – faster and livelier than that of anybody else of the age, even of 'Lumpy' Stevens. Almost every ball which Harris bowled rose over the wicket (it was then several inches shorter than the 28″ today, while the third stump was added early in Harris's career, around 1776). This was an exceptional ability, and one to be respected in the period before batting gloves. Nyren often saw him making the ball lift alarmingly: 'many a time have I seen the blood drawn in this way from a batter who was not up to the trick'. This damage caused a change of method among batsmen, who were now forced to 'get in', that is, to play well forward to scotch the bounce

*David Harris
(1755–1803)
Hambledon and Hampshire*

'His attitude when preparing for his run previously to delivering the ball would have made a beautiful study for the sculptor. Phidias would certainly have taken him for a model.' (John Nyren)

9

instead of waiting to be pinned in their crease. 'You were obliged to get in, or it would be about your hands, or the handle of your bat; and every player knows where its next place would be.'

Cricket was not then the effete pastime, played in lace cuffs, that some may have romantically considered it to be. It was already a virile sport of pleasure and pain, hard work and practice. Harris was so coached by John Nyren's father, Richard, that he once sent down 170 balls for a single run. On match days at Hambledon Harris would be up at six to select a pitch, since it was the custom for the home team's best bowler to make the choice. Old Lumpy would select a place where the ball would shoot, like the brow of a little hill, and would grin in triumph when he bowled out his man. Not Harris: 'he would choose a rising ground to pitch the ball against, and he who is well acquainted with the game of cricket will at once perceive the advantage that must arise from a wicket pitched in this way to such a tremendous bowler as Harris was'. He went, in short, for the extra bounce.

Harris died when still in his forties, and so severely troubled by gout that he had to spend his days in a wheelchair. Most of the Hambledon players lived to a great age, as befits men from the game's Old Testament. But Harris ended his career in sad circumstances, the first great bowler to do so and not the last. Bowlers through history have been less than celebrated. Yet the ball is initially in their hands: with them the action begins.

Career figures unknowable

W.G.GRACE

It is hard to believe that 'W. G.' was a great bowler as well as the first great batsman – and gamesman. But his figures in his early years equal or excel those of any contemporary and he remained, like Ian Botham in his later years, a great wicket-taker. At Lord's once, against Sri Lanka, Botham picked up a handful of wickets simply by bowling some resemblance of off-break, coupled with a deep animal hunger for success. Grace, one suspects, did much the same for most of his unparalleled career.

Under-arm bowling was being phased out when Grace entered first-class cricket in 1865, aged 16 when the season started. Experimenters had found during the preceding decades that the higher the arm was raised, the more numerous the possibilities. In 1835 round-arm had been recognised as legal, the hand to be raised no higher than the shoulder. Then experimenters again tried to raise the level of the arm and of bowling, until over-arm was permitted in 1864. The era of Harris was over, although one or two 'lobsters' lingered on.

Naturally bowlers could not alter their styles overnight. Grace himself had already learnt to bowl fastish round-arm on the pitch laid out in the orchard of Downend House near Bristol. As pitches were poorly prepared – if rollers existed on the major grounds, they were pulled by horses not machines, while the mower did not replace the scythe until the 1870s – a bowler did not have to do a lot beyond straight medium-pace to be effective. However, being the athlete he was, W.G. must have bowled faster than most in his youth, and he built up to a hundred wickets a season as the first-class programme expanded in the 1870s.

By the time he was 30 Grace was resorting more to artifice, if we can judge by the incomplete reports of the day (the chroniclers tended to describe what he did, not how). In the season of 1877, when he is stated to have been a slow bowler, he attained his second largest haul of 179 wickets, 17 of them in Gloucestershire's match against Nottinghamshire. The last seven batsmen whom he dismissed did not score a run as they kept holing out, despite themselves, to long-hops pitched outside leg-stump. Fielders on the square-leg boundary took catch after catch while the Doctor chortled in his beard.

It appears he was bowling leg-breaks in the main. Lord Harris wrote: 'I shall always hold that W.G. was the best and pluckiest field to his own bowling I ever saw. The ground he used to cover to the off – and with the leg-break on of course, the majority of straight balls went there – made him as good as a twelfth man.' A. G. Steel hints at top-spin as well: 'Never, as far as I know, did any bowler give the same peculiar flight to the ball as W.G. does, and well justified is the remark I have often heard him make of a newly-arrived batsman: "Oh, he's a young one, is he? I think I ought to do for him."'

Dr William Gilbert Grace (1848–1915) Gloucestershire, London County and England

*'The Champion' on the roof
of the pavilion at Lord's. His
best bowling was done before
Test cricket, or the action
photograph*

All this bowling was done, with superhuman energy, on top of the finest batting cricket had seen. When Grace hit up 344 for MCC against Kent, he had already bowled 77 four-ball overs in the county's innings of 473! After hitting 318 for Gloucestershire, Grace had bowled 36 overs and barely had time to take himself off before rain washed out the rest of Yorkshire's innings. His county possessed little other bowling – few professionals and no other amateur of note until C. L. Townsend – so Grace needed no second invitation to keep one end going.

And so he continued for the rest of his Olympian career, telling a batsman to look at a flock of birds which happened to be passing and chuntering to another to air his strokes – not unlike Mike Procter, Gloucestershire's latterday champion, when he bowled slow off-breaks. Even in the 1890s Grace was rated 'the best change bowler in England'. However, his figures in Test cricket – which came too late in his life to reflect his dominance of the game – suggest that international players were less gullible, if just as respectful.

He took over 50 wickets in 1901 when well past 50 himself, and some of those deliveries must have gently turned. Essentially, though, he triumphed by force of character, by being the Colossus he was; and when he retired after more than 40 seasons from the sport he had done so much to fashion, he had taken more wickets than anybody else. Even now, only five bowlers have exceeded the total set by W.G.

FIRST-CLASS CAREER (1865–1908)

1493 innings	105 not outs	54896 runs	average 39.55	126 hundreds
	2876 wickets	51545 runs	average 17.92	10–49 best

TEST RECORD (22 matches)

36 innings	2 not outs	1098 runs	average 32.29	2 hundreds
	9 wickets	236 runs	average 26.22	2–12 best

Series	Tests	O		M	R	W	Av
1880 v A	1	29.1	(4-ball)	10	68	3	22.66
1882 v A	1		did not bowl				
1884 v A	3	42	(4-ball)	28	38	3	12.66
1886 v A	3	10	(4-ball)	3	22	1	22.00
1888 v A	3		did not bowl				
1890 v A	2	14	(5-ball)	10	12	2	6.00
1891/2 in A	3	15.3		2	34	0	—
1893 v A	2		did not bowl				
1896 v A	3	13	(5-ball)	4	25	0	—
1899 v A	1	22	(5-ball)	8	37	0	—

F. R. SPOFFORTH

Frederick Robert Spofforth
(1853–1926)
New South Wales, Victoria
and Australia

'Like all the better kind of
Australians, he is not
distinguishable from an
English gentleman.' Thus
the magazine Vanity Fair, *in*
1878, in its caption to the
cartoon of Spofforth by Sir
Leslie Ward or 'Spy'

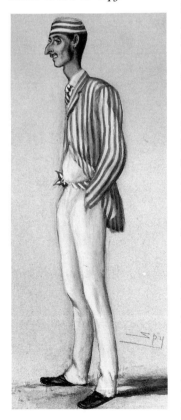

Frederick Spofforth was the first great bowler of cricket as we know it. Born on the outskirts of Sydney, he began bowling under-arm there, as that was still the fashion in Australia. But when he saw the English fast bowlers of the first touring team to Australia in 1863/4, he decided to embark on the new method and was the first to master it.

By 27 May 1878 Spofforth was ready to announce himself. To that point the first tour of England by white Australians had been no more of a success than that by Aborigines ten years before, and Englishmen did not conceive that 'the colonials' or 'Cornstalks' could possibly be their equal at cricket. Then at Lord's, on that single day, the Australians dismissed MCC for totals of 33 and 19 and won by nine wickets: other people could play the game after all! Spofforth clean-bowled W. G. Grace for a duck, and took ten wickets for 20 runs. 'The fame of Australian cricket' wrote Sir Pelham Warner, 'was established for all time.'

Accounts of Spofforth's bowling leave doubt as to its nature if not its quality. On the whole, if he has to be placed in one category, then it would have to be that of 'medium-paced off-cutter'. He bowled many opponents – through the gate, no doubt – and seven of his ten wickets in that epoch-making game were thus taken. Otherwise he would induce return catches with his slower ball, or have batsmen caught at short-leg – as early a reference as any to this type of attack. However, he could also be fast at that stage of his career, at least by the standards of the day. We know that when he got away from the wet pitches which prevailed that season, he bounced 'W.G'.

In Spofforth's character there was a strange contradiction. He was 6' 3", the champion bowler of his time, lean and immensely strong from his youthful days of horse-riding in the Australian bush. Yet he was of a nervous disposition, highly strung and hypochondriacal: it was well known that almost every throw-in to him would make him wring his hand. This characteristic, though, did not make him any less formidable in the eyes of batsmen. To them he was still 'the Demon', armed with a dark-moustached ferocity that must have been similar to Lillee's.

The Demon set great store by variation of pace and said that he tried to equip himself with every ball from fast to slow, using a wide range of grips but the same action. Already a considerable amount of thought was going into over-arm bowling, while there is a familiar ring to the report that Spofforth used to dig up the pitch with high-heeled boots for the benefit of his partner at the other end.

In 1882, in the sole Test match, the Demon had his finest hour with 14 wickets for 90 runs. All his nervous energy went into defeating England by seven runs in a game which set the Ashes series alight forever. His field on that occasion, incidentally, included no more than

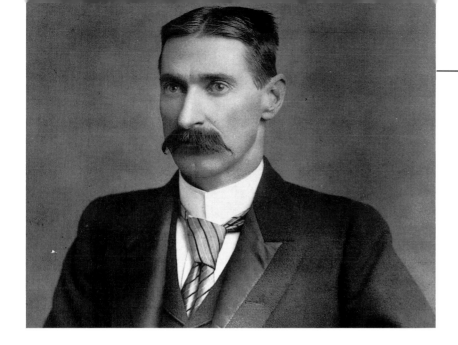

three men on the leg-side, two relatively close in and one out at long-on for the big hit. On the 1884 tour he was more effective still, with 207 first-class wickets at 12 apiece.

He was quite a businessman, too, as he left £164,000 in his will when he died in 1926. He had settled in England in 1888 and had become the managing director of a tea company. Spofforth, in fact, played several games for Derbyshire in the early 1890s when they weren't a first-class county (his father had been a northerner who emigrated to Australia from Yorkshire, whence the surname). He even headed the national bowling averages in 1896 when he played in the Scarborough Festival, demoniacal until the last.

FIRST-CLASS CAREER (1874/5–97)

| 236 innings | 41 not outs | 1928 runs | average 9.88 | 0 hundred |
| | 853 wickets | 12760 runs | average 14.95 | 9–18 best |

TEST RECORD (18 matches)

| 29 innings | 6 not outs | 217 runs | average 9.43 | — |
| | 94 wickets | 1731 runs | average 18.41 | 7–44 best |

Series	Tests	O	M	R	W	Av
1876/7 v E	1	44	9	111	4	27.75
1878/9 v E	1	60	25	110	13	8.46
1881/2 v E	1	66	17	128	1	128.00
1882 in E	1	64.3	33	90	14	6.42
1882/3 v E	4	244.1	93	408	18	22.66
1884 in E	3	192.1	79	301	10	30.10
1884/5 v E	3	194.1	84	306	19	16.10
1886 in E	3	168.3	73	260	14	18.57
1886/7 v E	1	12	3	17	1	17.00

Note: All of Spofforth's overs were 4-ball overs.

ALFRED SHAW

Alfred Shaw
(1842–1907)
Nottinghamshire, Sussex
and England

Alfred Shaw is the first Victorian bowler one feels able to refer to by his Christian name instead of his initials. He was only 5′ 6½″ tall and had a friendly bulk by the end of his career. In trousers held up with a belt nearer to his chest than his waist, and bedecked in the mandatory Victorian whiskers and sideburns, he looks more like a ship's stoker or a fireman than the finest medium-pacer of his age.

He was staggeringly economical, thanks to his strict adherence to line and length. For Nottinghamshire he often had analyses like 98.3 overs, 63 maidens, 62 runs and 12 wickets, which he recorded in a match against the Australians at Trent Bridge. They were four-ball overs at that stage of his career, but when the five-ball over was introduced in 1889, he still totted up the maiden overs as eagerly as Emburey. In the whole of his first-class career, Shaw bowled more overs than he conceded runs.

In his method Shaw would probably be now called a seamer, but he was essentially a length bowler who bowled on or just outside off-stump with as many as eight fielders on the off-side. His run-up consisted of half-a-dozen quick strides, and he said of himself: 'I really used to bowl faster than people thought I did, and I could make the ball break both ways, but not much. In my opinion, length and variation of pace constitute the secret of successful bowling.'

If Shaw were to play in limited-overs cricket today, he might possibly come in for some stick, as all modern bowlers have at one time or another. In other words, the batsmen of his heyday – the 1870s and 1880s – may have frequently allowed him to bowl. It is only with the advent of the Surrey batsmen W. W. Read and K. J. Key (who, significantly, batted on some of the best pitches at the Oval) that we hear of the pull to the leg-side as a counter to the off-side attack of Shaw and his emulator Attewell. Until then it was deemed unethical to hit an off-side ball (as opposed to a straight ball) to leg.

But there is no doubting the stamina of Shaw and ancients like him. In 1876 he became the first bowler to deliver more than ten thousand balls in a first-class season, and his total of 10723 remained a record until 'Tich' Freeman beat it in 1928. That is almost 1800 overs! Alec Bedser used to say that it was beneficial for a bowler to walk to work, and those players who were around before the motor-car became popular must have had a fitness which we don't possess in the sponsored age.

For many years Shaw was on MCC's groundstaff, but it was for Nottinghamshire against MCC that he performed one of his most admirable stints. In 1875 at Lord's he bowled 41.2 four-ball overs, 36 of them maidens (in his career nearly two-thirds of his overs weren't scored off), and took seven wickets for seven runs. He was truly 'the high priest of length'. He was also a professional captain of Nottingham-

OPPOSITE: *Shaw captured during his comeback years with Sussex when nearer to portliness than his prime. Note how relatively unprominent is the stitching of the ball beside him*

shire and led them to the championship in four successive seasons in the mid-1880s, besides captaining England when he jointly promoted all-professional tours of Australia.

Yet perhaps his most famous moments came when he returned to county cricket with Sussex at the age of 52. He was then in the employ of Lord Sheffield, and Sussex's coach, but was still better in the nets than their regular bowlers. So in 1894 he bowled 422 overs for them, for 516 runs and 41 wickets. And in the following season against Nottinghamshire at Trent Bridge, on a May day so cold that Ranjitsinhji kept his hands in his pockets and fielded the ball with his feet, Shaw sent down 100.1 five-ball overs in a total of 726. With sprained sinews in his foot he then bowled 58 overs unchanged against Lancashire before retiring finally. He became a publican, and had well earned a drink.

FIRST-CLASS CAREER (1864–97)

630 innings	101 not outs	6585 runs	average 12.44	0 hundred
	2027 wickets	24579 runs	average 12.12	10–73 best

Note: plus one wicket for which no analysis available

TEST RECORD (7 matches)

12 innings	1 not out	111 runs	average 10.09	—
	12 wickets	285 runs	average 23.75	5–38 best

Series	*Tests*	*O*	*M*	*R*	*W*	*Av*
1876/7 in A	2	163.3	96	146	8	18.25
1880 v A	1	46	23	63	2	31.50
1881/2 in A	4	65	36	76	2	38.00

Note: All of Shaw's overs were 4-ball overs.

C.T.B.TURNER

A hundred years before PBL Marketing tried to give Australian crick-eters a glamorous image, the publicity people of the day had labelled Spofforth 'the Demon' and Charles Turner 'the Terror'. A certain amount of 'hype' was involved. In our terms Turner was not fast at all: his speed was actually measured at Woolwich Observatory during a tour of England as 55mph. Yet he came quickly off the pitch and, as a result, Grace rated him the second fastest bowler he had ever faced.

Charles Thomas Biass Turner (1862–1944) New South Wales and Australia

Turner was not tall at 5′ 8″ but as a country boy from Bathurst in New South Wales he was tough and had extraordinarily strong fingers. In spite of a chest-on action, these fingers brought the ball back sharply from outside off-stump on pitches which had not been rolled or covered against rain. For this reason Turner was a more fearsome prospect in England, although in 1887/8 he took over a hundred wickets in the Australian season, the only man ever to have done so (this was shortly before their pitches were transformed by the heavy roller into 'shirt-fronts').

He was an artful customer too, like Spofforth, but unlike English bowlers of the time. The latter did not vary their pace, which is partly why the Australians were such a revelation when they first toured England. As R. H. Lyttelton wrote: 'Spectators rubbed their eyes at what they saw. ... On the hard dry wickets at Sydney and Melbourne, these bowlers had found out what English bowlers had not yet dis-covered, that to get batsmen out on modern wickets it was no good trusting to any assistance from the ground, but to your own head. They bowled differently, and they placed the field differently. They dispensed altogether with a long-stop, they bowled many balls off the wicket, and no two consecutive balls were bowled with similar paces.' Turner was renowned for using the crease as well, although it extended only three feet to either side of the wicket, as against 3′ 11½″ today.

Whatever the pitches, only a fine bowler could take 50 wickets in his first six Tests against England – as the Terror did. He reached a hundred wickets in his seventeenth (and last) Test, a record never surpassed and only equalled by Barnes. And he had stamina. In 1888, on his first tour of England, the Australians had almost no bowlers apart from Turner and the left-arm medium-pacer Ferris. In all games Turner delivered 2589.3 four-ball overs – that is more than 1700 six-ball overs – and he took 314 wickets. Of those, 283 were in first-class matches at 11.68 runs each (easily a record for anybody on any tour). At Stoke, on a pitch which 'played treacherously under the hot sun', Turner took nine of An England XI's wickets for 15: seven were bowled, two LBW, and the other run out. On another drying pitch at Hastings, Turner took 17 wickets for 50 against An England XI: one was stumped, two LBW, the rest bowled.

Turner's success in hitting the stumps leads one to question the standard of pad-play. In this regard a relevant anecdote concerns the Lord's Test of 1893 when Turner was on his last tour but still running through England's batting. When Shrewsbury was joined by Hon F. S. Jackson, the Nottinghamshire professional advised him to use his pads as a second line of defence against Turner; this was not something to be taken for granted. They did so, and bailed England out. But Turner would no doubt have found some other way to terrorise if he had lived in another era.

OPPOSITE: *The pair who carried Australia's bowling in the late 1880s, shortly before the roller arrived and 'sporting pitches' disappeared*

FIRST-CLASS CAREER (1882/3–1909/10)

261 innings	13 not outs	3865 runs	average 15.58	2 hundreds
	993 wickets	14147 runs	average 14.24	9–15 best

TEST RECORD (17 matches)

32 innings	4 not outs	323 runs	average 11.53	—
	101 wickets	1670 runs	average 16.53	7–43 best

Series	Tests	O	M	R	W	Av
1886/7 v E	2	179.3 (4-ball)	95	161	17	9.47
1887/8 v E	1	88 (4-ball)	50	87	12	7.25
1888 in E	3	168 (4-ball)	62	261	21	12.42
1890 in E	2	104 (5-ball)	50	159	6	26.50
1891/2 v E	3	155.4	52	338	16	21.12
1893 in E	3	175 (5-ball)	72	315	11	28.63
1894/5 v E	3	187.1	76	349	18	19.38

JOHNNY BRIGGS

John Briggs
(1862–1902)
Lancashire and England

Johnny Briggs was not quite the equal of his Yorkshire rival Bobby Peel according to most contemporary judges. He was, however, one of the best left-arm spinners. He took 97 Test wickets against Australia, and made six tours of that country (which suggests what fun touring already was). He would surely have completed his century against them but for the illness which beset him.

Reports written after Briggs' death at the age of 39 say that he had epilepsy like Colin Blythe, the left-armer who began his career at the time Briggs was finishing his. But contemporary accounts do not mention epilepsy; perhaps because this was still the Victorian age, he was usually said to have been struck down or simply indisposed. One source states that the illness which afflicted Briggs derived from a bad attack of sunstroke in South Africa; another that it originated in a blow he received when bowling at the Oval and a ball was hit straight back. An X-ray showed a bone pressing against the valve of his heart, so the spasms may have resulted from the blood not being able to circulate freely.

Briggs was a comedian too; Cecil Parkin's predecessor at Old Trafford. He would play to the gallery while fielding at cover-point, where he was outstanding, or when batting, which is partly why he never made the runs he promised to (not the last left-armer to have done that). His bowling, in contrast, tended to be mechanical, although he was short enough at 5' 5" to have flighted the ball. He focussed on line and length, and consequently was not as effective as Peel or the early Rhodes when the pitch was flat. His variation lay in the occasional ball turning into the right-hander – to call it a chinaman would be an anachronism. One contemporary asserted that Briggs could not be hit off his length in 'a month of Sundays', a phrase which rings ironically now.

He was born in Nottinghamshire, became a professional at Hornsea in east Yorkshire aged 13 – following in his father's footsteps – and was taken on Lancashire's staff at 16. He made his first-class début the following year – very young for those days – when he was virtually a specialist fielder. Then his batting developed (he went on to score a century for England) while only an occasional fastish round-arm bowler. It was in 1885 that he 'went to the front', as they used to say, and became a regular England all-rounder; he and Peel would often play and bowl together.

By 1899 Briggs had taken 94 wickets against Australia (it was irrelevant to him that he had taken 15 South African wickets in a game at Cape Town in 1889/90: nobody then considered it to have been a proper Test match). His county skipper MacLaren exerted his influence on the selectors and Briggs was brought in for the Headingley Test of that summer. Naturally he was very excited, the more so after taking three Australian wickets on the opening day. That evening he and some other

A more innocent, less worldly man than Bobby Peel, his contemporary and rival from over the Pennines

England players went to a music hall in Leeds. Briggs became deranged. Next day he was put on the train and sent to Cheadle Asylum where he stayed for nine months. He was let out for the 1900 season, and had recovered enough to take all ten wickets in a Worcestershire innings. But he was soon to go back to the asylum, and to die there.

356	**FIRST-CLASS CAREER (1879–1900)**
357	826 innings 55 not outs 14092 runs average 18.27 10 hundreds
	2221 wickets 35430 runs average 15.95 10–55 best
366	
367	**TEST RECORD (33 matches)**
368	50 innings 5 not outs 815 runs average 18.11 1 hundred
	118 wickets 2094 runs average 17.74 8–11 best

	Series	*Tests*	*O*	*M*	*R*	*W*	*Av*
378							
380	1884/5 in A	5	8 (4-ball)	3	13	0	—
394	1886 v A	3	134.1 (4-ball)	75	132	17	7.76
403	1886/7 in A	2	63 (4-ball)	25	97	5	19.40
414	1887/8 in A	1	did not bowl				
423	1888 v A	3	84.1 (4-ball)	42	94	12	7.83
430	1888/9 in SA	2	97.3 (4-ball)	51	101	21	4.80
438	1891/2 in A	3	116.3	31	268	17	15.76
440	1893 v A	2	120.1 (5-ball)	40	293	16	18.31
457	1894/5 in A	5	150.3	25	435	15	29.00
463	1896 v A	1	58 (5-ball)	26	123	3	41.00
460	1897/8 in A	5	190	56	485	9	53.88
471	1899 v A	1	30 (5-ball)	11	53	3	17.66

GEORGE LOHMANN

By all accounts George Lohmann had the quality of a Keith Miller or Ian Botham. He was a dashing batsman and person, a tremendous slip-catcher – the first of note in that position – and he was a medium-pacer of infinite resource. He also burnt himself out well before the age of 30 through playing far too much cricket.

Lohmann appeared in the Surrey nets one day in 1883 when he was 18. He had left school at 14 and learnt how to play cricket on Wandsworth Common, developing variations of pace of his own accord. He was a natural: two years after being taken on the Surrey staff as a colt he was bowling for England. W. G. Grace wrote of him: 'To a right-hand batsman he bowls on or just outside the off-stump, and breaks back very quickly, but now and then he puts in a very fast one with a break from leg. ... But the ball he has been as successful with as any is a simple, straight, good length one, without any break. The batsman expects something exceptional from him every ball, and never thinks he will treat him with such an easy one.' Like Botham, he would go round the wicket to disturb the batsman with a change of angle.

But Lohmann – 'neither fast nor slow man' as a piece of doggerel went – was over-bowled from the moment he was established as a sensation. We shouldn't think of staleness as a modern phenomenon. In the 1880s the Australians toured England every two years, and English sides returned the visits no less frequently. Indeed there were two tours there in successive winters, and Lohmann as the leading English bowler of the time naturally went on both. From the start of the 1886 season to the end of that of 1888 he bowled eight thousand four-ball overs, the equivalent of more than 5300 six-ball overs, and that was in first-class cricket alone, never mind the up-country games against 'odds' during the two Australian tours.

Widely admired for his blond, handsome looks, and something of a ladies' man by legend – he was not above diving onto the ground to impress the crowds – Lohmann probably did not have a way of life that conserved his energy for cricket. From 1886 to 1890 he bowled more first-class overs than anyone else, and for the last three seasons took over two hundred wickets. In 1891/2 he went to Australia again, and took eight for 58 from 43.2 overs in one Test innings. He played through the following summer, but broke down at the end of it, aged 27.

He was discovered to have TB and was sent by Surrey (by far the most caring county of the time) to South Africa to recuperate. He was unable to return until the 1895 season, after trying himself out as an amateur for Western Province in a Currie Cup match. In the winter of 1895/6 he returned to South Africa with Lord Hawke's team, partly for reasons of health, and played in some games which have subsequently been labelled Tests for no apparent reason (none of the games which

George Alfred Lohmann
(1865–1901)
Surrey, Western Province and England

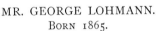

AGE 8.
From a Photo. by Southwell Brothers, Baker Street.

AGE 26.
*From a
Photo. by
George
Bradshaw,
Hastings.*

MR. GEORGE LOHMANN.

BORN 1865.

WE have no hesitation in saying that no cricketer has attracted more attention in cricket circles during the last few years than Lohmann, and that Surrey is greatly indebted to his excellent performances with the ball for its very high position among the counties. His rapid success was phenomenal. Since he first represented his county, in 1884, his

exceptional and enviable power of rising to the occasion, and the better the company the better he performs. He is an excellent batsman. In the field he is good anywhere, his quickness being almost electrical—and the amount of ground he covers, especially at short slip, is something remarkable. In 1892 Mr. Lohmann had to leave for South

From a Photo. by AGE 29. *F. Gow, Cape Town.*

Africa owing to ill-health, but two seasons afterwards, to the intense gratification of all, he returned to this country and again joined his popular team.

AGE 18.
From a Photo. by Stilliard & Co., Oxford.

bowling has been the theme of admiration in England, and very good judges in Australia have said that he is one of the best bowlers that have ever visited them. He has the

PRESENT DAY.
From a Photo. by Browne and Gradidge, Andover.

the South Africans played in England were recognised as Tests until 1907). Lohmann ran amok as Briggs had before him. He took nine for 28 at Johannesburg, and 35 wickets in three 'Tests' at 5.8 runs each!

He did not bowl his inspirational medium-pace again after the 1896 season. There was a dispute over terms with Surrey: Lohmann, then in South Africa, isn't the only professional to have wanted his county to pay his fare home. So he decided to settle in South Africa, and he was the manager of their tour to England in 1901. By the end of the year his health had further declined and he was dead at 36.

OPPOSITE: *How too much cricket can destroy a man: the 'present day' Lohmann is not 30 years older than the boy with Lord Fauntleroy curls*

FIRST-CLASS CAREER (1884–1897/8)

427 innings	39 not outs	7247 runs	average 18.67	3 hundreds
	1841 wickets	25295 runs	average 13.73	9–28 best

TEST RECORD (18 MATCHES)

26 innings	2 not outs	213 runs	average 8.87	—
	112 wickets	1205 runs	average 10.75	9–28 best

Series	Tests	O	M	R	W	Av
1886 v A	3	116.2 (4-ball)	55	191	13	14.69
1886/7 in A	2	110 (4-ball)	51	137	16	8.56
1887/8 in A	1	51 (4-ball)	31	52	9	5.77
1888 v A	3	94.3 (4-ball)	50	144	11	13.09
1890 v A	2	103.2 (5-ball)	56	137	9	15.22
1891/2 in A	3	188.2	71	289	16	18.06
1895/6 in SA	3	104 (5-ball)	38	203	35	5.80
1896 v A	1	33 (5-ball)	12	52	3	17.33

BOBBY PEEL

Robert Peel
(1857–1941)
Yorkshire and England

At Headingley in the members' stand hangs a picture of the Yorkshire XI of the 1890s. They all sport 'short back-and-sides' and a moustache, except for the fellow at the end of the row of players who are sitting. Bobby Peel alone among them has long sideburns. He must have been an individual, well before he was dismissed by the county for unbecoming conduct.

Given any sequence of cricketers of a particular type, people tend to think that the first of the line was the best. Of the five top left-arm spin bowlers England produced before the Great War – Peate, Peel, Briggs, Rhodes and Blythe – a few have claimed that Ted Peate was supreme, thanks to this tendency. In fact Peate, Peel's predecessor at Yorkshire, bowled with a low arm, concentrated on length and did not spin much. He mostly performed on wet, uncovered, northern pitches.

Peel, on the other hand, had a technique which allowed him to dominate on tours of Australia during the 1890s, when wickets became hard and true thanks to mechanical methods of preparation, as well as on helpful English pitches. He had that blessing: a strong, quick arm. Witnesses of the day describe how Peel would make the ball drop shorter than the batsman expected, so he had the power of over-spin as well as side-spin. Leveson-Gower praises 'the clever flighting of the ball for which Peel was so famous', not forgetting his quicker one with the arm.

These devices were almost superfluous when Peel first visited Aus-

The eyes suggest that Peel enjoyed occasional late nights and that some of Lord Hawke's Yorkshire reforms were necessary

tralia in 1884/5 and found that up-country batting techniques were as crude as the pitches: he took 321 wickets against teams like XXII of Ballarat at four runs each! Ten years later it was another story on the new shirtfronts, but Peel would still take the new ball for England in partnership with Richardson and rub the ball on the ground for a better grip. This series excited more interest in England and Australia than any hitherto. It stood at two games all before the final Test, when England drew deep into the reserves of their 13 players (one a lob bowler, another a reserve wicket-keeper) and won.

Peel was the hero of the First Test which was, according to *Wisden*, 'in some respects the most extraordinary in the history of the game'. Indeed, only Headingley 1981 can compare with it among Ashes Tests. Australia scored 586 first up, England followed on, and Australia had to score 177 to win. At the end of the fifth day they were 113 for two. Then it rained, although folklore has it that Peel was too deep in his cups to hear and was astonished on arriving at the Sydney ground to find it wet. Hung over or not, he bowled Australia out with the aid of Briggs for England to win by ten runs. Peel finished with six for 67 from 30 overs.

In 1896, the year before his disgrace, Peel played only one Test against Australia; he took six for 23 in the second innings, dismissed them for 44, and recorded his one hundredth Test wicket against them, the first Englishman to reach that landmark. The subsequent end, when it came, was that of a singular man. He got drunk again, too drunk to stand, but he insisted on presenting himself to the Yorkshire captain Lord Hawke on the field at the start of play – before, so legend has it, relieving himself against the sightscreen. For all that he lived to a fine age, and was not bitter, so it is said.

FIRST-CLASS CAREER (1882–99)

| 693 innings | 66 not outs | 12191 runs | average 19.44 | 7 hundreds |
| | 1776 wickets | 28758 runs | average 16.19 | 9–22 best |

TEST RECORD (20 MATCHES)

| 33 innings | 4 not outs | 427 runs | average 14.72 | — |
| | 102 wickets | 1715 runs | average 16.81 | 7–31 best |

Series	Tests	O	M	R	W	Av
1884/5 in A	5	390.2 (4-ball)	193	451	21	21.47
1887/8 in A	1	51.3 (4-ball)	23	58	10	5.80
1888 v A	3	110.2 (4-ball)	48	181	24	7.54
1890 v A	1	67 (5-ball)	34	87	6	14.50
1891/2 in A	3	94.5	43	128	6	21.33
1893 v A	1	22 (5-ball)	12	36	0	—
1894/5 in A	5	305.1	77	721	27	26.70
1896 v A	1	32 (5-ball)	14	53	8	6.62

TOM RICHARDSON

Thomas Richardson
(1870–1912)
Surrey, London County,
Somerset and England

Tom Richardson is the first fast bowler who can be called great. In the four years from 1894, including a tour of Australia, he took 1074 first-class wickets. He reached his one thousandth by the age of 26 and in 134 matches; his two thousandth by the age of 32 and in 327 games. All these records endure, while to this day no one has taken more wickets for Surrey, neither Lohmann nor Lock nor Laker.

If the standard of batting among tail-enders helped to flatter him, Richardson had hard, heavy-rollered pitches on which to bowl at the Oval and in Australia. This was a far cry from a generation before when, according to one authority, 'Jackson, Willsher and Tarrant had merely to bowl their fastest and straightest, and the batsman might any ball expect either a dead shooter or a body blow'. Moreover, Richardson had only one new ball per innings; and after rain, since covering was still non-existent, he could not stand up to take advantage of the spiteful turf like slow left-handers and even medium-pacers.

He was of gipsy stock, with bushy eyebrows, swarthy features and a luxuriant moustache. On Mitcham Common he learnt to bowl or rather, it seems, to throw because everyone complained when he entered first-class cricket in 1892. Somehow he learnt to straighten his arm, and kept out of the throwing controversy which often flared in those days when there was no visual proof. Then followed those wonderful few years of prolific wicket-taking for Surrey and England.

How fast was a fast bowler in that era? When the England wicket-keeper Dick Lilley first saw Richardson, he stood up to him, as was his custom to all bowlers, although he soon moved back. Another clue is that Richardson seldom used a fine-leg, yet he consistently brought the ball into the right-hander with his 'breakback'. There was no prominent seam on the ball to produce the sudden and unintentional 'nip-backer'. So Richardson hoisted his left arm and swept his right fingers across the ball to achieve a sort of off-cut.

In terms relative to his period Richardson was as fast as they came. Mercifully for batsmen, he pitched the ball up all the time and in some seasons half of his wickets would be bowled, clean or off the pad. In one of his finest hours, in the Lord's Test of 1896, he bowled six Australian batsmen in 11.3 overs from the pavilion end, routing them for 53. And they had only to get their front pad outside off-stump to keep the breakback out and avoid being LBW.

But if 'Honest Tom' wasn't outright fast, he undoubtedly had stamina. In those four great years he bowled the equivalent of five-and-a-half thousand six-ball overs. In the 1894/5 series against Australia he took 32 wickets without any pace support (one fast bowler per side was thought sufficient and Peel would open with him). The following summer he took the grand total of 290 first-class wickets, beating

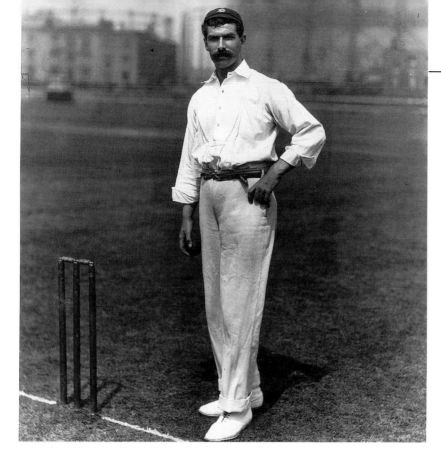

'Honest Tom' at the Oval in simple dignity, as if he had stepped from Gray's 'Elegy' or a Constable painting

Turner's 283 and setting a record which has since been surpassed only by Freeman. In 1896 his haul was 246, and in the next year 273.

It is good to know that he was at least being rewarded financially for these Herculean labours. He secured himself decent winter pay from Surrey of £100 while other pros had to fend for themselves. But he was soon rheumatic and over-weight as well as over-bowled. His form petered out rapidly and he left Surrey in 1904, moving to Bath where he kept a hotel and appeared for Somerset against the 1905 Australians. This was a pathetic mistake in the eyes of those who remembered him bowling with full steam up on English and foreign fields. After some years as a publican back in London he became another great bowler to die young, aged 41, while on holiday in France.

FIRST-CLASS CAREER (1892–1905)

| 479 innings | 124 not outs | 3424 runs | average 9.64 | 0 hundred |
| | 2104 wickets | 38794 runs | average 18.43 | 10–45 best |

TEST RECORD (14 MATCHES)

| 24 innings | 8 not outs | 177 runs | average 11.06 | — |
| | 88 wickets | 2220 runs | average 25.22 | 8–94 best |

Series	Tests	O	M	R	W	Av
1893 v A	1	67.4 (5-ball)	20	156	10	15.60
1894/5 in A	5	291.1	63	849	32	26.53
1896 v A	3	175.1 (5-ball)	58	439	24	18.29
1897/8 in A	5	255.5	50	776	22	35.27

HUGH TRUMBLE

Hugh Trumble
(1867–1938)
Victoria and Australia

One of the many fine photographs taken by E. Hawkins of Brighton, which froze turn-of-the-century cricketers into immortality, shows a 6′ 4″ Australian. He is standing in the bowling crease, right arm poised to deliver. He wears a cap, which fails to disguise his protruding ears, and a kind of cummerbund around his midriff. Difficult though it may be to conceive of this friendly giant as the leading wicket-taker in Anglo-Australian cricket, Hugh Trumble was such, and remained so until Dennis Lillee overtook his 141 wickets.

Taking over from Turner 'the Terror', Trumble led the Australian attack until 1903/4. He was a medium-pacer who could swing the new ball when everything clicked – and nobody then knew for certain how – but he was primarily an off-spinner or -cutter with a respected slower ball. He was, like Turner, more effective in England than at home. Indeed the method which Spofforth and Turner had pioneered, and which Trumble, Giffen and Noble emulated, was soon to die out on Australian pitches which were acquiring the consistency of iron. By the First World War it was appreciated that bowling in Australia had either to be fast or wrist-spin.

That was after Trumble's day. On his five tours of England from 1890 to 1902, Trumble took 603 first-class wickets at 16 runs each (and, being a limited batsman, he did the double in 1899). He was especially devastating on one of those sticky wickets which so often occurred in those times and which were defined by Ranjitsinhji in *The Jubilee Book of Cricket*, or more likely by his amanuensis C. B. Fry. A 'sticky' is 'usually the result of a heavy night's rain followed by a strong morning sun … and at times not even the bowler, though a good one, has the slightest idea what the ball will do. It may rise with a huge break over the batsman's head; it may shoot or keep uncommonly low; it may, wonderful to relate, break from leg after receiving an emphatic off-spin from the bowler's hand.'

Trumble, moreover, was renowned as an astute bowler – 'he is the most long-headed, observant and acute judge of the game' said an admiring Fry – and it may well have been he who popularised Spofforth's technique of bowling off-spin from round the wicket in conducive conditions. Blessed with immense hands and long fingers, he must often have found the ball doing too much when delivered over the wicket. He altered to round, brought up four or five close fielders on the leg-side, and aimed to have the batsman caught there, bowled or LBW.

When the immortal series of 1902 was held, Trumble was the bowler England were fighting. In the Old Trafford Test, which Australia won by three runs, Trumble took 11 wickets. At the Oval, when England won by one wicket, Trumble took 12. He might have taken one more in that most epic of Tests, for Hirst was hit on the pad by Trumble first

Thought has ever been a valuable commodity in cricket, so the pensive Trumble recognised

ball, from round the wicket, and several people were reported as feeling 'uncomfortable' about the reprieve. Hirst went on to 58 not out and to win the match with Rhodes.

Trumble played his last Test, indeed his last first-class game, against England in 1903/4. He not only ended with a hat trick but with seven for 28 on a rain-affected pitch. It was his second hat trick in Tests at his native Melbourne. Later he became secretary of the prestigious Melbourne Cricket Club, Australia's equivalent of MCC.

FIRST-CLASS CAREER (1887/8–1903/4)

344 innings	67 not outs	5395 runs	average 19.47	3 hundreds
	929 wickets	17134 runs	average 18.44	9–39 best

TEST RECORD (32 MATCHES)

57 innings	14 not outs	851 runs	average 19.79	—
	141 wickets	3072 runs	average 21.78	8–65 best

Series	Tests	O	M	R	W	Av
1890 in E	2	22 (5-ball)	8	45	2	22.50
1893 in E	3	105.2 (5-ball)	30	234	6	39.00
1894/5 v E	1	35.1	10	87	3	29.00
1896 in E	3	170.1 (5-ball)	58	339	18	18.83
1897/8 v E	5	232.2	57	535	19	28.15
1899 in E	5	192.2 (5-ball)	78	375	15	25.00
1901/2 v E	5	267.2	93	561	28	20.03
1902 in E	3	172.4	55	371	26	14.26
1902/3 in SA	1	34	4	127	0	—
1903/4 v E	4	199.4	59	398	24	16.58

J. T. HEARNE

Jack Hearne has taken more first-class wickets, 3061 of them, than any man bar Rhodes, Freeman and Parker, but the Middlesex medium-pacer is the least celebrated of all the huge wicket-takers. He might have taken quite a few more, too, if he had started county cricket before the age of 23. He was a Buckinghamshire man, however, from Chalfont St Giles, and had to move to London in 1888 and spend two years living there while working as a school groundsman before he qualified for Middlesex.

Warner says that after a notably long run-up, Hearne's 'beautiful method was a model for all time, his rhythm in action, lovely swing, and control of pace and length being as near perfection as any bowling could be'. He brought the ball in, probably more by cutting one side of the ball than spinning the whole of it. In this way he would accomplish, for Middlesex and MCC, all the damage required when pitches were

*John Thomas Hearne
(1867–1944)
Middlesex and England*

The last hat trick for England against Australia in England was taken by Hearne in 1899. His victims? Hill, Gregory and Noble

wet or crumbling (it was a help to Hearne, with his run-up, that from 1910 the bowler's footholds could be covered as the first exercise in pitch protection). Playing so often at Lord's, Hearne took 1719 wickets there; more than any other man.

But there was more to him than being a 'bad wicket bowler' who took nine wickets in an innings eight times. He demonstrated as much when he followed his 257 wickets in the 1896 season – he reached his one hundredth on 12 June, the earliest date recorded – by topping the England averages the next time they visited Australia. That was in 1897/8 when he took nine for 141 in the First Test at Sydney, and 20 wickets in the series for a badly beaten side, bowling 'with a steadiness beyond all praise' (*Wisden*). In Australia then, and in England too from 1899, the over consisted of six balls and this would have allowed a bowler like Hearne more scope for planning his attack.

He also toured South Africa in his early years and for six winters went to India as a coach, although he was there more to lend lustre to the Maharajah of Patiala's retinue. After these wanderings he settled down to become an essential part of Lord's and to take his annual one hundred wickets, which he did 15 times. Tom Hearne, MCC's head groundsman for a dozen years, was his uncle. Jack Hearne himself was on the groundstaff from 1891 to 1924, in addition to being a Middlesex professional until the First World War. He was as much a part of the furniture of Lord's as 'Young Jack' Hearne (no relation) or Patsy Hendren or Fred Titmus.

Men like Hearne helped to raise the status of professional cricketers by their example. He became the father figure to young Middlesex and MCC players, and is remembered for sitting at the head of the table with watch and chain at the pros' hotel, and carving the roast for all in due solemnity. He was so widely respected that he was the first professional ever to be elected to the Middlesex committee, in 1920. He did his work thoroughly and without ostentation, which may be why he is recalled so rarely today.

FIRST-CLASS CAREER (1888–1923)

919 innings	318 not outs	7205 runs	average 11.98	0 hundred
	3061 wickets	54352 runs	average 17.75	9–32 best

TEST RECORD (12 MATCHES)

18 innings	4 not outs	126 runs	average 9.00	—
	49 wickets	1082 runs	average 22.08	6–41 best

Series	Tests	O	M	R	W	Av
1891/2 v SA	1	8 (5-ball)	2	12	1	12.00
1896 v A	3	127.1 (5-ball)	56	211	15	14.06
1897/8 v A	5	217	66	538	20	26.90
1899 v A	3	199.3 (5-ball)	87	321	13	24.69

BILL LOCKWOOD

Not all English bowlers of the Victorian era were uncomplaining stalwarts of never-ending stamina, ready to bowl themselves into an early grave. Bill Lockwood was 'the best' fast bowler Warner ever faced, and 'the most difficult' in Ranji's eyes. In character Lockwood was very different from Tom Richardson, his partner in many a Surrey and England side. In his teens, Lockwood was a lace-worker in Nottingham – a blue-collar worker therefore, with his own ideas about his worth and status.

So it was that after a few games for Nottinghamshire, who were the leading county of the 1880s, Lockwood left them for Surrey and for greater opportunity. It was a move requiring considerable independence of thought and spirit in those still-feudal times. The qualification period was two years, enough to deter most men from moving from one first-class county to another. Furthermore, once Lockwood had fulfilled his qualification by residence, Surrey had revived and were developing into the leading county of the 1890s.

Lockwood therefore had barely any more scope when he made his début for Surrey in 1889 (the year, incidentally, when legislation was

William Henry Lockwood
(1868–1932)
Nottinghamshire, Surrey
and England

Practising his slower ball, presumably an off-break

revised to allow a bowler to change ends as often as he liked during an innings). But he made his way as a passable batsman until his bowling blossomed in 1892, when it was reported that 'he gets up very quickly and the balls come back at a great rate'. In this early stage of his career he was frequently criticised for pitching too short, so unlike the faithful Tom.

From 1892 to 1894 Lockwood attained 150 wickets a season but then, on the verge of greatness, he turned into a major disappointment. On the 1894/5 tour, when Richardson cried out for aid, Lockwood's performances were desultory. Nor did he do anything of note in the next three English seasons so that it appeared his career would finish without fulfilment. Hereabouts his wife died, as did one of his sons, and he was not very healthy himself. There was also his difficult personality. One of Lockwood's peculiarities was to run in, overstep the crease and hold on to the ball in order to embarrass the umpire when he shouted 'no-ball'.

But the most extraordinary phase of Lockwood's career was still to come. In 1898 he returned to the top, armed with a devilish slower ball. No fast bowler seems to have possessed anything so deceptive until Franklyn Stephenson in the 1988 season. Whereas Stephenson's slower ball was an off-break, Lockwood's sometimes turned from leg. In general he was said to have the ability to make the ball dip, which may be taken as an indication of inswing, or perhaps of occasional doubts about his action.

By 1902 Lockwood was beyond question England's premier pace bowler. In the Old Trafford Test that England lost by three runs, Lockwood took 11 for 76; at the Oval, five for 45 in Australia's second innings. At a mature 34 Lockwood had made it at last and, having silenced his critics, he retired two years later. He became a coach, until arthritis afflicted him so badly that he was confined to a wheel-chair. But he would still visit Trent Bridge, and tell those who listened that Richardson was a better fast bowler than he had ever been.

FIRST-CLASS CAREER (1886–1904)

531 innings	45 not outs	10673 runs	average 21.96	15 hundreds
	1376 wickets	25247 runs	average 18.34	9–59 best

TEST RECORD (12 MATCHES)

16 innings	3 not outs	231 runs	average 17.76	—
	43 wickets	884 runs	average 20.55	7–71 best

Series	Tests	O	M	R	W	Av
1893 v A	2	93 (5-ball)	27	234	14	16.71
1894/5 in A	5	123.2	31	340	5	68.00
1899 v A	1	55.3 (5-ball)	24	104	7	14.85
1902 v A	4	81.1	18	206	17	12.11

GEORGE HIRST

The history of swing can be no more precise a subject than the science of bowling it. However, it is widely agreed that during the 1890s George Hirst started to do – on and off – that which had only rarely been done before. Originally, when he had made his first-team début for Yorkshire at 18 in 1889, Hirst had tried to bowl fast; when he slowed down he found by experiment that the ball would sometimes swing, curve or curl into right-handed batsmen.

He decided to hold the ball lightly with his first two fingers, one on either side of the seam (not the thick-stitched thing it is now). For variety he would also mix in the occasional orthodox spinner. For a field he would have three short-legs and a fine-leg, as there was no restriction on the number of men behind the wicket on the leg-side until the 1950s. One of his short-legs, for Yorkshire and England, would be his colleague from Kirkheaton near Huddersfield, Wilfred Rhodes.

In county cricket Hirst achieved remarkable feats for season after season: in 14 of them he did the double, and in 1906 the one and only double double of two thousand runs and two hundred wickets. Pad-play was clearly still not advanced enough to counter these deliveries swinging in from outside off-stump towards the wicket. In 1906 against Somerset, Hirst took 11 wickets in addition to scoring a century in each innings. In 1910 he bowled eight Lancashire batsmen out of nine, for 23 runs. This was done at Headingley, so collapses there against swing are nothing new.

Even when playing against the Australians for Yorkshire, Hirst could be relied upon to be successful. At Headingley again, in 1902, Hirst captured five of their first six wickets for nine runs, tumbling the Australians out for a match-losing total of 23. But for England Hirst was not quite the omnipotent all-rounder he was in county cricket, except for one Birmingham day in 1902 when he took three for 15 and, with Rhodes, dismissed Australia for their record lowest total of 36.

This difference in success must have been partly due to the higher standard of pad-play at Test level and partly to the fact that Hirst was unable to make the ball swing in Australia where he played nine of his Tests. In 1897/8 he was given the new ball initially but could make nothing of it (a strain is mentioned as an excuse). In 1903/4 he was scarcely more effective until he found a wet pitch at Melbourne and took five for 48, when the ball was doing everything. At any rate in the first half of his career, it has to be concluded, Hirst did not possess sufficient technical mastery of his swing to be a force in all conditions.

In England it was another matter. In his thirty-eighth year he had a notably fine game against the 1909 Australians and dismissed nine of them for 86 in the Edgbaston Test: he may have mastered the technique by now. And there was always his batting to make him worth a place in

George Herbert Hirst
(1871–1954)
Yorkshire and England

Hirst, not knowing that posterity is watching, perversely goes round the wicket in slower style

the England team, and his mid-off fielding, and his popularity, and the affection he commanded. He may be considered the greatest of county cricketers.

FIRST-CLASS CAREER (1891–1929)

1217 innings	152 not outs	36356 runs	average 34.13	60 hundreds
	2742 wickets	51373 runs	average 18.73	9–23 best

TEST RECORD (24 MATCHES)

38 innings	3 not outs	790 runs	average 22.57	—
	59 wickets	1770 runs	average 30.00	5–48 best

Series	Tests	O		M	R	W	Av
1897/8 in A	4	99		18	304	2	152.00
1899 v A	1	35	(5-ball)	13	62	1	62.00
1902 v A	4	79		18	208	9	23.11
1903/4 in A	5	163.2		29	451	15	30.60
1905 v A	3	62		13	212	6	35.33
1907 v SA	3	87		28	185	10	18.50
1909 v A	4	143.4		27	348	16	21.75

BART KING

The first regular practitioner of swing was not an Englishman or an Australian or a South African. He was an American, Bart King, who learned the mechanics of swing from baseball. He then applied them so successfully that he acquired 390 first-class wickets at an average of 16, mostly on tours of England by the Philadelphians.

John Barton King (1873–1965) Philadelphia

King was an inswing bowler who delivered the ball from over his head so that it was already slanting in towards the right-hander. Other bowlers in England, most notably Hirst, had found that the ball would swing on occasional days – although through the 1890s the general practice continued to be rubbing the new ball in the dirt in order to obtain a better grip for breakbacks. King worked it all out and found the secret, such as it was: namely, that for consistent swing the bowler has to flick his fingers down the seam in the act of delivery, so that the ball rotates backwards during its flight. Otherwise the seam will not regularly stay upright.

King made his first impact at the age of 20 when the Australians visited Philadelphia on the way home from their 1893 tour of England. By then American interest in cricket had already contracted and survived in only the most Anglophile city. When the Philadelphians had toured England a while earlier, they had done little to suggest that they were much above club standard. One great bowler, however, launched two golden decades for the game in America when King routed the Australians by an innings.

In 1896, in three representative matches between Philadelphia and Australia (more entitled to be called Tests than some matches between South Africa and England), King took 15 wickets at 16 runs each: 'it was his baseball curves that upset our batsmen' said one Australian. In 1897 the Philadelphians were emboldened to undertake the first of their three first-class tours of England. Great was the sensation when King bowled Ranjitsinhji first ball with one that swung in late at the prince! King returned home with 72 wickets, then routed an English team led by Warner which had followed them to America: his nine for 25 on that occasion were his best innings figures.

By 1903 and their second major tour of England, the Philadelphians were at their peak. Of their 16 first-class matches they won seven and lost six. King was aged 30, stood 6′ 1″ tall and was superbly athletic; for an opening partner he had a fine supporter in Percy Clark. Their best performance happened at the Oval: King hit his one first-class century, as well as 98 run out, and took six wickets (the last within minutes of the scheduled close), to give the Philadelphians a prestigious win over Surrey. On the tour he had 78 wickets at 16 and was declared the equal of any all-rounder in England.

King, although 35, went a stage better on the Philadelphians' last

*An athletic, virile,
inswinging action*

tour in 1908 by heading the national bowling averages: his 87 wickets came in ten games at a cost of 11.01, astonishingly low. By then he had developed an outswinger for variation, albeit bowled with a revealingly low arm, while his yorker was as sharp as ever.

Naturally King was made plenty of offers by first-class counties in his time. But he declined them and, with King, cricket in America itself declined. By the time he died aged 92 (he was an amateur, and wealthy) the cricket clubs of Philadelphia had been made over to tennis, their original purpose long forgotten.

FIRST-CLASS CAREER (1893–1912)

111 innings	9 not outs	2047 runs	average 20.06	1 hundred
	390 wickets	6353 runs	average 16.28	9–25 best

NO TESTS

WILFRED RHODES

Wilfred Rhodes took more first-class wickets than anyone ever has, or ever will, unless one-day games are ranked as first-class. He alone has a total of over four thousand wickets. He alone has taken a hundred wickets in a season 23 times, thrice more than the next man. But there is a drawback to this longevity: people forgot how good Wilfred Rhodes was at his youthful peak. Had he died young, instead of continuing to bowl for 25 years and more, he might have been recognised as indisputably the greatest slow left-hander the game has seen.

Having made his début for Yorkshire in 1898 following Peel's enforced and hasty retirement, Rhodes dismissed 261 batsmen in 1900 and 251 more in 1901. But he was not able to play Test cricket in those two prime years of his, for the Yorkshire committee would not allow him and Hirst to tour Australia in the intervening winter. It was not until 1903/4, when he was already in relative decline, that he visited Australia and bowled more successfully than any English slow bowler has done there.

At Melbourne he had the assistance of an old-fashioned sticky. Still, he had eight chances missed off him as he took 15 wickets for 124: they were the best figures in Test cricket to that point. Then at Sydney, which was not a 'turner' in those days, he bowled 40.2 overs for 94 runs and five wickets as the Australian batsmen, led by Trumper, went on a rampage against the other England bowlers. Ominously, however, Rhodes had just scored an unbeaten 40 in England's innings, in a last-wicket stand of 130.

'Flight was his secret – flight and the curving line': so wrote Neville Cardus of Rhodes in one of his most lyrical essays. More prosaically, Rhodes actually spun the ball in his early years off a wart, which may have become a contributory factor in his decision to cease being a specialist bowler. In any event he started to open the batting for his county – not the last left-armer to have such aspirations, but Rhodes actually went on to open the batting for England as well, with Jack Hobbs. On England's triumphant 1911/12 tour of Australia, Rhodes was England's number two batsman in every sense, and did not take a single first-class wicket.

But the third part of Rhodes' career, after the First World War, was not the least amazing. He dropped down the order to number five for Yorkshire and so revived his bowling that he was the best slow left-hander again in the immediate post-war period, heading the national averages from 1919 to 1923 inclusive, as he had not done since 1901. No doubt the standard had temporarily fallen as a consequence of war. Nevertheless the figures speak eloquently. Past 40 himself when it was over, he took 828 wickets at 13 in the first six seasons thereafter.

It was sometimes said that Rhodes would only finger his sweater and

Wilfred Rhodes
(1877–1973)
Yorkshire and England

43

In his final season Rhodes tosses the ball up against Essex at Leyton. He knew that the ball flighted above the batsman's eye-level is more difficult to judge; his close fielders know his line and length will not falter

whisper throatily to his amateur skipper that he fancied 'hissen' when conditions were favourable. Be that as it may, he was never collared except on the rarest of occasions by Frank Woolley. Then in 1926 he returned again to the top of the national averages and, aged 48, did the double for the sixteenth, final and record-setting time. He was recalled by England's selectors (of whom he was one himself) for the Oval Test against Australia. Anti-climax? His 45 overs brought six wickets for 79, and victory, and the Ashes.

Yet there was even a fourth stage to his greatness. This happened when Yorkshire suddenly found themselves short of bowlers, after the sudden death of Roy Kilner. Rhodes had no chance to pick his moments now, and he passed 50 in October 1927. He still had three more seasons in the game, and one MCC tour to the West Indies when he represented England again at the age of 52, easily the oldest player in Test cricket. It was 30 years since his début, when 'W.G.' was in the same side.

In the West Indies, as George Headley found his feet, Rhodes still conceded less than two runs an over in marathon spells. The accuracy by then was embedded within him, although he was now reduced to spinning or simply rolling the ball off his thumb. In his last three years from the ages of 50 to 52, Rhodes averaged 1150 overs. The flight and the curving line remained intact. We will, for certain, never see his like again.

FIRST-CLASS CAREER (1898–1930)

| 1528 innings | 237 not outs | 39802 runs | average 30.83 | 58 hundreds |
| | 4187 wickets | 69993 runs | average 16.71 | 9–24 best |

TEST RECORD (58 MATCHES)

| 98 innings | 21 not outs | 2325 runs | average 30.19 | 2 hundreds |
| | 127 wickets | 3425 runs | average 26.96 | 8–68 best |

Series	Tests	O	M	R	W	Av
1899 v A	3	146.2 (5-ball)	37	341	13	26.53
1902 v A	5	140.5	38	336	22	15.27
1903/4 in A	5	172	36	488	31	15.74
1905 v A	4	110.3	21	314	10	31.40
1907/8 in A	5	157.4	42	421	7	60.14
1909 v A	4	79	9	242	11	22.00
1909/10 in SA	5	57	14	147	2	73.50
1911/12 in A	5	19	3	57	0	—
1912 v SA	3	4	1	14	0	—
1912 v A	3	21.2	6	60	3	20.00
1913/14 in SA	5	88.5	24	195	6	32.50
1920/21 in A	5	85.4	15	245	4	61.25
1921 v A	1	13	3	33	2	16.50
1926 v A	1	45	24	79	6	13.16
1929/30 in WI	4	256	92	453	10	45.30

BERNARD BOSANQUET

Bernard James Tindal
Bosanquet
(1877–1936)
Oxford University,
Middlesex and England

Bernard Bosanquet laid his claim to celebrity with the invention of the 'googly' rather than his execution of it. He had his good days with the ball, most notably in a couple of Tests against Australia, but he was not to be the leading exponent of the googly or 'bosie'. Nevertheless, the act of fathering a revolutionary type of delivery wins him the accolade of greatness.

At Oxford at the turn of the century Bosanquet represented the university at billiards and throwing the hammer, as well as winning his cricket blue in all three years. This was mainly for his hard-hitting batting (he was to score over 11,000 runs) rather than for his occasional medium-pace. As a natural athlete he also played a friendly game called 'Twisti-Twosti', which involved bouncing a tennis ball on a table and spinning it in such a fashion that your opponent could not catch it. From here, according to Bosanquet's own recollection in later life, emanated the ball which resembled a leg-break but turned into the right-handed batsman.

It is hard though to believe that Bosanquet was the first person ever to bowl a googly. Leg-spin, while never the most common form of slow bowling, had long been a feature of county cricket, and it is probable that at one time or another several leg-spinners came out with an

The artful Old Etonian demonstrates his leg-break, not his mystery ball, to the cameraman

46

unintended googly. Bosanquet's achievement was to develop it so that he could produce it at will.

At Oxford he confined his novelty to the nets, surprising a few county batsmen with it during the lunch interval. It was not until he left Oxford for Middlesex in 1900 that he unveiled his secret publicly and took a wicket with a googly which bounced four times before hitting the stumps. For a while he pretended that the ball was a complete and laughable accident so that the word would not spread, especially to the Australians. In this he was largely successful, such was the slowness of communication.

Bosanquet was taken on the 1903/4 tour of Australia, the first to be managed by MCC and not by a private individual. In the Adelaide Test he took seven wickets in a losing cause. At Sydney he took six for 51 in Australia's second innings to put England three–one ahead in the series: half his victims were stumped, including right- and left-handers. He was a match-winner again in the First Test of 1905 when Australia were dismissed for 188. While they blocked out Rhodes at one end, they went after Bosanquet at the other and eight of them fell to him for 107 runs. He played two more Tests without distinction: his length was frequently uncertain.

The bosie was naturally taken up in Australia, but it was popularised even more widely in South Africa by Reggie Schwarz, who played alongside Bosanquet for Middlesex before emigrating to South Africa. The invention went with him, and by 1907 when the South Africans made their first Test tour of England, they had four googly bowlers in Schwarz, Vogler, White and Faulkner. If the googly has subsequently not touched such heights again, thanks to the development in pad-play which these South Africans brought about, it should forever be a part of cricket.

Bosanquet lost his bowling altogether after 1905, although he kept playing for Middlesex periodically until 1919 and headed the national batting averages in 1908. He died a day short of his sixtieth birthday. He was the father of the newscaster Reginald Bosanquet as well as of the googly.

FIRST-CLASS CAREER (1898–1919)

382 innings	32 not outs	11696 runs	average 33.41	21 hundreds
	629 wickets	14974 runs	average 23.80	9–31 best

TEST RECORD (7 MATCHES)

14 innings	3 not outs	147 runs	average 13.36	—
	25 wickets	604 runs	average 24.16	8–107 best

Series	Tests	O	M	R	W	Av
1903/4 in A	4	103	7	403	16	25.18
1905 v A	3	58.4	3	201	9	22.33

COLIN BLYTHE

Colin Blythe
(1879–1917)
Kent and England

If Victor Trumper is the most romantic figure in Australia's cricket, Colin Blythe has to be the equivalent in England's. Blythe died at the age of 38 – a year older than Trumper was at his death – in action near Passchendaele in Belgium. He could have accepted the option of doing war work at home, which Hobbs and Rhodes and many other cricketers preferred. Instead, he joined the Kent Fortress Engineers and became cricket's most famous casualty of the Great War.

As a bowler, Blythe was of the most romantic sort: a slow left-arm spinner, he flighted the ball up to an off-side field among the marquees at Canterbury, and encouraged the batsman to play the game's classical strokes. There was nothing so unchivalrous as firing it in at leg-stump, although he is said to have commanded a nice quicker ball with the arm. The ball leaving the right-handed bat was still exceptional in Blythe's time as most of the bowling was done by exponents of breakbacks, inswingers, off-breaks and googlies. The slow left-handers had the going-away ball almost to themselves, and England had a fine lineage in Peel and Briggs, Rhodes and Blythe.

He dismissed more than 2500 batsmen in 15 seasons and a bit. The bit consisted of four games in 1899 when he made his début, aged 20, and took a wicket with his first ball (he had simply turned up at the nets one day, shyly asked for a bowl and made an immediate impression). His value to Kent can be seen even today on the flag flying at any of the county's matches. Most of their championship titles – four of them – were won between 1900 and the First World War, when Blythe was their leading bowler.

Blythe had his best game for Kent in 1907 against Northamptonshire, who had recently been the sixteenth county promoted to first-class status. Kent scored 254 on a wet Northampton pitch; then on the last of the three days, a Saturday, Blythe took ten for 30 in one innings, and seven for 18 in the next, as the home county gave, according to *Wisden*, 'a deplorable display'. Never before or since has anyone taken so many wickets in a day for so few runs. Only Jim Laker has recorded a better match analysis.

In Test cricket Blythe was not quite the bowler he was in the county game. On his two tours of Australia – the first in 1901/2, when Rhodes was not allowed to go by Yorkshire – he did some good work, but was not the equal of the Yorkshireman at his best. Again, on his two tours of South Africa he was not quite so effective on the matting as he might have been (he also toured America with Kent in 1903, the first overseas tour by a county). The strain of touring and Test cricket did not suit Blythe for, of course, he suffered from attacks of epilepsy.

His best series were at home where the strain was possibly reduced. At Headingley in 1907, in a close game with South Africa, his 15 wickets

Blythe here is firing in his quicker ball. Fry remarked that when Blythe did this on one particular occasion, it was the fastest bowling he faced!

for 99 runs gave England victory by 53. In 1909 he took 11 of Australia's wickets at Edgbaston, but was so severely taxed that he could not play at Lord's a fortnight later. He was therefore no longer an England player when the war came. But that did not make his loss any less grievous.

FIRST-CLASS CAREER (1899–1914)

| 587 innings | 137 not outs | 4443 runs | average 9.87 | 0 hundred |
| | 2503 wickets | 42099 runs | average 16.81 | 10–30 best |

TEST RECORD (19 MATCHES)

| 31 innings | 12 not outs | 183 runs | average 9.63 | — |
| | 100 wickets | 1863 runs | average 18.63 | 8–59 best |

Series	Tests	O	M	R	W	Av
1901/2 in A	5	175	63	470	18	26.11
1905 v A	1	32	11	77	4	19.25
1905/6 in SA	5	226.4	74	548	21	26.09
1907 v SA	3	100.3	26	270	26	10.38
1907/8 in A	1	31	6	88	1	88.00
1909 v A	2	91.3	19	242	18	13.44
1909/10 in SA	2	83	32	168	12	14.00

SYD BARNES

Sydney Francis Barnes
(1873–1967)
Warwickshire, Lancashire,
Wales and England

The master bowler is ready
to observe the back foot rule,
if few other conventions

Syd Barnes, to judge by all accounts, was the consummation of pre-Great War bowling. He combined the methods of Spofforth, Lohmann and Turner, and developed them to their highest extent. That is, he learnt to cut the ball both ways, and pitch it accurately, at medium-pace. Even when he was in his mid-fifties, touring teams considered him to be the best bowler in England.

Barnes made his first-class début in 1894, in one of four games for Warwickshire, when he was a straight fastish bowler. It was later that he decided, after much thought and experiment, that the new fashion of swing was technically inferior to cutting the ball, since it largely depended on the ball maintaining its shine. Outfields in his day were looked after by simple nature not fertilisers, and one new ball per innings was the rule until 1907. Then, in a far-reaching change, a second new ball was permitted after every two hundred runs. Barnes therefore held the ball with the first three fingers of his right hand, the second – for the most part – on top of the seam, one to either side and touching it. With this grip he delivered a leg-cutter which swerved into the right-hander before pitching, then broke away; or, less often, an off-cutter which did the reverse.

This technique understandably required years to perfect, but Barnes was able to give the necessary time to it when he turned pro in the Lancashire League in 1895. The greater financial security was another factor in his move, and the wish not to burn himself out in county cricket like Lohmann and Richardson were doing. In the League he improved to such an extent that Lancashire gave him two matches in 1899 and another in 1901, when he broke through with six for 70 in a Leicestershire innings. Nevertheless, it came as the biggest bolt from the blue in the history of England selection when a telegram was carried on to the field at Burnley, where Barnes was the professional, asking him if he would tour Australia that winter.

No committee could have been so imaginative. The selection was made by the Lancashire captain Archie MacLaren who organised the tour and led the team (and who had already been refused the services of Hirst and Rhodes by Yorkshire). Barnes' qualifications, to that point, were 13 first-class wickets at 37 runs each. Yet MacLaren knew what he was doing. Barnes took five for 65 in his first Test innings, and six for 42 and seven for 121 in the Second Test, before breaking down with knee trouble as a result of being over-bowled.

In 1902 Barnes was selected, by committee, for only one Test match, when he had six for 49 in one innings at Sheffield. That was the sole home Test for the finest right-arm bowler of his time until 1909: indeed, it was one of only ten home Tests for Barnes. He was branded a 'prima donna' who would not perform except when he was in the mood and

the price was right (he was known to pull out of a Gentlemen v. Players match, after the start, when he thought his match fee insufficient). It did not assist his image when after two seasons at Old Trafford he fell out in a public scene over terms and returned to league cricket, where he could earn £8 a week to Lancashire's £3.

The only county cricket Barnes chose to play thereafter was for

Staffordshire (he finished with far more wickets than anyone else in the history of the minor county game). This Achillean trait seemed to rule him out of contention for an England place and it did until 1907/8, when again several leading bowlers were unavailable for Australia (bowlers declining tours is nothing new). Barnes went and finished with 24 wickets for a losing team. Four years later Barnes enjoyed his finest hours in the company of F. R. Foster and finished with 34 wickets. Probably the finest of all happened at the start of the Melbourne Test when he dismissed Kellaway, Bardsley, Hill and Armstrong for one run in his first five overs.

In 20 Tests against Australia, Barnes captured 106 wickets, 77 of them in that country when massive totals were being made. That is more of a memorial than his 83 wickets in seven Tests against South Africa at an average of nine. Their batting did not add up to much beyond Herbie Taylor in 1913/14 when Barnes, on matting, took 49 of their wickets (a record for any series) in four Tests.

Barnes remained a league professional until his sixties. In 1928 and 1929, when he was 55 and 56, he even reappeared in a handful of first-class games, mainly for Wales against the visiting West Indians and South Africans. Had age withered him? He took 49 wickets for 13 runs each. He still had a long swing of the arm which he kept vertical in delivery. He still, with a peculiar mannerism, ran up with the ball in his left hand until the last moment. And he still moved the ball both ways at will, by actively cutting it. Since the 1960s, of course, as the seam has grown in size, any hack seamer has been able to move the ball around, both ways, like Barnes in his prime. It is therefore pointless to compare him with the moderns. Suffice it that he was the greatest bowler of his era.

FIRST-CLASS CAREER (1894–1930)

| 173 innings | 50 not outs | 1573 runs | average 12.78 | 0 hundred |
| | 719 wickets | 12289 runs | average 17.09 | 9–103 best |

TEST RECORD (27 MATCHES)

| 39 innings | 9 not outs | 242 runs | average 8.06 | — |
| | 189 wickets | 3106 runs | average 16.43 | 9–103 best |

Series	Tests	O	M	R	W	Av
1901/2 in A	3	138.2	33	323	19	17.00
1902 v A	1	32	13	99	7	14.14
1907/8 in A	5	273.2	74	626	24	26.08
1909 v A	3	155.3	52	340	17	20.00
1911/12 in A	5	297	64	778	34	22.88
1912 v A	3	62	26	122	5	24.40
1912 v SA	3	128	38	282	34	8.29
1913/14 in SA	4	226	56	536	49	10.93

AUBREY FAULKNER

The googly developed by Bosanquet, and the leg-break which was already common currency, were brought together by a group of South African bowlers shortly after the turn of the century. In 1907 the South African touring party to England contained no fewer than four wrist-spinners. One was Albert Vogler, who was highly successful, but who subsequently had a dreadful tour of Australia (drink was the suspected cause); another was Gordon White, mainly a batsman; the third was Reggie Schwarz, who had been at Cambridge without gaining a cricket blue (how many do that and yet take 55 Test wickets?), and had then played with Bosanquet in the Middlesex team before leaving for South Africa to be the secretary to the millionaire Sir Abe Bailey. The fourth, and 'the most difficult of all' on his day, according to 'Plum' Warner, was Aubrey Faulkner.

George Aubrey Faulkner (1881–1930) Transvaal and South Africa

Faulkner seated, far left, next to A. C. MacLaren, whose XI alone beat the 1921 Australians, after being dismissed for 43 at Eastbourne. Faulkner then hit 153 and took six for 63 in the sensation of the season

Born in Port Elizabeth, Faulkner represented Transvaal when 21 but did little out of the ordinary as an all-rounder until the Headingley Test of 1907. There he took six wickets, including those of Hayward, J. T. Tyldesley, Braund and Jessop, for 17 runs. Like his fellow googly bowlers he was, rather interestingly, thought to be more efficient on rain-affected pitches than hard ones. He then acquired a real taste for batting, of which his country had more urgent need, and by application as much as talent became the pick of his side. The 732 runs which he scored in South Africa's first series in Australia in 1910/11 left him with little energy for bowling.

Faulkner accomplished the double in 1912, the year of the highly original Triangular Tournament when South Africa, Australia and England played each other three times each in England, in Test matches. In addition to his thousand runs that season, Faulkner totalled 163 wickets at an average of 15 (it was another wet summer). In the Oval Test against England he had seven for 84. As well as a quicker ball which was often a 'yorker', he must have commanded considerable over-spin as he could make the ball hasten off the pitch.

That was his penultimate Test match, for in 1913 he moved to England and did not play for South Africa except in one emergency in 1924, by which time the country had lost much of its pre-war strength. During the war Faulkner rose to the rank of major and won a DSO. In peacetime he opened the first coaching establishment for the public in London, the Faulkner School of Cricket, and inculcated the methods which had made him one of the finest of all-rounders (he was the first to record two hundred runs and eight wickets in a Test). All his career was spent in playing 'up hill' against stronger opposition, too. In 1930 he joined the list of cricket suicides when he poisoned himself with gas at his indoor school.

FIRST-CLASS CAREER (1902/3–1924)

| 197 innings | 23 not outs | 6366 runs | average 36.58 | 13 hundreds |
| | 449 wickets | 7826 runs | average 17.42 | 7–26 best |

TEST RECORD (25 MATCHES)

| 47 innings | 4 not outs | 1754 runs | average 40.79 | 4 hundreds |
| | 82 wickets | 2180 runs | average 26.58 | 7–84 best |

Series	Tests	O	M	R	W	Av
1905/6 v E	5	119.4	34	272	14	19.42
1907 in E	3	73	11	218	12	18.16
1909/10 v E	5	209.1	45	635	29	21.89
1910/11 in A	5	124	13	514	10	51.40
1912 v A (in E)	3	66.1	7	194	4	48.50
1912 in E	3	95.3	14	260	13	20.00
1924 in E	1	17	0	87	0	—

FRANK FOSTER

In the decade before the First World War two young and dashing amateur all-rounders burst upon the English scene. The first was Jack Crawford who played for Surrey, and almost topped the national bowling averages, while still at school. He soon emigrated to Australia and dropped out of cricket prematurely. The second all-rounder was Frank Foster, who was chosen for Warwickshire shortly after leaving Solihull School. Foster should be rated the better medium-paced bowler of the two on the strength of his Test record and because he was left-handed.

Foster employed what we would consider an unusual procedure: he bowled, loose-limbed and whippy, off an eight-pace run – but not over the wicket. He always bowled round, and from wide out in the crease, so that he was doing the very opposite of slanting the ball across the

Frank Rowbotham Foster
(1889–1958)
Warwickshire and England

Foster braced for a spinner rather than the inswinger that was his stock ball

right-handed batsman. Sometimes he would make the ball swing in; in any event he aimed at leg-stump, pretty incisively too. In 1911 he hit the stumps 74 times out of 116 victims – and he not only topped Warwickshire's batting and bowling averages, and did the double, but led them to their first championship at the age of 22!

This incisiveness suggests that pad-play was still at a rudimentary level among many county cricketers. In Test cricket the standard was higher but Foster still hit the stumps 25 times out of 45 Test wickets. He also had the support of packed leg-side fields, and he engaged in leg-theory 21 years before it became an emotive word in Australia. Foster usually had four short-legs, two in front of the wicket and two behind, with a fine-leg to back them up. On the 1911/12 tour of Australia, Foster finished with 32 Test wickets to Barnes' 34.

He was consistency itself in that series, taking seven wickets in three of the Tests, six in another and five in the last. One was a leg-side stumping by his Warwickshire team-mate 'Tiger' Smith to dismiss Clem Hill, but the majority of his victims were bowled as they underestimated his speed and played back. In the following summer he took eight more South African wickets to give him 40 from his first half-dozen Tests. But it was the horribly wet season of 1912 that made the Triangular Tournament a disaster, and Foster barely bowled in the three remaining Tests of his brief career.

Before the age of 26 he had played his last game in first-class cricket, for he suffered a bad motor-cycle accident during the First World War. By then he had achieved the double a second time, had scored 305 not out (Warwickshire's highest innings), and been acclaimed as the best young captain since W. G. Grace. Fate was harsh – or was it? – in forcing him to retire while still at his dashing peak.

FIRST-CLASS CAREER (1908–14)

263 innings	17 not outs	6548 runs	average 26.61	7 hundreds
	718 wickets	14879 runs	average 20.72	9–118 best

TEST RECORD (11 MATCHES)

15 innings	1 not out	330 runs	average 23.57	—
	45 wickets	926 runs	average 20.57	6–91 best

Series	Tests	O	M	R	W	Av
1911/12 in A	5	276.4	58	692	32	21.62
1912 v A	3	39	18	50	2	25.00
1912 v SA	3	92.1	32	184	11	16.72

CECIL PARKIN

Cecil Parkin was one of cricket's rebels. When he began in 1906, the Victorian age was over, and professionals were not always recognising an amateur as a superior simply because of his accent and the Mr in front of his name on the score card. Like Barnes and Parker, Parkin was caught up in the tension as the age-old social fabric unwound; and he was not reluctant to kick against the pricks.

Certainly he was born on the wrong side of the river, if not of the tracks, as far as Yorkshire were concerned. He came from the Durham side of the River Tees, the son of a station master; so after one appearance for Yorkshire he disappeared into the leagues until the First World War. He was a pace bowler at first, a rather skinny one. But the old leg-spinner C. L. Townsend lived in Parkin's home town of Norton-on-Tees, and during the long periods of practice which a pro's job allowed, Parkin mastered the leg-break, then the googly. His hero was Syd Barnes, and he too wanted to be a fully equipped medium-pacer.

Parkin's growing reputation in the Lancashire League (he was later to be suspended from the Central Lancashire) brought him an invitation to play for Lancashire in 1914. Already 28, he took his chance and 14 Leicestershire wickets at Liverpool for 99 runs. *Wisden* reported that he broke both ways 'on the quick side of medium' and that 'a player of remarkable powers has been found'.

But Parkin's basic delivery, when he settled down after the war, was the medium-paced off-break from round the wicket to a short-leg field. It was only a basis though; he augmented it with his leg-break and googly, his swinger and yorker, so that setting a field for him was an impossibility when the batsman got on top. Parkin was hopelessly in love with experiment and variety, conjuring and fun. He must have been the Derek Randall of bowlers.

While a league pro in 1919 and 1920, playing for Lancashire in mid-week, Parkin was selected for the 1920/21 tour of Australia. If a record of 16 wickets at 41 wasn't outstanding, he was nevertheless the leading wicket-taker for an enfeebled England, as he was again in 1921. In the following four seasons he was probably at his peak, playing full time for Lancashire and twice taking two hundred wickets. But he was to play only one more Test match, against South Africa at Edgbaston in 1924.

That was the occasion when South Africa were dismissed for 30 by Maurice Tate and Arthur Gilligan. Parkin, although still widely regarded as England's premier bowler, never got on in that innings and was sparingly used in the second. He voiced his disappointment publicly about Gilligan's captaincy; or rather, the 'ghost' of his newspaper column vented all of Parkin's frustration for him without any discretion. The outburst effectively ended Parkin's Test career. He soon returned to the leagues where he was better able to indulge his comic, tragic traits.

Cecil Harry Parkin
(1886–1943)
Yorkshire, Lancashire and
England

FIRST-CLASS CAREER (1906–26)

| 239 innings | 33 not outs | 2425 runs | average 11.77 | 0 hundred |
| | 1048 wickets | 18434 runs | average 17.58 | 9–32 best |

ABOVE: *Parkin delivering what looks to have been an off-break for Lancashire in 1921*

TEST RECORD (10 MATCHES)

| 16 innings | 3 not outs | 160 runs | average 12.30 | — |
| | 32 wickets | 1128 runs | average 35.25 | 5–38 best |

Series	Tests	O	M	R	W	Av
1920/21 in A	5	211.2	29	670	16	41.87
1921 v A	4	121.5	21	420	16	26.25
1924 v SA	1	16	5	38	0	—

JACK GREGORY

*Jack Morrison Gregory
(1895–1973)
New South Wales and
Australia*

When Jack Gregory entered first-class cricket in 1919 it was still common practice for a batsman to dispense with a glove or two. Gregory often batted without them, but such was the impact of his bouncy bowling that by the dramatic end to his career in 1928/9 batting gloves were *de rigeur*.

Gregory took to fast bowling quite naturally as he was an all-round athlete. Besides being a fine left-handed hitter with the fastest Test century in terms of time to his name, and an exceptional slip-catcher (his 15 catches in the 1920/21 series against England has yet to be beaten by a non-keeper), he was outstanding at rugby, sprinting and hurdling. The hurdling came into his bowling when he leapt at and into the crease for the sake of bounce; his run-up was a modest 12 paces.

*Even in his last season
Gregory could make the ball
bounce enough to hit
Chapman, England's
captain, during the Brisbane
Test of 1928/9*

When the Australian Imperial Forces (AIF) were casting around Europe to find a fast bowler for the team which was to play the 1919 season in England, Gregory was no more than an artilleryman and a batsman with an insignificant record in Sydney grade cricket. He had, however, the right physique at 6′ 3½″; and he had the right pedigree since he was the nephew of Australia's first Test captain, Dave Gregory of Scottish origin. He duly made his first-class début in 1919 and took 131 wickets. When the AIF team went on to visit South Africa, Gregory was still fearsome (his best figures of nine for 32 came against Natal), and he had 198 wickets under his belt before he made a first-class appearance in Australia.

To judge by the archive film we have of him, Gregory was not fast by the standards of today because he did not put a lot of body into his bowling and follow-through. But what matters is that he was too much for the English batsmen of his post-war day, unused to cricket as they were, let alone to pace bowling. In the 1920/21 series his 23 wickets led the first five–nil thrashing in Test annals. In 1921, now firmly united with his hunting partner Ted McDonald, Gregory took 17 more wickets in the first three victories before the Australians sat on their lead. This tour was followed by another visit to South Africa where he hit his 70-minute century. He had been through three years which were crowded by any standard.

The reaction occurred in 1922 when Gregory had to have a knee cartilage removed. He was never the same bowler again, although he carried on until the First Test of 1928/9 when his knee went to pieces and he limped from the field forever. He enjoyed a long retirement as a recluse on the coast of New South Wales. But for a few short years his cricket had generated an electric quality.

FIRST-CLASS CAREER (1919–1928/9)

173 innings	18 not outs	5661 runs	average 36.52	13 hundreds
	504 wickets	10580 runs	average 20.99	9–32 best

TEST RECORD (24 MATCHES)

34 innings	3 not outs	1146 runs	average 36.96	2 hundreds
	85 wickets	2648 runs	average 31.15	7–69 best

Series	Tests	O	M	R	W	Av
1920/21 v E	5	208.2	29	556	23	24.17
1921 in E	5	182.2	35	552	19	29.05
1921/2 in SA	3	115.4	29	284	15	18.93
1924/5 v E	5	208.4 (8-ball)	22	816	22	37.09
1926 in E	5	105	20	298	3	99.33
1928/9 v E	1	41	3	142	3	47.33

TED McDONALD

Edgar Arthur McDonald
(1891–1937)
Tasmania, Victoria,
Australia and Lancashire

Ted McDonald was by no means the first overseas player to be invited to play county cricket. Quite apart from Spofforth, the Australians Midwinter and Ferris had joined Gloucestershire before the turn of the century; Sammy Woods had gone to Somerset; Trott and Tarrant to Middlesex, and Alan Marshal to Surrey. But McDonald was the first overseas star to be signed by a county.

For a fast bowler, he spent a considerable time reaching that status. Born in Tasmania, McDonald left his native Launceston under some kind of cloud – he was, until his death in a road accident, always a bit of a lad – and moved to Melbourne. He was developing as a bowler (and as a footballer and rugby player) when the war came, causing the Sheffield Shield to be suspended from 1915 to 1919. By the 1920/21 series he was in the Australian side, partnering Gregory, but took only six wickets in three Tests, owing partly to poor slip-catching.

In the 1921 series he broke the shoulder off one bat and took 27 wickets (against Gregory's 19) to extend to eight the sequence of Australian victories over England. Early on that tour, at Leicester, a photographer captured one of the game's great actions. Like Holding, McDonald had the capacity to ghost over the grass in his run of 15 paces, without leaving any trace. He could swing the ball both ways, or whip his wrist to produce some added pace. Like a later Lancastrian fast bowler he was double-jointed, and could clasp his hands in front of him, bring them over his head and rest them on his behind. His extraordinary arm-span, from fingertip to tip, was 6′ 4″.

Nelson of the Lancashire League signed him after the tour. Then the idea grew that since McDonald was residing in Lancashire he would qualify for the county in two years. The county bought him up for the fine sum of £500 a year, with an almost free house thrown in, to compensate him for no longer being eligible for Australia. He was worth it too, although he was 33 before he played county cricket. Between 1924 and 1931 he took 1053 wickets for Lancashire and won them four championships. Nobody has taken more wickets in a season for the county than McDonald's 198 in 1925.

While in the league and with Lancashire, McDonald learnt to accommodate himself to slow and wet pitches. He eventually bowled medium-paced off-breaks from round the wicket very presentably. But he was forever, in spirit, a fast bowler – moody, sardonic, a little like John Snow, seldom bothered to clean up cheap tail-enders. However, when confronted with Bradman in 1930, he lengthened his run, posted five slips, made the ball fly, and knocked his leg-stump out of the ground when the Boy Wonder had made nine. McDonald was 38 then, yet he was built perfectly for his job.

So how fast was he? It would be against the grain of all other athletic

Who could say that this man with the streamlined delivery – McDonald at Leicester in 1921 – would not have been a marvel in any age?

advances in this century if bowlers had not become faster with time. Perhaps McDonald was fast-medium by our standards, although anything must have seemed quick to English batsmen after four seasons lost to war. What is certain is that McDonald caused as much apprehension among batsmen of his day as Harold Larwood, Frank Tyson, and Malcolm Marshall all did in theirs.

FIRST-CLASS CAREER (1909/10–1931)

| 302 innings | 47 not outs | 2663 runs | average 10.44 | 1 hundred |
| | 1395 wickets | 28966 runs | average 20.76 | 8–41 best |

TEST RECORD (11 MATCHES)

| 12 innings | 5 not outs | 116 runs | average 16.57 | — |
| | 43 wickets | 1431 runs | average 33.27 | 5–32 best |

Series	Tests	O	M	R	W	Av
1920/21 v E	3	126	10	392	6	65.33
1921 in E	5	205.5	32	668	27	24.74
1921/2 in SA	3	149	48	371	10	37.10

CHARLIE PARKER

Charles Warrington
Leonard Parker
(1882–1959)
Gloucestershire and England

Around the turn of the century appeared a particular figure in the English first-class scene: the grammar school product who, by force of circumstance, had to play cricket as a professional. He had reached the same level of education as many amateurs, and post-1962 (when amateur status was abolished) he would have become a county captain in time. But in those days of rigid class divisions he was condemned to subservience.

Such a cricketer was Charlie Parker, a farm labourer's son who was educated at Cheltenham Grammar School. Furthermore, he rose to be the third highest of all wicket-takers in the first-class game with a wealth of illustrious feats to his name. Yet he was chosen but once to bowl his left-arm spin for England, against Australia in 1921, when he took two for 32 off 28 overs. He was not alone, of course, among professionals in feeling frustration at amateurs who sent their men over the top; but he was one of the few to vent it openly.

Parker first appeared for Gloucestershire in 1903; had he been born a decade or two later he might have been able to turn amateur like Wally Hammond of Cirencester Grammar. He was medium-paced until the war during which he served in the ranks of the Royal Flying Corps, and heard about the Russian Revolution – not without approval. After the war he cut down his pace but still pushed the ball through as he spun it, not flighting it like Rhodes. Always with a cap on and his sleeves unbuttoned, he then bowled at one end for Gloucestershire for season after season.

He was the first to achieve six hat tricks, two of them against Yorkshire, and one of them when he hit the stumps with five consecutive balls, only for the second to be called a no-ball. Seven times he captured 15 or more wickets in a match, a number surpassed by Freeman alone; nine times he took either nine or ten wickets in an innings, a number never exceeded. The week after his England début he took all ten against Somerset. But he never played for England again.

However, there was that famous Headingley Test of 1926 when Australia were sent in on a damp wicket, only for Macartney to hit a century before lunch. Parker had been chosen for the England party but was left out, to Australian consternation, in favour of Roy Kilner who was a defensive left-hander without Parker's power of spin. It is fairly certain that Parker was omitted because Warner, a selector that year, did not like his insubordination (is there something about left-arm spinners?). There was a hushed-up incident later, when Parker grabbed Warner in a Bristol hotel lift and threatened the *éminence grise* of English cricket.

Parker remained prolific until he was 50 and beyond: 1500 overs and two hundred wickets was about par for his seasonal course, even when Tom Goddard started to harvest his share at the other end. Together

From the fact that Parker gets in nice and close to the stumps here, one may deduce that the pitch is not offering a lot of spin

they would run amok at Bristol, Cheltenham and Gloucester, without receiving national attention. Parker, after a spell as a coach with Gloucestershire and at Cranleigh School, died in the unmerited obscurity which he never overcame during his life.

FIRST-CLASS CAREER (1903–35)

954 innings	195 not outs	7951 runs	average 10.47	0 hundred
	3278 wickets	63817 runs	average 19.46	10–79 best

TEST RECORD (1 MATCH)

1 innings	1 not out	3 runs	average —	—
	2 wickets	32 runs	average 16.00	2–32 best

Series	Tests	O	M	R	W	Av
1921 v A	1	28	16	32	2	16.00

The uncompromising mien well caught in 1929

MAURICE TATE

Several of the best spin bowlers have initially tried their hand at pace – Parker, Goddard and Rhodes, for example – before slowing down. It is rare for a man who has been bowling off-spin for ten years suddenly to change to a higher gear; rarer still for him to transform himself into the best medium-pacer of his generation.

Maurice Tate was not a complicated man by nature. When he was taken onto the Sussex groundstaff in 1912, he bowled slow-medium off-breaks largely because – one suspects – his father had done so. Maurice played a few county games before the war. Afterwards he used his powerful physique mainly for batting, and bowled his off-breaks – the odd quicker ball mixed in – part-time.

During the 1922 season all this changed, though the exact circumstances of time and place are disputed. In any event, by the end of the season Tate found himself running in with half-a-dozen paces, rocking back, banging down a size 11 boot and making the ball fizz off the pitch, sometimes swinging away as well. He used the same run-up as in his off-spinning days, about eight yards; it was one of his peculiarities to turn round clockwise at the start of his run, the opposite way to most right-arm bowlers.

Now that he was what we would call a 'seamer' in so many words, Tate was established at the best bowler in England. From 1923 to 1925 he did the double of a thousand runs and two hundred wickets (on only four other occasions in history has that been accomplished, including Hirst's double double). On his Test début against South Africa in 1924 he had eight wickets for 115. It was with renewed hope, based on the belief that some young bowlers had at last arrived, that MCC set off that winter to regain the Ashes.

Tate played his part to the full, but as England went down four–one the Yorkshire left-hander Kilner was the only other bowler of note (incidentally, Kilner bowled his slow left-arm over the wicket to a leg-side field, taking 17 wickets in three Tests). Otherwise, on the heartless turf, Tate alone stood between England and vast Australian totals. He took 38 out of England's 94 wickets in that series, more than any Englishman has managed in Australia. He often came off the pitch so rapidly that his keeper, Strudwick, had to stand back; and he varied his pace instinctively by means of his bodyswing. Yet he was at times in dreadful pain from a toe injury caused by the bone-hard grounds, and always had to wear a canvas girdle to support his stomach and lower back.

If he never achieved figures like those again, Tate remained England's first-choice bowler for another half-dozen years and took three times as many wickets during his Test career as the next England bowler. He remained the leader of Sussex's attack until 1937, making a fresh Hove

Maurice William Tate
(1895–1956)
Sussex and England

morning something to be dreaded when he was hitting 'the deck' hard. But then he suffered a fate similar to that of Alec Bedser, to whom he was so often compared.

Both carried England's attack in the years of post-war feebleness on willing shoulders, to be elbowed aside when a generation of outright fast bowlers grew up. Tate was taken on the 1932/3 Bodyline tour but was not wanted in Jardine's game-plan. Sussex treated their faithful cart horse more shamefully still so that he never had anything to do with the county again. Tate's fifties found the great, cheerful, lion-hearted bowler working in a Butlin's holiday camp. His opponents, at least, always respected him.

OPPOSITE: *Tate bowls for the Players against the Gentlemen at the Oval in 1925. The feet were huge. And (below) pulling his first pint as a Rotherfield landlord in 1950*

FIRST-CLASS CAREER (1912–37)

970 innings	102 not outs	21717 runs	average 25.01	23 hundreds
	2784 wickets	50571 runs	average 18.16	9–71 best

TEST RECORD (39 MATCHES)

52 innings	5 not outs	1198 runs	average 25.48	1 hundred
	155 wickets	4055 runs	average 26.16	6–42 best

Series	Tests	O	M	R	W	Av
1924 v SA	5	217.2	68	424	27	15.70
1924/5 in A	5	316 (8-ball)	62	881	38	23.18
1926 v A	5	208.3	64	388	13	29.84
1928 v WI	3	127	43	246	13	18.92
1928/9 in A	5	371	122	697	17	41.00
1929 v SA	3	162	43	333	10	33.30
1930 v A	5	280.1	82	574	15	38.26
1930/31 in SA	5	189.2	58	341	14	24.35
1931 v NZ	1	39	15	37	4	9.25
1932/3 in NZ	1	40	17	47	2	23.50
1935 v SA	1	31.3	7	87	2	43.50

GEORGE GEARY

George Geary
(1893–1981)
Leicestershire and England

George Geary was the pick of a group of professional bowlers who kept one end going between the wars for their unfashionable counties. His partner at Leicestershire, Ewart Astill, was another member of the group; so were the Hampshire pair of Alec Kennedy and Jack Newman; Jack Mercer of Glamorgan was another. They varied their pace around medium according to circumstances, for they had to bowl all day, rain or shine.

Strong, sturdy and controlled, Geary was medium-fast with a new ball and could swing it away after a brief run-up. Given the old ball he used his large hands for off-breaks or -cutters. But what set him apart was his leg-cutter, which once had Bradman caught at slip. While

Inswinger, off-cutter, leg-cutter: Geary was ready to bowl anything, on a good length, naturally

Kennedy was picked for only one series, and that effectively on a B tour to South Africa; while Astill had two such series, and Newman and Mercer never played for England at all, Geary was always in contention for the major Tests against Australia.

One of 16 children of a Barwell bootmaker, Geary had a career more laudable for the fact that his leg was badly damaged by a propeller during the war (after one hundred wickets in 1914), so that he had to miss two seasons. In 1928 he had to have an operation on his right elbow; happily he recovered for the winter tour to Australia. There he headed the Test bowling averages and bowled a spell of 81 overs in one innings for five wickets and 105 runs. It is worth noting that England's attack for those timeless Tests consisted of no more than four bowlers – Tate, Larwood, Geary and White – with Hammond lending an occasional hand.

On a tour of South Africa the previous winter, before the matting disappeared from there, Geary had cut the ball around so much as to take 12 for 130 in one Test and to be compared with Barnes. In helpful conditions he can't have been dissimilar. For Leicestershire against Glamorgan in 1929 he took all ten wickets from 16.2 overs in return for 18 runs.

It is well known that on his retirement Geary was appointed coach at Charterhouse, and that the young Peter May was one of his charges; less so that after retiring from Charterhouse at 65 he went to the nets at Rugby School, could not resist taking his coat off, and kept on bowling there until he was 76. He was renowned as a cheerful and considerate man. He deserved to keep going – with a plastic hip – in his longest spell of all, until the age of 87.

FIRST-CLASS CAREER (1912–38)

820 innings	138 not outs	13504 runs	average 19.80	8 hundreds
	2063 wickets	41339 runs	average 20.03	10–18 best

TEST RECORD (14 MATCHES)

20 innings	4 not outs	249 runs	average 15.56	—
	46 wickets	1353 runs	average 29.41	7–70 best

Series	Tests	O	M	R	W	Av
1924 v SA	1	11	5	21	0	—
1926 v A	2	74.3	15	188	3	62.66
1927/8 in SA	2	77.3	18	180	12	15.00
1928/9 in A	4	240.3	70	477	19	25.10
1929 v SA	2	108.3	46	189	7	27.00
1930 v A	1	35	10	95	1	95.00
1934 v A	2	88	17	203	4	50.75

TICH FREEMAN

Alfred Percy Freeman
(1888–1965)
Kent and England

Nobody better illustrates the changing nature of first-class cricket than 'Tich' Freeman. He was the second highest wicket-taker of all time: for eight consecutive years in the late 1920s and early 1930s he captured well over two hundred wickets a season; in 1928, uniquely, he took over three hundred wickets. And he did it all with leg-breaks and googlies.

There are more extraordinary statistics, such as that he took as many as 15 wickets in a match nine times, more often than anybody else. But not the least interesting is that he did not enter county cricket until the age of 26, and then the war eliminated the next four seasons. Thus, by the time he was 30, he had to his name 29 wickets for Kent. But this long wait at least allowed him to develop fully, unlike so many young leg-spinners who are superb in their teens then lose their skill when they mature.

This 5′ 2″ eastender had two other advantages: one was a strong and sinewy arm. The other was his very lack of height. Being so tiny he was able to release the ball upwards, and therefore had a natural teasing loop, unlike the tall spinner. Freeman's method could not have been better designed for the county cricket – as opposed to the Test cricket – of his period.

The breakdown of Freeman's dismissals is revealing. Almost an eighth of his wickets – 484 of them – came from stumpings (so many indeed that Kent's keeper Les Ames would make almost as many stumpings as catches in a season). Another half of Freeman's wickets were either bowled or LBW. The first figure suggests that batsmen did not deal very effectively with his leg-break, the second with his googly. For all but Freeman's last two seasons a right-handed batsman couldn't be dismissed LBW if the ball pitched outside his off-stump. In other words, a little of the modern technique of playing forward with the bat just behind pad might have largely scotched him.

To account for Freeman's relative lack of success at the highest level it is also necessary to understand the nature of the opposition he faced in county cricket. Many a county captain between the wars had to fill up his side with amateurs from club cricket and other part-timers like schoolmasters and even schoolboys. This sort of player, unrefined in footwork, was cannon-fodder for Freeman. Against the major counties of the day he wasn't anything like so devastating: against Surrey, for instance, his bowling average was 26, against Lancashire 24, whereas he rolled over the players of lowly Leicestershire and Northamptonshire for 11 runs each.

It was the same to a large extent in Test cricket. He ran through the inexperienced West Indians of 1928 when they made their first Test tour. The next summer the South Africans, never at their happiest against wrist-spin, again fell to Freeman until the final Test when he

conceded 169 runs for no wicket. On his two tours of Australia he fared well enough in state games but, as an English 'roller', he couldn't turn enough to worry the best batsmen. His eight wickets in 1924/5 were expensive; in 1928/9, just after setting his 304-wicket record, he wasn't given a game. It was never thought worthwhile to pit Freeman against the extraordinary phenomenon of Don Bradman. Indeed he did not get another game for England after 1929.

On the other hand, against anyone but the best (Bradman, Duleepsinhji, Hobbs) Freeman came the nearest there has been to an automatic wicket-taker. Against them he did enough to put his name into the record books with some feats that will never be surpassed.

FIRST-CLASS CAREER (1914–36)

716 innings	194 not outs	4961 runs	average 9.50	0 hundred
	3776 wickets	69577 runs	average 18.42	10–53 best

TEST RECORD (12 MATCHES)

16 innings	5 not outs	154 runs	average 14.00	—
	66 wickets	1707 runs	average 25.86	7–71 best

Series	Tests	O		M	R	W	Av
1924/5 in A	2	121	(8-ball)	16	459	8	57.37
1927/8 in SA	4	132.3		29	399	14	28.50
1928 v WI	3	140		50	302	22	13.72
1929 v SA	3	188.1		47	547	22	24.86

JACK WHITE

*John Cornish White
(1891–1961)
Somerset and England*

Jack or 'Farmer' White took more wickets than any other amateur barring W. G. Grace (if he can be called such). Yet White's reputation largely rests on what his slow left-arm accomplished on England's 1928/9 tour of Australia, when his 25 wickets were taken on pitches as kind as concrete. He is remembered for little else, although for Somerset he took a hundred wickets in 14 seasons, almost twice as often as the next man, Arthur Wellard, who did it eight times. White was a modest man, readier to talk about horse-racing than his successes, but tough and unsympathetic. Let it not be said that amateurs cannot play as hard as anyone.

In England, White was unfailingly effective but not outstandingly special: he simply bowled from one end for Somerset for summer after summer just as Parker did for the county to the north. He took his hundred or so (never more than 168) and made an unspectacular début for England in 1921, as so many others did. On English pitches he did not have the spin of Parker or the flight of Rhodes. From the age of 17 and his Somerset début in 1909 he hardly spun the ball at all.

While bowling for Somerset in 1926, White exhibits the amount of body that goes into slow bowling

However he was indefatigably accurate, and it was therefore a thoughtful piece of selection that led to White visiting Australia in Percy Chapman's team. He had a farmer's constitution and required it on

pitches still prepared – but not for much longer – with soil from Bulli Creek and designed to last. The final Test, when White led England in Chapman's absence, went on for eight days, the longest in history to that point. As England's stock bowler in the series he bowled a huge number of overs, pushing the ball through on off-stump or just outside, tying the batsman down, not losing his length by striving for spin, while Larwood, Tate and Geary took turns at the other end.

White enjoyed a Brisbane sticky. Then came the hard part. In consecutive innings White took one for 64 from 57 overs; five for 107 from 56.5 overs; five for 130 from 60 overs; eight for 126 from 64.5 overs; and two for 136 from 75.3 overs. In the innings when he had eight wickets, Australia were chasing 349 to win at Adelaide. Only White's nerve and accuracy kept them short of their goal by 12 runs.

As Somerset's captain he was no source of encouragement to the youth of his side, and he may not have been a very good England selector in 1929 and 1930 (the selection committee up till then always included an active player or two). But as an England bowler in Australia, where the temperament was nearer his own, he was liked for his unaffected manners. M. A. Noble wrote that White was the man who won that Ashes series: 'one of the most tireless workers with muscle and brain that this or any other England team has ever possessed'.

FIRST-CLASS CAREER (1909–37)

765 innings	102 not outs	12202 runs	average 18.40	6 hundreds
	2356 wickets	43759 runs	average 18.57	10–76 best

TEST RECORD (15 MATCHES)

22 innings	9 not outs	239 runs	average 18.38	—
	49 wickets	1581 runs	average 32.26	8–126 best

Series	Tests	O	M	R	W	Av
1921 v A	1	36	7	107	3	35.66
1928 v WI	1	27.3	10	53	3	17.66
1928/9 in A	5	406.4	134	760	25	30.40
1929 v SA	3	129	52	187	5	37.40
1930 v A	1	53	7	166	3	55.33
1930/31 in SA	4	148	43	308	10	30.80

CLARRIE GRIMMETT

Clarence Victor Grimmett (1891–1980) Wellington, Victoria, South Australia and Australia

If any young spin bowler should think that he is not receiving sufficient encouragement to become a Test cricketer, he should take heart from the life and times of Clarrie Grimmett. He had to move away from Dunedin, in the South Island of New Zealand, where he was born, to Wellington, where he was brought up, close to the Basin Reserve ground; thence across the Tasman to Sydney; then on to Melbourne and eventually Adelaide, where he finally found acceptance for his wrist-spin at the age of 32. Not discouraged, he went on to break the existing record aggregate of 189 Test wickets held by Barnes; to become the first bowler to take two hundred Test wickets; and to take more first-class wickets than any other bowler who has not played county cricket.

Grimmett had to emigrate to Australia, where he found a job as a sign-writer, because the Plunket Shield offered very limited scope. Bowling for Wellington he might get three first-class games a season, if picked. This was not enough for such an insatiable theorist and practiser. On the Melbourne leg of his journey he laid out a turf pitch in his back-yard and taught his dog to fetch the balls for him. Grimmett may have spent more time bowling in nets than anyone, even Geary.

He was as famous for his low bowling arm as for his fox-terrier. At Trent Bridge, once, a cameraman filmed over after over by Grimmett so that he has been better captured than any of his predecessors or contemporaries. This film confirms that he was almost round-arm, like a mid-Victorian. He usually bowled in the baggy green cap which had cost him so much single-minded devotion to acquire, and his stock ball was the leg-break. But among a host of variations in grip and trajectory he pioneered the 'flipper', that ball which is made to spin backwards so sharply as it goes through the air that it skids off the pitch, probably to catch a batsman LBW. He kept his googly for left-handers in the main, as the wrist movement involved led him to toss the ball higher, which he was loath to do.

When Australia first called on his services in 1924/5, Grimmett made no mistake: 11 English wickets for 82 runs. Soon he was half of Australia's attack, as crucial to their bowling as Bradman was to their batting. In the 1930 series in England, where he found the turf more responsive than at home, he had 29 wickets and 25 more in 1934. Over his Test career he averaged nearly six wickets per game.

By the 1935/6 visit to South Africa he was more devastating than ever – 44 wickets in the series, more than anyone bar Barnes and Laker. Yet that was the end! It is said that Bradman had it in for him; certainly anno Domini didn't. As late as 1939/40, when he was 49, the little wizened magician was taking 73 wickets for South Australia in the Sheffield Shield season, another record. After so many years of waiting, he was determined to enjoy his success while it lasted.

FIRST-CLASS CAREER (1910/11–1940/41)

| 321 innings | 54 not outs | 4720 runs | average 17.67 | 0 hundred |
| | 1424 wickets | 31740 runs | average 22.28 | 10–37 best |

TEST RECORD (37 MATCHES)

| 50 innings | 10 not outs | 557 runs | average 13.92 | — |
| | 216 wickets | 5231 runs | average 24.21 | 7–40 best |

Series	Tests	O	M	R	W	Av
1924/5 v E	1	31.3 (8-ball)	5	82	11	7.45
1926 in E	3	194	59	414	13	31.84
1928/9 v E	5	398.2	96	1024	23	44.52
1930 in E	5	349.4	78	925	29	31.89
1930/31 v WI	5	239.2	60	593	33	17.96
1931/2 v SA	5	306	108	557	33	16.87
1932/3 v E	3	147	41	326	5	65.20
1934 in E	5	396.3	148	668	25	26.72
1935/6 in SA	5	346.1	140	642	44	14.59

Note how much closer than his contemporaries Grimmett got to the stumps, in this case at Leyton in 1930. With his low arm he was bowling wicket to wicket

HAROLD LARWOOD

*Harold Larwood
(1904–   )
Nottinghamshire and
England*

We have the word of Sir Leonard Hutton that Harold Larwood was the best and fastest bowler he faced, and the most beautiful in action. And quite conceivably he was the best fast bowler the world had seen until that stage, although the Australian Ted McDonald – who finished before Hutton began – had his advocates.

On the Bodyline tour, Larwood routed the Australian batsmen as never before on their own hard grounds. Bouncers had been an occasional weapon in the hands of Gregory and McDonald, and of Cotter and Jones – the Australian fast bowler at the turn of the century who was called for throwing. When Larwood bowled in 1932/3 the bouncer became frequent, and so threatened chests, heads and the game's well-being that a law against intimidating the batsman had to be quickly passed. Jardine's Bodyline strategy, I have to say, was unethical by the standards of the day – a phenomenon 50 years ahead of its time. Bodyline was exactly what Lillee and Thomson bowled in their prime. The West Indians – and anybody else capable of doing so – have also bowled Bodyline except for the leg-side fields.

But there is another point about Larwood's bowling in the understanding of that historic controversy, and it has been something of a sacred cow, unmentionable until now: surviving film shows Larwood bending his back for one bouncer, and doing the same to his elbow. Of course, while he may possibly have been the first fast bowler to do this when summoning up an 'effort ball', he was certainly not the last. A few fast bowlers, otherwise perfectly legitimate, will privately admit that they throw the odd quicker ball, at times without knowing what they do.

By one means or another Larwood on the Bodyline tour enjoyed an ascendancy which he had never before known in his Test career. He so softened up Ponsford and Woodfull, McCabe and Bradman, that 16 of his 33 wickets in the series were actually bowled. Until then a bouncer had been something a batsman was normally expected to hook. Larwood's quicker bouncer – he seems to have had a legitimate version, too – was altogether different in kind to anything before. His would reach Les Ames on the up, while other bouncers died around the keeper's feet.

Larwood came from the classic fast bowling background: he was the son of a Methodist miner in Nuncargate and a miner himself until he was taken on the Nottinghamshire staff at 18. Work underground as a pit-pony boy strengthened his back for the tasks ahead, but the miner cannot afford to be a big man. Larwood, we should not forget, was 5′ 7½″ tall.

Above ground Larwood, like the young Fred Trueman, was tended as carefully as a thoroughbred colt since England then had no other fast

bowler. He made his début for England in 1926 and helped them to win the final Test of the series, and the Ashes, as Trueman did in 1953. His first of only two overseas tours was to Australia in 1928/9 when his wickets cost 40 runs each. In 1930 his four wickets in three Tests cost 73 runs each. Even doped marled pitches and the name of Bradman are not sufficient to account for such undistinguished figures. His success on the next tour of Australia represents a vast leap forward.

In the course of his finest hours Larwood damaged his left foot so badly, by pounding it against the concrete, that he missed the next season and was not the same bowler again. But he publicly declared that he didn't want to play against Australia in 1934. He was tired of the controversy that raged around his head – and he had only been carrying out the instructions which Jardine had given to him and Voce. In 1936 the flame flared, off a short run, but was soon extinguished.

After the Second World War, Larwood and his family emigrated to a better life in Australia. There the great bowler was mainly welcomed and honoured because people realised that he did what he did under orders. However, the television series called *Bodyline*, nationalistically pro-Australian, led to a spurt of hate mail. An old man deserved better, especially one who had in his time extended the frontiers of fast bowling.

FIRST-CLASS CAREER (1924–38)

438 innings	72 not outs	7290 runs	average 19.91	3 hundreds
	1427 wickets	24994 runs	average 17.51	9–41 best

TEST RECORD (21 MATCHES)

28 innings	3 not outs	485 runs	average 19.40	—
	78 wickets	2216 runs	average 28.41	6–32 best

Note: Elsewhere, Larwood's Test bowling figures are erroneously given as 78 wickets, 2212 runs, average 28.35

Series	Tests	O	M	R	W	Av
1926 v A	2	95	19	252	9	28.00
1928 v WI	2	50	13	114	6	19.00
1928/9 in A	5	259.1	41	728	18	40.44
1929 v SA	3	102.4	34	186	8	23.25
1930 v A	3	101	18	292	4	73.00
1931 v NZ	1	did not bowl				
1932/3 in A	5	220.2	42	644	33	19.51

BILL VOCE

That Bill Voce's name will be forever associated with Bodyline is in many ways unfortunate for him. He was not by any means at his best or fastest during the series in Australia in 1932/3. Yet the film we have of that series shows Voce bowling rather ponderously – he was handicapped by injury and missed the Fourth Test – at a pace we would now consider medium. He was better than that.

William Voce
(1909–84)
Nottinghamshire and
England

When he made his first-class début in 1927, Voce was actually a medium-pace left-arm spinner and kept relapsing into that mode during his career. He hailed from the same area of the Nottinghamshire coalfield as Larwood, and was playing for Annesley Colliery Second XI when recommended to the county by one of their many miner-cricketers Fred Barratt (Joe Hardstaff senior and Sam Staples were others).

It was only in 1928 that Voce started to inswing the ball at greater speed and thereafter combined the two styles, with pace for preference. Thus in his second Test in 1929/30 he took 11 wickets against West Indies on the matting at Port-of-Spain. On this occasion he was bowling his medium-paced spinners from his unusual height with a natural nip off the pitch. The next winter he was England's leading bowler in South Africa with 23 wickets. He had played in nine Tests abroad before making his home début, and this was the pattern for his whole career. Only five of his 27 Tests were at home, at the rate of one per series, and none of them against Australia.

Politics had most to do with that omission. In 1934 at Trent Bridge, in the game between Nottinghamshire and the Australians, Voce took eight for 66 in the tourists' first innings. He did not bowl in their second. 'Strained side' the county officials stated. 'Strained relations, more likely' said Larwood.

As his partner declined, Voce was over-bowled, batted too much, and suffered from poor slip-catching. In those days it was reckoned to be good going if every other chance was held. Nevertheless Voce reached a peak on the 1936/7 tour of Australia when he dominated the first two Tests with 17 wickets for 133 runs. As well-built as Bedser, he hit the pitch hard, but for actual speed he was rated no faster than Bowes by the Australian observer, Ray Robinson. Scantly supported, Voce nearly but not quite prevented Bradman from bouncing back to win the rubber.

He did not make a clean break as Larwood did. Instead he toured Australia after the Second World War for a third time when a stout 37, which again did nothing for his reputation. As Nottinghamshire's coach he played odd games for them up till 1952. By then there was little in Voce's bowling to remind batsmen of the days when he and Larwood would go for a few lunchtime pints at a Trent Bridge pub and, on the way back to bowl, make playful bets between themselves as to who would make the first direct hit of the afternoon session.

Voce works up so much pace, when bowling for the Rest of England at the Oval in 1932, that the non-striker is most reluctant to get to the other end

FIRST-CLASS CAREER (1927–52)

525 innings	130 not outs	7590 runs	average 19.21	4 hundreds
	1558 wickets	35961 runs	average 23.08	8–30 best

TEST RECORD (27 MATCHES)

38 innings	15 not outs	308 runs	average 13.39	—
	98 wickets	2733 runs	average 27.88	7–70 best

Series	Tests	O	M	R	W	Av
1929/30 in WI	4	188.2	35	584	17	34.35
1930/31 in SA	5	250.4	65	561	23	24.39
1931 v NZ	1	42	12	100	0	—
1932 v I	1	29	9	51	5	10.20
1932/3 in A	4	133.3	23	407	15	27.13
1932/3 in NZ	2	32.3	6	62	5	12.40
1936 v I	1	40	10	86	1	86.00
1936/7 in A	5	162.1 (8-ball)	20	560	26	21.53
1937 v NZ	1	43.1	10	115	5	23.00
1946 v I	1	26	8	46	1	46.00
1946/7 in A	2	44 (8-ball)	12	161	0	—

AMAR SINGH

His may not be a familiar name but this Indian medium-pacer had won praise from all who had seen him by the time of his early death. As a 21 year old on India's 1932 tour of England, Amar Singh took 111 first-class wickets at an average of 20, and *Wisden* said of him: 'Better bowling than his in the second innings of the Test match has not been seen for a long time, and more than one famous old cricketer said afterwards that Amar Singh was the best bowler seen in England since the war'.

A Hindu, not a Sikh, he was born in Rajkot in north-western India – which was fortunate for him because it was where Ranjitsinhji went to school and one of the main areas of cricket activity as a consequence. His elder brother was L. Ramji, an all-out pace bowler for India. Before touring England, Amar Singh was coached in India by the Australian Frank Tarrant, but nothing could fully have prepared him for an experience so strange. One of the few advantages Amar Singh had was to have played in communal cricket, where the atmosphere was like a Test match as Hindus tried to defeat Muslims or Parsis.

He had an ungainly run-up; his action was chest-on; and he was utterly inexperienced. Yet none of this prevented him bowling outswing and inswing with fizz off the pitch. 'Physically built like a whip, Amar Singh's bowling was like the cracking of one' says another account. He had wiry muscles in his back and shoulders, and a wrist – underneath buttoned sleeves – that was full of snap. The standard comparison was with Tate, but Amar Singh could also off-cut the ball on worn or matting pitches.

He was the first to take a hundred wickets in the Ranji Trophy, and his first-class career average stands out among Indian bowlers for being less than 20. If his Test figures are not so impressive, then many of All-India's games in the 1930s were not classified as Tests; moreover he was dead at 29. Still, at Lord's in 1936, he took four for ten in his first nine overs, and six England wickets in all (Gubby Allen the least of them as a batsman) for 35 runs; and in the Madras Test of 1933/4 he had seven for 86 off 44.4 overs. As one example of his bowling at the top level but outside Tests, Amar Singh took 11 for 96 against Lord Tennyson's MCC team of 1937/8 to give India victory by an innings.

He was a fine all-rounder as well, an aggressive hitter who habitually scored at a run a minute, and was the first Indian to become a star in the Lancashire League. But on the outbreak of war he had returned to Jamnagar, where he was playing for the late Ranji's state team, when he suffered a fatal attack of pneumonia.

Ladhabhai Nakum Amar Singh
(1910–40)
Patiala, Western India, Nawanagar, Hindus and India

FIRST-CLASS CAREER (1930/31–39/40)

149 innings	12 not outs	3338 runs	average 24.36	5 hundreds
	498 wickets	9199 runs	average 18.47	8–23 best

Cricket contained novelty in the days when a country could tour England with every player a newcomer

TEST RECORD (7 MATCHES)

14 innings	1 not outs		292 runs	average 22.46		—	
	28 wickets		858 runs	average 30.64		7–86 best	

Series	Tests	O	M	R	W	Av
1932 in E	1	72.1	23	159	4	39.75
1933/4 v E	3	163.5	39	382	14	27.28
1936 in E	3	127.4	33	317	10	31.70

BILL O'REILLY

If Spofforth was the finest bowler of cricket's early years, and Barnes the pick between him and the First World War, Bill O'Reilly was *the* bowler of the inter-war period. Like Spofforth and Barnes, and Lillee later, he had the savage intensity of the champion bowler, the primitive hostility of the hunter tracking his prey until he succeeds. O'Reilly bowled with a grudge for he had the sense of injustice that an Australian country boy felt towards the city, that an Irishman in Australia felt towards the Anglo-Saxon, and that a bowler had in the days when pitches were covered and made for batsmen.

Like nobody else, O'Reilly took 20 wickets or more in four consecutive Ashes series, from 1932/3 to 1938. In 19 Tests against England he claimed 102 wickets, and he did it all in an idiosyncratic way for he was as much his own man in leg-spin as he was in other walks of life. Hailing from the same region of New South Wales as his contemporary Bradman, he did not know the luxury of being coached since all the cricket facilities were then concentrated in the capital city of each state. He had to work out his own grip, and forever after he held the ball with his first two fingers, the last two being tucked between it and the palm of his hand. It meant that he was a roller, not a ripper like Arthur Mailey, but he turned the ball enough on all except the truest wickets (except that he would not have called them that).

He was classified early on as a medium-pacer, by Bradman among others; he was certainly brisk for a leg-spinner and liked the wind behind him, another oddity. The run-up was theatre in itself: a long, bucketing approach to wind up for the act of delivery, then a bit of a stoop on a bent right knee at the vital moment. This too the Sydney coaches wanted to correct but 'the Tiger' was having nothing of it. He was given two games for New South Wales in 1927/8, then forgotten. He qualified as a schoolmaster, like his father before him, and was sent back up-country, out of selectorial sight and mind. But there in the bush, if not the wilderness, he streamlined his googly and gave it more bounce or venom than his leg-break. When he returned to the city he was picked again for his state in 1931/2 and recognised for the original talent that he was.

O'Reilly's first series against England was renowned for Bodyline: the fact that he took ten wickets to send England to their one defeat has been forgotten, so too the fact that he finished with only six fewer wickets than Larwood and bowled 383.4 eight-ball overs. In 1934 he took 28 of England's wickets, including three of the best in four balls at Old Trafford, the nearest he ever got to a hat trick. In 1936/7 his swag was another 25 wickets, and in 1938 at the Oval he alone stood between England and a total of a thousand. By then England's right-handed batsmen, especially Wally Hammond whom he had long shackled, had decided to take guard on or outside leg-stump; and on over-marled

William Joseph O'Reilly (1905–   )
New South Wales and Australia

85

The original caption to this photograph was, quite understandably, 'O'Reilly, the Australian fast bowler'

pitches O'Reilly could do little but maintain line and length, curse beneath and over his breath, and bide his time.

He did play one more Test after the war when 40, but the game was not recognised as such until a couple of years afterwards – and he routed

New Zealand so decisively that the two countries didn't meet again for almost 30 years. In Sydney grade cricket he routed almost everyone to top the averages for 12 seasons. Nobody was more respected if he was on your side, or feared if he was an opponent.

FIRST-CLASS CAREER (1927/8–45/6)

167 innings	41 not outs	1655 runs	average 13.13	0 hundred
	774 wickets	12850 runs	average 16.60	9–38 best

TEST RECORD (27 MATCHES)

39 innings	7 not outs	410 runs	average 12.81	—
	144 wickets	3254 runs	average 22.59	7–54 best

Series	Tests	O	M	R	W	Av
1931/2 v SA	2	90.4	28	174	7	24.85
1932/3 v E	5	383.4	144	724	27	26.81
1934 in E	5	333.4	128	698	28	24.92
1935/6 in SA	5	250.2	112	460	27	17.03
1936/7 v E	5	247.6 (8-ball)	89	555	25	22.20
1938 in E	4	263	78	610	22	27.72
1945/6 in NZ	1	9	6	33	8	4.12

BILL BOWES

William Eric Bowes
(1908–1987)
Yorkshire and England

Bill Bowes was one of the finest medium-pacers in English conditions, comparable with Derek Shackleton or Tom Cartwright or Les Jackson. Indeed Bowes and Maurice Tate, by their successes, did much to shape the subsequent pattern of English bowling.

Being an arm bowler – that is, with little body in his follow-through – he was not rated a good prospect for overseas tours. He was chosen only for the Bodyline tour of Australia and New Zealand, and it is a measure of his pace that when Don Bradman went to pull his first ball in the Melbourne Test, from Bowes, he got a bottom-edge and played on. In New Zealand shortly afterwards, in greener conditions, Bowes took six for 34 in the Auckland Test, but the level of cricket was not high: New Zealand's best batsman, Dempster, turned up late for the start; all of Bowes' six victims were bowled, and Hammond helped himself to 336 not out in 318 minutes.

At home, on a cloudy morning at Bramall Lane or Park Avenue or

Not much of a follow-through but the maximum control, of body and ball, in lieu of pace

Headingley, Bowes was another proposition. On the MCC groundstaff (he was exceptional in reaching Yorkshire that way) he had learnt inswing and outswing; coming into the Yorkshire side in 1929 he was taught everything else there was to know. For his wedding present Bowes was given a barometer by the all-rounder Emmott Robinson, to know when a wet wicket was in the offing. He and Verity were so thoroughly tutored by Rhodes and Robinson that they became as masterly as the masters. If Yorkshire supply more bowlers than any other county to this volume, it is largely because their collective wisdom used to be passed on.

Bowes was never found wanting by England so long as the match was at home. Even Bradman could not seriously disrupt his length, accuracy and movement. When Bradman hit 304 at Headingley, Bowes looked intrepidly back through his spectacles and responded with six for 142 from 50 overs, while his colleagues took three wickets for over four hundred runs. In the next Test at the Oval, while Bradman hit 244 and 77, Bowes had four for 164 and five for 55. In all three of those innings he had Bradman's wicket, twice bowled. His Test average of 22 is very low for a bowler of the high-scoring thirties; but too often someone of greater pace, like Allen, Clark, Farnes or Gover, was preferred as a spearhead.

He had a large, almost Viking, but none too strong physique which had to be nourished with two raw eggs every morning. As a prisoner-of-war Bowes could not afford the loss of four-and-a-half stone; he was not so substantial as a shadow of his former self when he gamely returned for two more seasons after the Second World War. Thereafter he was popular as a cricket correspondent, and one of the most fondly regarded of old England players.

FIRST-CLASS CAREER (1928–47)

326 innings	148 not outs	1530 runs	average 8.59	0 hundred
	1639 wickets	27470 runs	average 16.76	9–121 best

TEST RECORD (15 MATCHES)

11 innings	5 not outs	28 runs	average 4.66	—
	68 wickets	1519 runs	average 22.33	6–33 best

Series	Tests	O		M	R	W	Av
1932 v I	1	44		18	79	6	13.16
1932/3 in A	1	23		2	70	1	70.00
1932/3 in NZ	1	21		5	38	6	6.33
1934 v A	3	144.3		27	483	19	25.42
1935 v SA	4	178.4		43	412	14	29.42
1938 v A	2	75.4		12	188	10	18.80
1939 v WI	2	70	(8-ball)	16	176	11	16.00
1946 v I	1	29		8	73	1	73.00

HEDLEY VERITY

Hedley Verity
(*1905–43*)
Yorkshire and England

As a slow-medium left-arm spinner Hedley Verity has been consistently compared with Derek Underwood. But, unlike Underwood, Verity for the whole of his career could enjoy pitches that were uncovered, except at the ends, once a match had started. Equipped with this method he was the 'Deadly' of his day. In an era of timeless Tests and Bradman's batting, Verity averaged less than 15 runs per wicket, the lowest by any major bowler since the First World War.

Although he soon appeared for Yorkshire Second XI as a batsman and distinctly medium-paced bowler, Verity was 25 before he made his first-class début for them. His apprenticeship was mostly spent as a professional in leagues in Yorkshire and Lancashire, which may also account for his pushing the ball through with little flight. Yet he immediately filled Rhodes' boots.

In his first full season he was selected for England, ahead of White or Parker. The next season he took all ten wickets in an innings for the *second* time, and for ten runs – the cheapest 'all ten' in history. It was a genuine performance too, not a matter of a succession of tail-enders and club batsmen getting stumped. Nottinghamshire had led Yorkshire on first innings and their batting went so deep that their number 11 was Sam Staples, who had done the double. Eight of the wickets fell to catches, mostly around the bat.

Bill Bowes recorded how he and Verity used to be lectured every evening by Rhodes and Robinson. They were told to write down in a notebook all their observations of players and their weaknesses, of pitches and umpires. In many ways the standard of county cricket has improved, but there is not the same transmission of knowledge that there was in Verity's time. Too many alternative amusements exist to distract.

On unresponsive pitches, especially overseas, Verity was often criticised for pushing the ball through automatically: so he was the fore-runner of the modern slow left-armer. On these occasions he saw himself as the stock bowler, set about doing his job well and normally did so – the only slip-ups coming when Frank Woolley or the South African Jock Cameron adjusted to his predictability of length and pace. Verity's basic variation was an even quicker ball with the arm, often a yorker.

But these odd moments were nothing compared to his hours and years of supremacy. For Yorkshire he was forever taking seven for 20 or eight for 40, figures of which today's spinner may only dream. For England he had a triumph at Lord's in 1934 when firstly he caught-and-bowled Bradman on a dry pitch, then trapped the Australians on a wet if not sticky one, so that in a single day he took 14 wickets for 80 runs off 44.3 overs. Bradman in his second innings was caught off a cross-batted swipe at Verity, born of frustration. Strangely, Verity's success was achieved from the pavilion end.

Thorough and methodical in his private life as well as his cricket, Verity prepared for war by studying military tactics. Although a professional, he was commissioned as a captain in the Green Howards – times had changed since the days of Colin Blythe – and he was leading his men into action in Italy when fatally wounded. He was 38, the same age as his predecessor. But Verity had perhaps more life and more cricket in him. In his final innings he had taken seven Sussex wickets for nine runs.

Balance and strength – albeit slightly stiff – exemplified by Verity in the 1933 match between Yorkshire, the Champion County, and the Rest of England

FIRST-CLASS CAREER (1930–39)

| 416 innings | 106 not outs | 5603 runs | average 18.07 | 1 hundred |
| | 1956 wickets | 29146 runs | average 14.90 | 10–10 best |

TEST RECORD (40 MATCHES)

| 44 innings | 12 not outs | 669 runs | average 20.90 | — |
| | 144 wickets | 3510 runs | average 24.37 | 8–43 best |

Series	Tests	O	M	R	W	Av
1931 v NZ	2	34.4	12	85	4	21.25
1932/3 in A	4	135	54	271	11	24.63
1932/3 in NZ	1	26	8	64	1	64.00
1933 v WI	2	79.1	28	153	7	21.85
1933/4 in I	3	157.5	61	387	23	16.82
1934 v A	5	271.2	93	576	24	24.00
1935 v SA	4	172	78	250	12	20.83
1936 v I	3	114.1	44	228	15	15.20
1936/7 in A	5	195.7 (8-ball)	57	445	10	44.50
1937 v NZ	1	39	20	81	2	40.50
1938 v A	4	154.1	53	354	14	25.58
1938/9 in SA	5	283.2 (8-ball)	89	552	19	29.05
1939 v WI	1	30 (8-ball)	7	54	2	27.00

LEARIE CONSTANTINE

Lord Learie Nicholas Constantine (1901–71) Trinidad, Barbados and West Indies

Learie Constantine was possibly not the best fast bowler to have been produced by the West Indies before the Second World War. Herman Griffith and George Francis were formidable forerunners of the West Indian fast bowlers of today, while we have the word of C. L. R. James that George John should be accorded the title. But John was nearing 40 when he was taken on the 1923 tour of England and given his only regular experience of first-class cricket. Through lack of opportunity he, like many another, could not demonstrate to the world how good he was.

Nor was Constantine great by any analysis of his Test figures. He was given 18 opportunities but could not make a lot of them. At times he kept his place in the West Indies team on the strength of his fielding, electric as it was, and in the hope that he would come off with a burst of hitting. He did so at Lord's in 1928 when he enjoyed the match of his life against Middlesex, scoring 86 and a century in little more than an hour for each. But that sort of thing doesn't happen in Test cricket; so in batting too he was a disappointment until the last series of his career.

The fact is that Constantine took a long time to fulfil his potential as a bowler and when he did, in his and the decade's late thirties, it was as a medium-pacer. As a fast bowler, which he was during the 1920s, he was too short to obtain much bounce and relied on pace, and variations of it. He ran in energetically from 19 yards, sleeves buttoned to the wrist, and looked skywards in the moment before delivery. But the results, save when he did the double in 1928 (the only tourist to achieve this since the Great War apart from Mankad), were seldom out of the ordinary. On his own he could not uphold the bowling of a weak, faction-ridden team as George Headley could its batting, although he was effective as a first change behind Martindale and Hylton in 1934/5.

The year of 1929 marked the start of the turning point: Constantine then became the first black cricketer to be given a professional post in the Lancashire League, and in the subsequent decade (during which he won the league for Nelson eight times) his bowling matured. As a pro he had to bowl from one end throughout an innings, so he was forced to modify to medium-pace while retaining a faster ball, if needs be a bouncer. Indeed in 1933 he and Manny Martindale were ordered to bowl Bodyline at England, and did so from round the wicket at Jardine, though it was a waste of energy on a typically slow Old Trafford pitch.

If anything, Constantine would attempt too much variation, especially slow googlies, and he was criticised on this score during the Lord's Test of 1939. But in the last two Tests he was more disciplined and took 11 wickets, including his best Test figures, and 103 wickets on the tour at an average of 17. Constantine therefore was great in that he trod alone

Always experimenting, Constantine goes round the wicket, as he did when trying Bodyline against England in 1933

where no black cricketer had gone before. He showed the three W's and Sobers and the whole subsequent line of fast bowlers how to earn a living by playing cricket in England, and how to acquire an all-purpose, controlled technique at the same time. Thereby he opened up the largest reserve of talent the game has known.

FIRST-CLASS CAREER (1921/2–45)

| 197 innings | 11 not outs | 4475 runs | average 24.05 | 5 hundreds |
| | 439 wickets | 8991 runs | average 20.48 | 8–38 best |

TEST RECORD (18 MATCHES)

| 33 innings | 0 not outs | 635 runs | average 19.24 | — |
| | 58 wickets | 1746 runs | average 30.10 | 5–75 best |

Series	Tests	O	M	R	W	Av
1928 in E	3	71.4	19	262	5	52.40
1929/30 v E	3	163.4	42	497	18	27.61
1930/31 in A	5	127.3	15	407	8	50.87
1933 in E	1	25	5	55	1	55.00
1934/5 v E	3	114.1	36	197	15	13.13
1939 in E	3	71.3 (8-ball)	8	328	11	29.81

TOM GODDARD

*Thomas William John
Goddard
(1900–66)
Gloucestershire and England*

Only Charlie Parker has bowled more overs and taken more wickets for Gloucestershire than Tom Goddard, and only Parker among the leading all-time wicket-takers has been less regarded by the England selectors. Goddard may not have been a man of comely or even attractive aspect, but he took a hundred wickets in 16 seasons and he was the most prolific of all off-spinners.

Goddard was a convert from pace bowling, like many a spinner, who requires physical strength as much as a fast bowler. He took one of his six hat tricks during his years with this method, which lasted until 1927 (another hat trick occurred in South Africa in one of his eight Tests). The following season the county saw no further use for him, which would have been the end of his career but for his captain Bev Lyon getting him onto the MCC groundstaff to practise the off-spin which Goddard had occasionally tried in the nets. He certainly had an enormous hand to turn to it; he had the height to make his off-breaks bounce towards his short-legs; and he had nip off the pitch, if not flight through the air.

Having seen the light on the St John's Wood Road, Goddard returned to Gloucestershire in 1929 to take 184 wickets. In 1930 he claimed the wicket – 'how wuz thaat?' – which gave his county a tie against the

An exemplary high action, side-on, with plenty of shoulder. But he takes a long delivery stride: to loop the ball you need to spend time on the front foot

Australians at Bristol, and he won his first cap at Old Trafford. He fared presentably but it was his last Test until 1937, his big year, when his 248 wickets included 17 in a day against Kent at Bristol, and six for 29 when he scuppered New Zealand.

In return for his long wait to become an established bowler – he was 28 when he broke through – Goddard saw several developments during his career which aided the off-spinner's lot. One was that the habitually slow pitches at Bristol were sprinkled with sand, simply to help him, Parker and Sinfield – there being no TCCB pitches subcommittee busily laying down requirements. In 1939 Goddard had 84 wickets at Bristol alone at knockdown prices, and another year when Somerset were dismissed for 25 (Goddard took five wickets for four in three overs), their captain likened the strip to Weston-super-Mare's beach. Cheltenham's conditions weren't exactly adverse either, as both Parker and Goddard had a slope in their favour.

Another incentive for off-spinners (and inswingers) was provided in 1935 when the far-reaching change in the LBW law was made. Henceforth, as today, a ball pitching *outside* off-stump could win a decision, providing the pads were in line with the wickets and the ball would have hit. Slow off-spinners had been few until then – as opposed to the Lohmann, J. T. Hearne type – but now with Goddard and the new law they proliferated. In 1939 a further encouragement was given to bowlers by widening the wicket from eight to nine inches.

Goddard's 238 wickets in 1947 remains the most in a season since the war. A little dour in character, as you'd expect from his flight, he kept on bowling – without curing the revealingly long stride which preceded his quicker ball – until he went off to his carpet and furniture business at the age of 52. He returned next season when the county were short. But for pleurisy, and insufficient responses to his booming 'how wuz thaat?', he would have reached his coveted target of three thousand wickets.

FIRST-CLASS CAREER (1922–52)

775 innings	218 not outs	5234 runs	average 9.39	0 hundred
	2979 wickets	59116 runs	average 19.84	10–113 best

TEST RECORD (8 MATCHES)

5 innings	3 not outs	13 runs	average 6.50	—
	22 wickets	588 runs	average 26.72	6–29 best

Series	Tests	O	M	R	W	Av
1930 v A	1	32.1	14	49	2	24.50
1937 v NZ	2	60.4	20	143	8	17.87
1938/9 in SA	3	105 (8-ball)	26	282	8	35.25
1939 v WI	2	20.6 (8-ball)	2	114	4	28.50

*Old glory: Sobers in his last
Test series in England*

*Gibbs in his last Test series, and
the arm is still high*

Trueman side-on as ever, even when playing for Derbyshire in 1970

John Snow's Test trial at Worcester in 1974

OPPOSITE *Stars like Chandra inspired the subcontinental boom of the 1970s*

Perfection

Magnifique, but it's not spin bowling

The unrelenting hunter

In 1974/5 Thommo ushers in the brave new world of cricket with a throat ball to Greig

OVERLEAF *Roberts recording his best Test figures of seven for 54, at Perth in 1975/6*

ERIC HOLLIES

Eric Hollies was one of those leg-spinners of a peculiarly English type: one who went for accuracy first, spin second (though enough to make the ball drift into the right-hander), and was therefore a stock bowler suitable for all the eventualities of his day. This was as well because in 1946, when Warwickshire had only three professionals, Hollies had to bowl so much that he took more wickets (180) than anyone else in a season for the county.

Hollies began as a very slow leg-breaker – his father was a lob bowler – but, endlessly cheerful chap though he was, the assault he suffered at the hands of Hammond in his second county match (one for 150) persuaded him to push the ball through. He had been forced to move from Old Hill in his native Staffordshire to qualify by a year's residence for Warwickshire. But it was worth the wait as he ended up with most wickets for the county, 2201.

*William Eric Hollies
(1912–81)
Warwickshire and England*

One of the slowest of slow bowlers, nevertheless with a full, sweeping follow-through. Without it a ball sits up to be hit

By 1934/5 – it's significant that he was established before the change in the LBW law which stimulated off-break bowling – he was being selected for England in the West Indies. At Georgetown he recorded seven for 50, four of them leg-before, thanks to the top-spinner which was his principal variation (one of the umpires was a 'neutral', the Australian Arthur Richardson). He would have made his home Test début the next summer but after his name had been announced, a Warwickshire team-mate burst into his hotel bedroom one night under the mistaken impression that it was his own, and sat down on Hollies' neck.

The pain in it must have lasted some while since Hollies did not represent England again for 12 years. Then, against South Africa in 1947, he saved a match with his batting, although he played for a quarter of a century without making a 50 and registered more wickets than runs in his first-class career.

With his second ball at Don Bradman from over the wicket at the Oval in 1948, he bowled the greatest of run-makers. This was the googly which Hollies ill disguised and seldom used (left-handers were therefore his special bane as Leyland was for O'Reilly). Bradman however, in the tourists' match against Warwickshire, had appeared not to spot the one googly Hollies gave him in his first innings so that the bowler, on Dollery's advice, kept it up his sleeve and reserved it for the great occasion of Bradman's farewell.

In 1946 Hollies did something which no doubt appealed to his sense of practical joking by taking all ten wickets against Nottinghamshire without assistance: seven bowled, three LBW. If he didn't do much in Australia in 1950/51, he was not the first English leg-spinner to fail to turn the ball there; and he would have subsequently gone to the West Indies again if his dentist had allowed. In 1956 he captained Warwickshire for a season, but found it difficult even to set a field for himself.

FIRST-CLASS CAREER (1932–57)

616 innings	282 not outs	1673 runs	average 5.00	0 hundred
	2323 wickets	48656 runs	average 20.94	10–42 best

TEST RECORD (13 MATCHES)

15 innings	8 not outs	37 runs	average 5.28	—
	44 wickets	1332 runs	average 30.27	7–50 best

Series	Tests	O	M	R	W	Av
1934/5 in WI	3	93	24	217	10	21.70
1947 v SA	3	149.2	46	331	9	36.77
1948 v A	1	56	14	131	5	26.20
1949 v NZ	4	175	54	385	10	38.50
1950 v WI	2	119	38	268	10	26.80

JACK COWIE

It wasn't easy to become an international-class cricketer if you were born in New Zealand – or in the West Indies or the Indian subcontinent for that matter – before the Second World War. After a maiden series in 1929/30 New Zealand played one Test a year on average through the 1930s. Apart from a two-Test visit from South Africa, the only country they played before the war was England.

In domestic cricket the opportunities for New Zealanders were equally scant. The four first-class provinces played each other once a year over the Christmas holidays – and that was it! The games did last four days,

John Cowie (1912–   )
Auckland and New Zealand

Even in April 1949 the Bull could summon an occasional roar

but that still added up to a maximum of 72 hours of first-class cricket per year. To produce a top-class bowler in such circumstances was unlikely, but that was accomplished in the person of Jack Cowie.

Known as 'the Bull' because he was built and appealed like one, Cowie took 114 wickets on the 1937 tour of England and, *Wisden* opined, 'might have been termed a wonder of the age' if he had been Australian. As it was, he was a part-time amateur in a weak side, deprived of proper support when Tom Pritchard, equally pacey, was ignored by the New Zealand selectors. Thirteen years later, Pritchard was taking 172 wickets in a season for Warwickshire.

Cowie was more of a batsman and leg-spinner in Auckland school cricket, until a neighbouring school took an unexpected first innings lead and Cowie was stirred to try something drastic. Dour and determined, he thenceforth rolled back to his mark, turned, ran in and hit the deck hard – and often the batsman's thigh as well. He had an outswinger and a breakback. He did not drink or smoke; and he reckoned he was no-balled twice in the whole of his first-class career.

In 1937 at Lord's he dismissed Len Hutton on his Test début for nil and 1. At Old Trafford he took ten wickets, and 19 in the three-Test series. He was 25, at his peak, more hostile than outright fast – and he was not to play another Test for eight years. But on the way home he had Bradman caught behind in Australia for 11 and bowled McCabe for 12 and nil, to add to the wicket of Hammond which he had on their first acquaintance.

When Cowie returned to England in 1949 his Test career amounted to five matches, and the four more he played that summer completed it. For a 37 year old in high-scoring drawn matches he did not do badly, attacking the stumps when age and strained leg-muscles allowed. He was still rated the equal of any pace bowler in England.

FIRST-CLASS CAREER (1932/3–49/50)

104 innings	29 not outs	762 runs	average 10.16	0 hundred
	359 wickets	8001 runs	average 22.28	6–3 best

TEST RECORD (9 MATCHES)

13 innings	4 not outs	90 runs	average 10.00	—
	45 wickets	969 runs	average 21.53	6–40 best

Series	Tests	O	M	R	W	Av
1937 in E	3	139.5	30	395	19	20.78
1945/6 v A	1	21	8	40	6	6.66
1946/7 v E	1	30	4	83	6	13.83
1949 in E	4	147.1	23	451	14	32.21

DOUG WRIGHT

Environment and training seem to have important effects upon cricketers, if not more so than genes. After Aubrey Faulkner had set up his coaching school in London, he inspired and instructed a number of young bowlers who might not have otherwise taken to leg-spin. Ian Peebles, Freddie Brown, Peter Smith and Doug Wright all attended the converted garage in Walham Green and took lessons from the Aristotle of all-rounders until his death.

But nature also played her part in making Wright into the fastest of leg-spinners (with the possible Edwardian exception of Tom Wass of Nottinghamshire). For training alone cannot make a man run in 15 yards, hop along until a last kangaroo leap, then spin a ball with his wrist as well as his fingers at medium-pace. Wright was *sui generis*, a bigger spinner than Tommy Greenhough, faster than Bill O'Reilly. He was able to stop a batsman pushing forward automatically by the simple expedient of giving him a bouncer.

Into this freakish, and delicate, machinery inconsistency was built. From his Kent début in 1932 he was forever variable, all long-hops and full-tosses one day, a match-winner the next, and there was no advance

*Douglas Vivian Parson Wright
(1914–   )
Kent and England*

A photograph as rare as that of the last dodo: an English leg-spinner bowling in 1962, when Wright turned out for the Lord's Taverners

warning of which it would be. In his first Test against Australia in 1938 he got right on top, until Stan McCabe knocked more daylights out of him than anyone else in his innings of 232. In his third Test, the low-scoring Ashes decider at Headingley, Wright took five for 64, which nicely compared with O'Reilly's ten for 122.

This pattern did not alter. In Australia in 1946/7 he had one for 169 in one Test innings (although bowling finely), and seven for 105 in another. He had his fruitless days – yet captured more hat tricks, seven, than anyone in history (five of them before the war). But was the disparity in his performances determined by the factor of luck? Not perhaps entirely. Wright spun one way or the other: he rarely bowled a surprise straight ball like Lohmann had, or a top-spinner to hit the stumps, like Freeman. His leg-break was so devilishly good that it would more often than not miss the bat's edge, which Hollies by contrast would have gently brushed. If the batsman did get a nick, the ball would frequently fly past keeper and slip.

For Wright, therefore, the human world was too fallible a place when Kent's fielders were having an off-day on a slow pitch, and opponents were not skilled enough to get a touch. On other days he could be blessed with a hint of the divine, as when he ran through Gloucestershire with nine for 47. He is the sort of bowler you would want in your all-time England party if not team, to play against Bradman and friends on a perfect pitch up above.

FIRST-CLASS CAREER (1932–57)

703 innings	225 not outs	5903 runs	average 12.34	0 hundred
	2056 wickets	49307 runs	average 23.98	9–47 best

TEST RECORD (34 MATCHES)

39 innings	13 not outs	289 runs	average 11.11	—
	108 wickets	4224 runs	average 39.11	7–105 best

Series	Tests	O		M	R	W	Av
1938 v A	3	120		20	426	12	35.50
1938/9 in SA	3	134	(8-ball)	19	526	9	58.44
1939 v WI	3	51	(8-ball)	4	214	6	35.66
1946 v I	2	41		7	150	4	37.50
1946/7 in A	5	240.2	(8-ball)	23	990	23	43.04
1946/7 in NZ	1	13		1	61	0	—
1947 v SA	4	183.2		50	484	19	25.47
1948 v A	1	40.3		12	123	2	61.50
1948/9 in SA	3	86	(8-ball)	11	316	9	35.11
1949 v NZ	1	28		1	114	1	114.00
1950 v WI	1	53		16	141	5	28.20
1950/51 in A	5	103	(8-ball)	6	500	11	45.45
1950/51 in NZ	2	58		7	179	7	25.57

VINOO MANKAD

'Vinoo' Mankad was the first of India's spinners to win fame abroad. An earlier left-hander, Baloo, had taken over a hundred wickets in all matches on the All-India tour of England in 1911; of the mercurial Jamshedji, Wilfred Rhodes, who coached in India, reputedly said: 'no team would make a hundred if I had his power of spin.' But Mankad was the first to establish an international reputation when he did the double on the 1946 tour of England, the only tourist since 1928 to have done so.

He was lucky to have been born in Jamnagar, the capital of the state of Nawanagar, where Ranjitsinhji and Duleepsinhji lived. At the local school he was coached in batting by Duleep, and in bowling by Albert Wensley, one of several Sussex professionals who wintered in India thanks to the connection with Ranji. Theirs was a precocious pupil. At 20, Mankad was in India's team for the unofficial Tests against Tennyson's 1937/8 touring team, and he headed the batting and bowling averages.

As a batsman, often an opener, Mankad could be an adventurer. As a bowler he was relentlessly accurate, tireless and persistent, rather than a great spinner and experimenter. He would take three walking paces, then three quicker strides, in a straight run-up to the crease. If he had a weakness, it was that he bowled from too wide of the crease with too low an arm; but on hard wickets, when he had to be India's day-long stock bowler, this method did not prevent him flighting the ball up on off-stump to a battery of off-side fielders. Discouraged at school by Wensley from trying the chinaman, he had a deceiving, quicker arm-ball.

It did not help Mankad that he was 29 before he could make his Test début on the 1946 tour of England, nor that he played for a weak bowling side, nor that his fielders were fallible. There is a world of difference between coming on at a hundred for no wicket and a hundred for four. Only in one series was Mankad on top, against a below-strength England in 1951/2, when he took 34 wickets at 16. In one Test innings his 76 overs brought him four wickets for 58. His 12 wickets for 108 at Madras gave India their first Test victory (five stumpings in the match also constituted a record for him).

For the rest he had to labour long and hard, and it is a measure of his success that he conceded little more than two runs an over in his Test career (his experience as a league professional must have come in useful here). As compensation he often enjoyed himself with the bat and hit two Test double-centuries. The Test record opening stand is still his; and he performed the double of one thousand runs and one hundred wickets in 23 Test matches, fewer than anyone until Botham came along.

Mulvantrai Himatlal
Mankad
(*1917–78*)
Western India, Nawanagar,
Hindus, Maharashtra,
Gujerat, Bengal, Bombay,
Rajasthan and India

Perhaps the most memorable moment during Mankad's finest hour. In the Lord's Test of 1952 he hit 72 and 184 and took five wickets in 97 overs

FIRST-CLASS CAREER (1935/6–61/2)

359 innings	27 not outs	11566 runs	average 34.83	26 hundreds
	781 wickets	19159 runs	average 24.53	8–35 best

TEST RECORD (44 MATCHES)

72 innings	5 not outs	2109 runs	average 31.47	5 hundreds
	162 wickets	5236 runs	average 32.32	8–52 best

Series	Tests	O		M	R	W	Av
1946 in E	3	139.5		40	292	11	26.54
1947/8 in A	5	174	(8-ball)	21	630	12	52.50
1948/9 v WI	5	272.3		52	744	17	43.76
1951/2 v E	5	370.5		151	571	34	16.97
1952 in E	3	173		68	386	9	42.88
1952/3 v P	4	265.2		100	514	25	20.56
1952/3 in WI	5	345		102	796	15	53.06
1954/5 in P	5	263.2		130	399	12	33.25
1955/6 v NZ	4	167.1		66	329	12	27.33
1956/7 v A	3	125.4		29	313	11	28.45
1958/9 v WI	2	93		18	262	4	65.50

RAY LINDWALL

As comparisons are odious, it is enough to say that Lindwall was the finest fast bowler between Larwood and the generation of Trueman, Tyson and Statham. His name, bracketed with Miller's, came to inspire in Englishmen the same awe as those of Gregory and McDonald. Yet he had barriers to overcome before he became Australia's highest wicket-taker, ahead of Grimmett. He was 24 before he could make his Test début, because of the war; during it, while he served with the army in the Pacific, he was badly debilitated.

Raymond Russell Lindwall
(1921–   )
New South Wales,
Queensland and Australia

Nature, though, had endowed him with an athlete's body, if not a large one: he was just under six feet tall and weighed 12 stone in his prime. He was equally good at rugby league when a young man in his native Sydney, before giving it up for fast bowling. These physical qualities enabled him, like Lillee, to make a comeback in his late thirties which was modestly successful.

To the modern eye Lindwall had an exceptionally low arm. Yet it did not stop him swinging the ball away, or indeed into the right-hander, which he learnt to do when he was Nelson's professional in the Lancashire League. Far from being a handicap, Lindwall's low arm gave him an advantage when delivering a bouncer, for it would skid towards the chest or throat rather than bounce harmlessly over the top. The yorker too was more potent in his hand, for the batsman would think it was aimed at a good length, only to find it kept coming like a torpedo. Half his wickets on the 1948 tour of England – 43 out of 86 – were bowled.

If that tour saw Lindwall's fastest hours – and he had six for 20 at the Oval – then he lost little of his effect when moderating his pace in return for extra craft. He had the subtlest change of pace – that yorker would often be quicker – and while the inswinger remained occasional, his outswinger was exceptionally brilliant in that he could direct it at middle-and-leg (many an outswing bowler can start it on off-stump but loses the swing if he aims straighter). In 1953 he took 26 Test wickets, against 27 on the previous tour. By 1956 he was considerably slower and made little impression on the turning pitches: he personally thought the Stuart Surridge balls used in that series, and which Jim Laker enjoyed so much at Surrey, did not favour swing.

At home he became the first star to move north to Queensland and the sun. But it wasn't a big-dollar signing like the ones that took Jeff Thomson and Allan Border from Sydney to Brisbane: Lindwall had simply married a Queenslander. And there he worked hard to regain the place he had lost in 1956. In early 1959 he was recalled, at the age of 38, and took seven wickets against England, with a handful more to follow on a tour of the subcontinent. Subsequently this truly modest, unflamboyant fast bowler has run a flower shop.

Was Lindwall faster than Holding or Marshall? Almost certainly not.

Not really as batsmen will remember him but in a pastoral setting – indeed under the pastoral eye of Revd D. S. Sheppard – at Arundel in 1956

He may even have been a yard slower. However, Lindwall dragged his back foot a long way – no-balls were then judged on the basis of the bowling, not popping, crease – and he was therefore a yard closer than the moderns when he finally delivered. The end result must have been pretty similar.

FIRST-CLASS CAREER (1941/2–61/2)

270 innings	39 not outs	5042 runs	average 21.82	5 hundreds
	794 wickets	16956 runs	average 21.35	7–20 best

TEST RECORD (61 MATCHES)

84 innings	13 not outs	1502 runs	average 21.15	2 hundreds
	228 wickets	5251 runs	average 23.03	7–38 best

Series	*Tests*	*O*	*M*	*R*	*W*	*Av*
1945/6 in NZ	1	17	4	29	2	14.50
1946/7 v E	4	122.1 (8-ball)	20	367	18	20.38
1947/8 v I	5	113.4 (8-ball)	23	304	18	16.88
1948 in E	5	222.5	57	530	27	19.62
1949/50 in SA	4	94.4 (8-ball)	13	248	12	20.66
1950/51 v E	5	99.3 (8-ball)	11	344	15	22.93
1951/2 v WI	5	154 (8-ball)	19	484	21	23.04
1952/3 v SA	4	134.7 (8-ball)	18	383	19	20.15
1953 in E	5	240.4	62	490	26	18.84
1954/5 v E	4	130.6 (8-ball)	28	381	14	27.21
1954/5 in WI	5	176	25	637	20	31.85
1956 in E	4	100.1	29	238	7	34.00
1956/7 in P	1	43	16	64	1	64.00
1956/7 in I	3	114.1	45	199	12	16.58
1958/9 v E	2	66 (8-ball)	9	209	7	29.85
1959/60 in P	2	59	17	122	3	40.66
1959/60 in I	2	82	23	222	6	37.00

KEITH MILLER

Keith Ross Miller
(1919–   )
Victoria, New South Wales,
Nottinghamshire and
Australia

The most astonishing point about Keith Miller and his character – which was the key to his bowling – is that he did not come from Sydney originally but from Melbourne. To Australian cricket, Melbourne is what the north is to England – the home of the game's more defensive, stoical form. Perhaps climate, and the degree of latitude, determine in both cases. In any event, only Melbourne could have raised Woodfull and Ponsford and Lawry, while Sydney – hotter, freer and more flamboyant – was the home of Trumper and McCabe and Walters.

Yet Miller was born in Melbourne, went to school there and learnt to play Australian Rules (a sport based in Victoria) to the highest standard. He did not, naturally, like the approach to cricket there, especially that of Woodfull who taught at his school. Nevertheless he had graduated to the Victorian team as a batsman when the war came. Once it was over he moved to New South Wales where he could, so to speak, air all his strokes: outside cricket he could cut a dashing figure at the races, in classical music halls and in the cockpit of fighter-planes (he was named after the early aviators Keith and Ross Smith).

It was not until after the war that Miller took up bowling in earnest (it is so easy to forget that he was initially a batsman, who hit 41 first-class centuries), and now his dare-devilry could be fully displayed. He had Botham's shoulders and sense of adventure, fine rhythm and a love of variety. Tossing his hair back into place after each ball, he might bowl a googly in his opening over, as fast as it is possible to bowl one; the next ball might be delivered off a run of five paces, although his full run-up was barely more than Sunday League length. Unlike Lindwall he had a high action, and when it was combined with his natural virility, a fuller follow-through than Jack Gregory, and with his hostility when in the mood, he was the most aggressive of his era.

Miller was helped, too, by the frequency of new balls in his time. Until 1946 it was the practice for a new ball to be available after every lot of two hundred runs had been scored in an innings. From 1946 to 1949 in England the change was made to after 55 overs, presumably to assist bowlers in a high-scoring period. This suited Lindwall and Miller ideally. Then until 1955, a slight alteration was made in England to 65 overs. (As the number of overs was not recorded on scoreboards in those days, a white flag had to be displayed after 55 overs, a yellow one after 60 overs, and both together after 65.) Throughout his fast-bowling career Miller was formidably equipped.

He was also a useful bowler of medium-paced off-breaks from round the wicket. His best Test figures, seven for 60, came on his début in 1946/7 when he bowled off-breaks on a sticky Brisbane pitch. If he had played county cricket – or more than one game for Nottinghamshire – he would surely have improved this facet of his game, as well as his

A curious, if not unique, combination of orthodox technique and unorthodox temperament

defensive batting technique. But then he would not have been Keith Miller, the instinctive cavalier.

FIRST-CLASS CAREER (1937/8–59)

| 326 innings | 36 not outs | 14183 runs | average 48.90 | 41 hundreds |
| | 497 wickets | 11087 runs | average 22.30 | 7–12 best |

TEST RECORD (55 MATCHES)

| 87 innings | 7 not outs | 2958 runs | average 36.97 | 7 hundreds |
| | 170 wickets | 3906 runs | average 22.97 | 7–60 best |

Series	Tests	O	M	R	W	Av
1945/6 in NZ	1	6	2	6	2	3.00
1946/7 v E	5	122.3 (8-ball)	15	334	16	20.87
1947/8 v I	5	72 (8-ball)	14	223	9	24.77
1948 in E	5	138.1	43	301	13	23.15
1949/50 in SA	5	135 (8-ball)	17	390	17	22.94
1950/51 v E	5	106.6 (8-ball)	23	301	17	17.70
1951/2 v WI	5	128.3 (8-ball)	16	398	20	19.90
1952/3 v SA	4	90.1 (8-ball)	17	241	13	18.53
1953 in E	5	186	72	303	10	30.30
1954/5 v E	4	88.4 (8-ball)	28	243	10	24.30
1954/5 in WI	5	188.2	37	641	20	32.05
1956 in E	5	205.1	44	467	21	22.23
1956/7 in P	1	29	9	58	2	29.00

BILL JOHNSTON

William Arras Johnston
(1922–   )
Victoria and Australia

Bill Johnston and Alan Davidson are widely considered the two best left-handed bowlers Australia have had in this century, with similar records to their credit. If Davidson was the better swing bowler, Johnston was the more accomplished when he turned his hand to spin. No change in run-up was required on Johnston's part: whether bowling his medium-pace swing or his orthodox spin, he had a run-up of seven, rather gangling, elbow-swinging strides.

That his name is one of the least known of the great bowlers does not mean that he wasn't highly effective for a decade after the Second World War. The leading wicket-taker on the 1948 tour – when Bradman's Australians were hailed as the strongest team of all time – was Johnston with 102 wickets. In the Tests he equalled Lindwall's haul of 27 although, as a genial and big-hearted soul, he was trying to allow Lindwall to overtake McDonald's record (for a fast bowler in England) of 29 wickets when he picked up the last three wickets of the series himself. A whimsical fellow who never lost his temper, Johnston was worked so hard during the summer that he sometimes had to go straight from spinning the old ball to swinging the new.

Who was Australia's leading wicket-taker against South Africa in 1949/50, against England the following year, and against England again in 1954/5? Neither Lindwall nor Miller, but Johnston in every instance. He had of course an immense advantage in having them as an opening pair fit to expose the late or middle order, so that he could swoop like a vulture on the carrion; and new balls were frequent. Nevertheless, Johnston recorded his best Test figures of six for 44 against South Africa when he opened the bowling himself.

For all the brevity of his run-up Johnston was able to put snap into his bowling by flicking a left wrist which had been strengthened – the story goes – by milking cows when he was a boy on his father's farm in western Victoria. His whole left arm was a sturdy limb in fact, for it once threw a baseball 132 yards in a competition with American base-ballers. Like every 'bush' cricketer who wants to succeed, Johnston had to move to his state capital, and by the time the Second World War was over he had risen through the Melbourne grade ranks to the Victorian team. A year later he was making his Australian début.

His career was disturbed by a couple of bad injuries. One was caused by a car accident in South Africa: this was, however, providential for the Australians since they were then able to send for Miller as a replacement (Miller had originally been omitted from the party, it is said, because Bradman wanted to cut him down to size). The second injury was in the nets at the start of the 1953 tour when Johnston damaged his right leg, had to change his action and couldn't bowl flat out in the series (instead he achieved a first-class tour batting average

of 102). If Johnston – Australia's leading wicket-taker in three series against England – had not been injured, England that summer might well not have won back the Ashes.

FIRST-CLASS CAREER (1945/6–54/5)

| 162 innings | 73 not outs | 1129 runs | average 12.68 | 0 hundred |
| | 554 wickets | 12936 runs | average 23.35 | 8–52 best |

TEST RECORD (40 MATCHES)

| 49 innings | 25 not outs | 273 runs | average 11.37 | — |
| | 160 wickets | 3826 runs | average 23.91 | 6–44 best |

Series	Tests	O	M	R	W	Av
1947/8 v I	4	84 (8-ball)	24	182	16	11.37
1948 in E	5	309.2	91	630	27	23.33
1949/50 in SA	5	160.5 (8-ball)	31	392	23	17.04
1950/51 v E	5	153.7 (8-ball)	29	422	22	19.18
1951/2 v WI	5	171.7 (8-ball)	25	508	23	22.08
1952/3 v SA	5	266.7 (8-ball)	59	737	21	35.09
1953 in E	3	174	67	343	7	49.00
1954/5 v E	4	141.4 (8-ball)	37	423	19	22.26
1954/5 in WI	4	53	9	189	2	94.50

ALEC BEDSER

Alec Victor Bedser CBE
(1918–   )
Surrey and England

When Alec Bedser dropped out of Test cricket in 1955, he had set a new world record of 236 Test wickets (surpassing Grimmett). For a decade he had been not only England's spearhead but most of the spear as well: their shock and stock bowler. In the post-war years Hutton at least had Compton for company; Bedser had only spasmodic spells from Wright for support. But he did have an advantage denied to his successors.

It is a surprisingly widespread misconception that the restriction on the number of leg-side fielders was introduced as a result of Bodyline. In fact, the antidote devised by the Australians shortly afterwards was the intimidatory clause. The restriction to five fielders on the leg-side, with no more than two behind the wicket, was not brought into English county cricket until 1957. It was designed to stop negative bowling on and outside leg-stump to a packed leg-side field, and was successful in its aim. But the new law also served to hamper true inswing and off-spin bowlers by robbing them of some of their most important fielders. Bedser did well to enjoy his Test career before 1957 and to retire in 1960. It may not only have been as a result of age that his average went from 18 to 24 to 28 in his last three seasons.

In the early stage of Bedser's career the inswinger was his sole weapon. It did however have the merit of 'going' late in its flight, and given an unlimited number of leg-side fielders he was able to take 11 wickets in each of his first two Tests against India in 1946. Under the prevailing law, he could station three backward short-legs, and a fine-leg to stop anything which passed them.

But as he bowled and practised, Bedser found that by holding the ball across the seam in his massive hand he could summon up a leg-cutter with the same action. He then developed at least two forms of cutter, one for wet wickets and another for dry. The slower one could turn like a big leg-spinner. At times he might feel inclined to bowl a whole over of leg-cutters without an inswinger.

His stamina and insatiable appetite for bowling would have been astounding in any era. These qualities, along with an inswinger that was always effective against left-handers (his Australian 'rabbit' Arthur Morris fell 18 times to him in 20 Tests), carried him through to his peak years of the early 1950s when his leg-cutter was primed for action. What is more, Bradman had gone by then although 'Big Al' was persevering enough to take his wicket in five successive confrontations, thrice to catches at backward short-leg.

In 1950/51 the other England bowlers managed 49 wickets between them against Bedser's 30. In 1953 he took 39 wickets, the others 52. At Trent Bridge his haul was 14 wickets for 99, the only improvement he made on the figures in his opening two Tests. Then, like Tate before

112

him, his reward for carrying the flag for so long was to be dropped on the following tour of Australia.

In his 15 years he averaged over a thousand first-class overs. But it should be added that he only chose to go on four MCC tours in that time, so he had the winter off to recuperate more often than not. When it mattered though, which was then in Tests against Australia, his lion-heartedness was never found wanting.

FIRST-CLASS CAREER (1939–60)

576 innings	181 not outs	5735 runs	average 14.51	1 hundred
	1924 wickets	39279 runs	average 20.41	8–18 best

TEST RECORD (51 MATCHES)

71 innings	15 not outs	714 runs	average 12.75	—
	236 wickets	5876 runs	average 24.89	7–34 best

Series	Tests	O	M	R	W	Av
1946 v I	3	144.2	33	298	24	12.41
1946/7 in A	5	246.3 (8-ball)	38	876	16	54.75
1946/7 in NZ	1	39	5	95	4	23.75
1947 v SA	2	111.1	24	233	4	58.25
1948 v A	5	274.3	75	688	18	38.22
1948/9 in SA	5	206.5 (8-ball)	37	554	16	34.62
1949 v NZ	2	85	19	215	7	30.71
1950 v WI	3	181	49	377	11	34.27
1950/51 in A	5	195 (8-ball)	34	482	30	16.06
1950/51 in NZ	2	84	26	138	2	69.00
1951 v SA	5	275.5	84	517	30	17.23
1952 v I	4	163.5	57	279	20	13.95
1953 v A	5	265.1	58	682	39	17.48
1954 v P	2	74.5	28	158	10	15.80
1954/5 in A	1	37 (8-ball)	4	131	1	131.00
1955 v SA	1	41	3	153	4	38.25

BOB APPLEYARD

Few cricketers have had a more extraordinary career than Bob Appleyard. For Yorkshire in 1950 he played two first-class games at the age
of 26. The next season he headed the national averages with two hundred
wickets, 43 more than anyone else, at 14 runs each. Owing to tuberculosis
he was confined to one more game in the next two seasons. He then
returned in 1954 to take 154 wickets at 14, which brought him second
place in the averages and a trip to Australasia (ahead of Jim Laker),
when he topped the Test and tour averages. Yet it was all over by 1958
when Yorkshire decided not to re-engage him.

Robert Appleyard
(1924–   )
Yorkshire and England

*Warming up at Perth on the
1954/5 tour, and (overleaf)
not so warm in Switzerland
when recuperating the winter
before*

Appleyard was the last and probably, at his peak, the best of a line of Yorkshire medium-paced off-spinners, beginning with Schofield Haigh and continuing through George Macaulay and Frank Smailes to Appleyard. They delighted in pitches which were left uncovered during a game or which began wet (and as Yorkshire used to play at so many grounds outside their Headingley headquarters, they could issue tacit instructions for the hose to be used in preparation, then protest that they had no control over the matter!). The last three could also take the new ball and produce some lively swing, for Appleyard began in the Bradford League as a pace bowler.

Appleyard's stock ball however was the one that turned from the off, bounced – he had a high arm and was almost 6' 2" – and carried from the bat as likely as not to one of his short-legs. Of these he might have as many as five, while two fielders were often enough to patrol his off-side. In 1951 he spun the ball with his second and third fingers. After the operation to remove part of his TB-affected lung, he had to change his grip to the first and second fingers, so as to lessen the strain on his side.

Then there would be the quick yorker; the outswinger which carried to slip; and a slower ball which possessed a tremendous loop. This armoury made him formidable on dry pitches, too. In Australia when the Ashes were at stake, he took Australia's first three wickets for 13 runs one evening with the aid of some footmarks, only to be prevented by Tyson and Statham next morning from completing the job. In New Zealand he helped himself to four wickets for seven when that country was dismissed for the lowest Test score of 26.

Appleyard had the remarkable average of 15 for his truncated career. He might have been greater still if he had been healthier, easier to handle, and had started younger; but he is still up there with the best.

FIRST-CLASS CAREER (1950–58)

145 innings	54 not outs	776 runs	average 8.52	0 hundred
	708 wickets	10965 runs	average 15.48	8–76 best

TEST RECORD (9 MATCHES)

9 innings	6 not outs	51 runs	average 17.00	—
	31 wickets	554 runs	average 17.87	5–51 best

Series	Tests	O	M	R	W	Av
1954 v P	1	47.4	13	123	7	17.57
1954/5 in A	4	79 (8-ball)	22	224	11	20.36
1954/5 in NZ	2	36	12	80	9	8.88
1955 v SA	1	47	13	78	2	39.00
1956 v A	1	30	10	49	2	24.50

SONNY RAMADHIN

Cricket has known other 'mystery' bowlers like Jack Iverson and John Gleeson, but none has created such an immediate sensation as Sonny Ramadhin. After only two first-class games the short and slim East Indian from Trinidad was chosen for the 1950 tour of England. In four Tests, in cap and buttoned-down sleeves, he took 26 wickets and in partnership with Alf Valentine gave West Indies their first victories in England.

In Ramadhin's day novelty was a potent asset which is denied a bowler now. Those who went out to bat against him in 1950 had not seen film of his bowling on television or on video, or been able to analyse it in slow motion. They were venturing into the unknown. Even seven years later the same applied to many English batsmen, until they discovered an antidote to Ramadhin, or a poison.

This unfamiliarity was crucial since there was nothing inherently outstanding about the balls he delivered. Ramadhin gripped the smooth part of the ball with only his middle finger on the seam; he aimed at off-stump or an inch or two outside, and with a quick twirl of his right arm usually produced an off-break. Sometimes, however, without any change of action, it was a leg-break or a ball that went straight on. The Australians went after him aggressively after being unable to decipher him for one Test. In his second Test against Australia, Ramadhin took one for 196 – and an awful lot of punishment from Hassett and Miller.

The mysterious element was essential because the off-break would skid, rather than bounce, as it turned. 'Ram' was short, 5′ 4″, and he did not bowl with a full arm-swing: his right hand began its arc by his legs. Thus is was that May and Cowdrey were able to pad him out at Edgbaston in 1957 after Ramadhin had bewitched seven batsmen for 49, and England had started their second innings 288 runs behind. They could push forward with bat and pad to everything since the ball, not bouncing, would not carry to short-leg. Aiding and abetting them was the LBW law of the time which allowed a batsman to kick away a ball pitching outside off-stump without playing a stroke, so long as the pad at the moment of contact was outside the line.

Ramadhin was deflated as any man would be after 98 overs at Edgbaston. Only five more wickets fell to him in the entire series. In 1950, it is true, he had bowled 81.2 overs in an innings against England, but on that occasion he had five wickets and a victory to justify the effort. His rewards thereafter were modest, although he had a tolerably satisfactory season for Lancashire in 1964.

Subsequently there has been nothing so romantic as this tale of the little East Indian, the first to represent West Indies. He was born in a small village in central Trinidad, the son of labourers in the sugar-cane fields. At school he batted but he did not bowl until he was 16 and a

Sonny Ramadhin
(1929–   )
Trinidad, Lancashire and
West Indies

Sonny and son in 1971, in northern England not southern Trinidad

golf caddy. His bowling then secured him the patronage of an official in the island's oil fields and transformed his life. It is a story that cannot be repeated in the television age, partly because the slow-motion replay means every bowling action is subjected to the closest scrutiny.

FIRST-CLASS CAREER (1949/50–65)

| 191 innings | 65 not outs | 1092 runs | average 8.66 | 0 hundred |
| | 758 wickets | 15345 runs | average 20.24 | 8–15 best |

TEST RECORD (43 MATCHES)

| 58 innings | 14 not outs | 361 runs | average 8.20 | — |
| | 158 wickets | 4579 runs | average 28.98 | 7–49 best |

Series	Tests	O	M	R	W	Av
1950 in E	4	377.5	170	604	26	23.23
1951/2 in A	5	232.3 (8-ball)	53	695	14	49.64
1951/2 in NZ	2	100	44	166	12	13.83
1952/3 v I	4	232.4	96	471	13	36.23
1953/4 v E	5	304.3	133	559	23	24.30
1954/5 v A	4	139	33	380	5	76.00
1955/6 in NZ	4	184.4	76	316	20	15.80
1957 in E	5	261.3	78	547	14	39.07
1958/9 in I	2	44.5	15	91	2	45.50
1958/9 in P	2	70.3	28	121	9	13.44
1959/60 v E	4	248.3	83	491	17	28.88
1960/61 in A	2	37 (8-ball)	4	138	3	46.00

ALF VALENTINE

When the West Indian selectors were picking their party for the 1950 tour of England, they made quite an adventurous choice in going for Ramadhin. But as he had taken as many as 12 wickets in the two trial games which constituted his entire first-class experience, Ramadhin was a conservative selection compared with that of the gawky left-arm spinner. Alf Valentine had taken two wickets for 190 runs in his two first-class games before he was selected to tour; and since he went on to capture 33 wickets in the four Test matches in England, he can be accounted the most inspired selectorial coup since Syd Barnes.

Valentine had, however, spun the ball sharply on the coir matting at Port-of-Spain in the trials; and although Jeff Stollmeyer scored 261 against him, the selectors believed his spin would 'go' on all surfaces. They were right. In the week before his Test début at Old Trafford, Valentine's figures against Lancashire were eight for 26 and five for 41. In the Test itself Valentine claimed England's first eight wickets, to be denied immortality by Hollies and Berry, the feeblest of bats! Even so,

Alfred Lewis Valentine (1930–   )
Jamaica and West Indies

Leaning forward prematurely Valentine won't obtain much bounce but that ball should turn. Unorthodox wrist position too, cf Bedi and Underwood

119

his performance was statistically the best by a West Indian in Test cricket to that point.

He kept on spinning the ball, and landing it accurately, so long as his fingers were uncalloused and supple. Once they lost their bite – well before his 1963 tour of England – Valentine was 'gone' as a cricketer since his two attributes were accuracy and spin. He had no loop to speak of since he delivered the ball from a chest-on position with a lowish arm, and pushed it through relatively quickly. The corkscrew break was his chief merit and it was enough to secure him the wickets of the best players of spin in 1950 – Hutton's thrice in six innings, Compton's once in two.

The old Glamorgan pace bowler Jack Mercer, when coaching in Jamaica, had encouraged the teenaged Valentine to develop his spin. Having been born in Kingston, the myopic youth was then playing his club cricket in Spanish Town outside the capital. He was never anything but a bowler (batting was the only thing he did right-handed, and perhaps that was a mistake). Even a pair of National Health glasses of extra strength in 1950 couldn't 'up' the rest of his game.

Valentine was never bowled as much as in his maiden series: 422.3 overs in four Tests, including a then-record of 92 in one innings, many of them delivered in 90 seconds. In Australia, while the home batsmen went after Ramadhin, Valentine continued his success with 24 wickets. He was only 23, and in his 19th Test, when he took his one hundredth wicket for West Indies. If there wasn't much to come, he had already given the game something different to remember.

FIRST-CLASS CAREER (1949/50–64/5)

142 innings	48 not outs	470 runs	average 5.00	0 hundred
	475 wickets	12451 runs	average 26.21	8–26 best

TEST RECORD (36 MATCHES)

51 innings	21 not outs	141 runs	average 4.70	—
	139 wickets	4215 runs	average 30.32	8–104 best

Series	Tests	O	M	R	W	Av
1950 in E	4	422.3	197	674	33	20.42
1951/2 in A	5	217.1 (8-ball)	42	691	24	28.79
1951/2 in NZ	2	113.4	55	153	8	19.12
1952/3 v I	5	430	179	828	28	29.57
1953/4 v E	3	190.5	81	378	7	54.00
1954/5 v A	3	140	42	349	5	69.80
1955/6 in NZ	4	201.4	99	283	15	18.86
1957 in E	2	26	4	88	0	—
1957/8 v P	1	45.2	9	124	3	41.33
1960/61 in A	5	170.4 (8-ball)	42	533	14	38.07
1961/2 v I	2	72	39	114	2	57.00

JIM LAKER

In method Jim Laker was the ideal off-spinner. By the end of his Test career the perfect action had given him control of the ball and usually of the batsman. He wasn't too fast through the air, like many off-spinners today; and he wasn't so slow that the batsman could get after him. In baggy, turned-up trousers he may look a dated figure in the photographs and film-clips we have of him taking his 19 wickets at Old Trafford in 1956, but his bowling was of the kind that is effective throughout the ages.

James Charles Laker
(1922–86)
Surrey, Essex and England

Yet here we must be careful not to put on the rose-tinted spectacles. There is the temptation, when looking back at cricketers, to think they were always at their best; we forget their ups and downs, the years they were written off. In Laker's case particularly we have to assess with fresh eyes – and come to terms with – the startling fact that until his year of triumph he was not a regular in the England side.

He started well, after growing up as a batsman and pace bowler in Yorkshire. In army cricket during the war he practised off-spin, and after a promising first full season with Surrey in 1947 he was bowling it for an inexperienced MCC team in the West Indies that winter (why Bedser, Compton, Edrich, Washbrook and initially Hutton declined to tour is another story). When rain fell in Barbados he cashed in on it to take seven for 103 on his Test début. In spite of straining stomach muscles there in the second innings, he persevered through the tour to be the pick of an inadequate attack.

The first crack showed in 1948 when the Australians hit nine sixes off him in one session of a warm-up game and never permitted him to settle. At Headingley, Laker was England's only specialist spinner when the tourists chased 404 on the last day – and England bowled 20 overs an hour to lose by seven wickets. Laker had Bradman dropped, which must have been something of a disappointment, but *Wisden* reported that the off-spinner 'was erratic in length'. Hereabouts the belief grew that he was a little lacking in heart. Having played his first seven Tests in a row, Laker was selected for only 17 more in the next eight years.

It is said that at Surrey, Stuart Surridge had to use blandishments when the going got tough. By chance or perhaps by design, that wasn't often the case at the Oval in the 1950s when the pitches were coated with a top dressing which cracked and encouraged spin (Eric Bedser would often be called up for off-spin away from home when the batsmen were well set). Another incentive was the Surridge ball used at the Oval then, palpably larger as it was than the other half-dozen brands.

Laker, in truth, was not at his best in a struggling team, and as England were that until the early to mid-1950s, Tattersall and Appleyard, McConnon and even the youthful Titmus, were frequently preferred. Laker was seen as a ground bowler: except in 1950 he would

always play the Oval Test. In 1951 there he took ten South African wickets. In 1953, when the Ashes were won, Laker and Lock had their first fruitful partnership. Yet he still wasn't chosen for the 1954/5 tour of Australia.

It was when English cricket fully recovered its strength after the war that Laker came into his own. In 1956, when England had runs on the board and a penetrative opening pair, he moved in to take 46 wickets in the series and, at Old Trafford, to surpass the previous record of 17 for a first-class match. Some of the Australians were rather deficient in technique as they never saw wet pitches at home. The leg-trap which Laker enjoyed (Alan Oakman had five catches) would be impossible today. But with 'all-ten' in a Test, he was still the first to climb Everest.

Laker stayed on top until he returned home early from his first and last tour of Australia, and he retired from Surrey at the end of 1959. (Coincidentally, the next season saw the limitation of five leg-side fielders extended from county cricket to a Test series in England for the first time.) After a break of two seasons from Surrey, whom he had left under a cloud that eventually cleared, he played three part-time seasons for Essex as an amateur. When the moment was right – which sadly, it often was not – he was in all probability the best of off-spinners.

OPPOSITE: *Between base camp and cricket's Everest: Laker pivots and bowls on the Old Trafford dust-bowl of 1956, when he finished with 19 wickets for 90*

FIRST-CLASS CAREER (1946–64)

548 innings	108 not outs	7304 runs	average 16.60	2 hundreds
	1944 wickets	35791 runs	average 18.41	10–53 best

TEST RECORD (46 MATCHES)

63 innings	15 not outs	676 runs	average 14.08	
	193 wickets	4101 runs	average 21.24	10–53 best

Series	Tests	O	M	R	W	Av
1947/8 in WI	4	186.4	48	548	18	30.44
1948 v A	3	155.2	42	472	9	52.44
1949 v NZ	1	32	6	89	4	22.25
1950 v WI	1	31	9	86	1	86.00
1951 v SA	2	111	30	208	14	14.85
1952 v I	4	90.3	33	189	8	23.62
1953 v A	3	58.5	11	212	9	23.55
1953/4 in WI	4	221.1	84	469	14	33.50
1954 v P	1	32.2	17	39	2	19.50
1955 v SA	1	60.4	31	84	7	12.00
1956 v A	5	283.5	127	442	46	9.60
1956/7 in SA	5	145.1 (8-ball)	46	324	11	29.45
1957 v WI	4	246.2	99	448	18	24.88
1958 v NZ	4	131	67	173	17	10.17
1958/9 in A	4	127.6 (8-ball)	24	318	15	21.20

JOHNNY WARDLE

John Henry Wardle
(1923–85)
Yorkshire and England

Johnny Wardle was the finest left-arm bowler of unorthodox spin England has bred. He was also one of the best orthodox spinners. In these two styles he took over a hundred Test wickets at 20 runs apiece, the lowest average for any regular Test spinner since the First World War. But – and it is a large but – he was not the first slow left-hander to have difficulties with officialdom, for he clashed with the authorities as vehemently as Peel or Parker. (Nor was he the last to do so.)

Wardle's talent was such that he could produce his chinaman at will and without any practice. Confronted with a tenacious tail-ender he could spontaneously place it on a length and bend it between the right-hander's bat and pad. He did not betray his intention: the ball started its life behind his back whatever its type, so the effect was usually as immediate as the surprise. Most finger-spinners need hours to rehearse their wrist-spin – if they can bowl it at all. Wardle's googly did not turn nearly so much, merely from middle- to off-stump, but that was usually sufficient.

Presented with the problem of what to bowl, when and at whom, Wardle normally opted for safety. Yorkshire's tradition that wrist-spinners are an expensive and frivolous luxury, like fur-coats, may have had something to do with it. More influentially, Yorkshire's attack was thin in the early 1950s when Appleyard was ill, and before Trueman and Illingworth had matured. Wardle became not a Tribe or a Walsh, his Australian contemporaries in the Midlands, but a long-spell stock bowler in county cricket.

Arthur Milton isn't quite sure either whether Wardle has slipped in a chinaman

Calling on the strength he had built up working underground, Wardle in 1952 delivered more six-ball overs than anybody in a season bar Freeman – 1857 of them. He also bowled more maidens than anybody in a season since the six-ball over came into being – 810 of them. A spinner now does not bowl that many overs in a year.

Overseas, on tour for England, Wardle had altogether more scope for his unorthodoxy. Ray Illingworth estimates that less than a quarter of Wardle's total wickets were taken with wrist-spin; but on the 1956/7 tour of South Africa over half of his 90 wickets were. South Africans had never enjoyed wrist-spin: Grimmett averaged 14 there, O'Reilly 13 and Wardle 12. In a strong batting side, and coming on after a couple of good fast bowlers, Wardle was at the top of his class.

In England, Tony Lock was preferred to Wardle as a rule. Lock was given 49 Tests, Wardle 28, and this rankled especially since Lock's bowling during that period was seldom as far above suspicion as Caesar's wife. (Wardle was also such a robust left-handed hitter that he could be considered an all-rounder at a pinch.)

He was a testy fellow withal, adored by the crowds who watched his antics, dreaded by the young fielders who waited under the catches off his bowling. The divisions had long been established, and his contract with Yorkshire terminated, before he put his name to some newspaper articles so outspokenly critical that MCC withdrew his invitation to tour Australia in 1958/9. A stormy petrel, one who needed wider seas than a team game would allow.

FIRST-CLASS CAREER (1946–67/8)

527 innings	71 not outs	7333 runs	average 16.08	0 hundred
	1846 wickets	35027 runs	average 18.97	9–25 best

TEST RECORD (28 MATCHES)

41 innings	8 not outs	653 runs	average 19.78	—
	102 wickets	2080 runs	average 20.39	7–36 best

Series	Tests	O	M	R	W	Av
1947/8 in WI	1	3	0	9	0	—
1950 v WI	1	47	16	104	2	52.00
1951 v SA	2	95.5	39	171	5	34.20
1953 v A	3	155.3	57	344	13	26.46
1953/4 in WI	2	83.3	23	187	4	46.75
1954 v P	4	142.5	82	176	20	8.80
1954/5 in A	4	70.6 (8-ball)	15	229	10	22.90
1954/5 in NZ	2	76.3	43	116	5	23.20
1955 v SA	3	165.4	77	273	15	18.20
1956 v A	1	27	9	59	1	59.00
1956/7 in SA	4	139.6 (8-ball)	37	359	26	13.80
1957 v WI	1	22	5	53	1	53.00

FAZAL MAHMOOD

Fazal Mahmood
(1927–)
Northern India, Punjab,
Lahore and Pakistan

There may not have been a more difficult stock ball to play than Fazal's leg-cutter when delivered on a coir matting pitch stretched tight – and no doubt loosened when the home team batted, so as to make it more easy-paced. Delivered by a burly man of powerful shoulders, this leg-cutter would swerve in through the air and zip away past the bat. Syd Barnes bowled it, but few others have.

To some extent Fazal has suffered unfairly for his reputation as a mat bowler. True, he did take 55 wickets in ten Tests on mat, including 12 wickets on the jute at Lucknow to give Pakistan their first Test victory; and 12 more wickets on coir matting at Dacca to give Pakistan their first Test victory over West Indies; and 13 wickets on the Karachi coir to give Fazal his best Test figures and Pakistan their first victory over Australia. But he also had 84 wickets in 24 Tests on turf, including 12 for 99 at the Oval in 1954 to give Pakistan their first win over England; and eight for 118 at Port-of-Spain to send West Indies to an innings defeat.

Fazal was known as the Bedser of Pakistan, quite misleadingly in some ways. Both were big strong medium-pacers, but Bedser was essentially an inswing bowler with an occasional leg-cutter. Fazal was almost solely a cutter of the ball, from leg and (less often) from the off. He himself will say, of course, that he bowled many other types of delivery. He is ever ready to recount at length, his piercingly bright eyes alight, how he dismissed Len Hutton at the Oval with an elaborate series of leg-cutters aimed progressively wider of off-stump. But he was a master of his kind, so it's sad that the England players of 1954 should have tried to disparage Pakistan's victory by saying that they wanted to finish the game on the fourth evening by quickly hitting off the 168 runs England chased to win. That doesn't explain how England fell behind on first innings, when Fazal took six wickets, four caught behind by Imtiaz.

Fazal was coached by his father, a professor at Islamia College in Lahore and president of the college cricket club. At first Fazal bowled a leg-break but converted it into a faster leg-cutter during his teens at the college, which was part of Punjab University. Allied to this skill was the relentless determination that a Pathan ancestry brings to a sturdy Punjabi physique. Officially born in 1927, he was playing first-class cricket before Partition and but for it would have toured Australia with India in 1946/7.

OPPOSITE: *Midway to a sensation, Fazal ascends the Oval steps after helping to dismiss England for 130 in their first innings of the 1954 Test match*

Without Fazal's bowling, even more so than Hanif's batting, Pakistan might not have attained Test status or been able to justify it so rapidly. Fazal saw his country through the first decade of growing pains; he had 'gone' by Pakistan's 1962 visit to England when he was sent for as a replacement in mid-tour (which again throws doubt on his official date

of birth as he was supposedly no more than 35). Thereafter he was a police detective in Lahore, never a person to be treated lightly.

FIRST-CLASS CAREER (1943/4–63/4)

146 innings	33 not outs	2602 runs	average 23.02	1 hundred
	460 wickets	8792 runs	average 19.11	9–43 best

TEST RECORD (34 MATCHES)

50 innings	6 not outs	620 runs	average 14.09	—
	139 wickets	3434 runs	average 24.70	7–42 best

Series	Tests	O	M	R	W	Av
1952/3 in I	5	229	74	512	20	25.60
1954 in E	4	165	50	408	20	20.40
1954/5 v I	4	216.2	94	329	15	21.93
1955/6 v NZ	2	57	22	92	5	18.40
1956/7 v A	1	75	28	114	13	8.76
1957/8 in WI	5	320.2	105	764	20	38.20
1958/9 v WI	3	143.3	47	333	21	15.85
1959/60 v A	2	96.2	32	213	11	19.26
1960/61 in I	5	160.3	63	239	9	26.55
1961/2 v E	1	63	23	98	0	—
1962 in E	2	113	25	332	5	66.40

TONY LOCK

Tony Lock's career had three phases, and if his claim to being called a bowler at all in the second of them is questionable, it is incontestable that in the final phase he was a great one. By then he was representing and captaining Western Australia, and training the young Dennis Lillee who eventually – but only eventually – exceeded Lock's number of wickets for the state. Not so much of a prophet in his native country, Lock is recognised as the finest left-arm spinner the Sheffield Shield has seen.

Lock changed to Australian citizenship by naturalisation, yet there was always something Aussie about his temperament. He began in cricket as a fast bowler; he had reddish hair before it fell out; his appeal was a deafening roar; and no spin bowler has been more aggressive, unless it was O'Reilly. This aggression, when properly channelled, made Lock the foremost short-leg of his period, before shin-pads and boxes and helmets were worn. He was also an inspiring captain of Leicestershire as well as Western Australia. But when he went all but wicket-less at Old Trafford in 1956, his frustration at seeing Laker clearing up the Australians impelled him to fire in the ball ever faster and shorter.

His early years contained no hint of the trouble to come. Taken on to the Surrey staff before he was 17, Lock was a slow and flighty bowler in the 1940s who needed to acquire more spin to have an international future. During the winter of 1951/2 he became a different proposition. He was appointed the winter coach of an indoor school with a low ceiling where he was forced to push the ball through, and now he discovered he could spin it sharply. In fact, this method made him impossible to play on a pitch of any assistance to him, since the only possible scoring shot was the back foot force when he dropped short. However, on a hard unhelpful pitch, such as in Australia in 1958/9, batsmen could hit him safely through the line.

Lock became quicker and quicker during the 1950s: batsman after batsman found his stumps demolished, probably by a yorker, before he could raise bat or eyebrow. Square-leg umpires began to raise their right arms as well. A week after his England début in 1952 Lock was called when bowling for Surrey against the Indians: Fred Price, the old Middlesex keeper, called his quicker ball three times. England's response? To pick him for the following Test. In 1953 the Australians departed muttering about being thrown out by Lock at the Oval. That winter in the West Indies, Lock was no-balled again in two matches. This was only the second occasion on which a bowler had been called for throwing in a Test match (Jones, the Australian fast bowler, was the first in 1897/8).

Lock was lucky that the slow-motion replay had yet to reach cricket. Seasons came and went, Lock was reported to have modified his action,

Graham Anthony Richard Lock
(1929–   )
Surrey, Leicestershire, Western Australia and England

Lock's action in the 1952 week when he was called for throwing and chosen for his England début

and in the meanwhile touring sides were mown down. In the 1957 Oval Test he took 11 West Indian wickets for 48 runs; against the 1958 New Zealanders he took 34 wickets for seven runs each! In the 1955 and 1957 seasons he bagged over two hundred wickets, the last person to reach that milestone. But nowhere was he more effective than on the matting of Pakistan where he took 81 first-class wickets for ten apiece on a B tour.

Only when Lock saw a film of his action in New Zealand in 1958/9 did he realise what he was doing, and set about changing his action again without losing his spin. Thereafter he did most of his work abroad. He first wintered in Western Australia in 1962/3, and did them proud until 1970/71. Cursing and chuntering, yet an old-fashioned sportsman, Locky proved that in slow bowling ripeness is all. Only Shackleton has taken more wickets among living bowlers.

FIRST-CLASS CAREER (1946–70/71)

812 innings	161 not outs	10342 runs	average 15.88	0 hundred
	2844 wickets	54709 runs	average 19.23	10–54 best

TEST RECORD (49 MATCHES)

63 innings	9 not outs	742 runs	average 13.74	—
	174 wickets	4451 runs	average 25.58	7–35 best

Series	Tests	O	M	R	W	Av
1952 v I	2	15.3	7	37	4	9.25
1953 v A	2	61	21	165	8	20.62
1953/4 in WI	5	296.5	88	718	14	51.28
1955 v SA	3	174	65	353	13	27.15
1956 v A	4	237.2	115	337	15	22.46
1956/7 in SA	1	26 (8-ball)	11	38	2	19.00
1957 v WI	3	114.2	59	163	15	10.86
1958 v NZ	5	176	93	254	34	7.47
1958/9 in A	4	126.2 (8-ball)	25	376	5	75.20
1958/9 in NZ	2	74.5	40	113	13	8.69
1961 v A	3	107	33	250	3	83.33
1961/2 in I	5	306.3	124	628	22	28.04
1961/2 in P	2	166	71	336	10	33.60
1962 v P	3	98	32	241	6	40.16
1963 v WI	3	91.5	24	230	6	38.33
1967/8 in WI	2	69	11	212	4	53.00

BRUCE DOOLAND

Bruce Dooland
(1923–80)
South Australia,
Nottinghamshire and
Australia

There may not have been a more valuable overseas player in county cricket. Nottinghamshire, certainly, cannot say that Sobers or Hadlee exceeded Bruce Dooland in value. In five seasons for them – from 1953 to 1957 – this friendly Australian with a strong arm, developed by pitching at baseball, took 770 wickets at 18.86; and he was bowling on the old Trent Bridge featherbeds in a weak side with minimal support. Such a feat sets him apart from his fellow Australian wrist-spinners in county cricket of the 1950s, men like Tribe and Walsh, McCool and McMahon.

It is a different game for a spinner if he has to come on after his side has been tumbled out and the opposition opening batsmen are going strong. Nottinghamshire had fallen into this sort of scenario when Dooland was registered to save them. In the previous ten seasons – Larwood and Voce and the Gunns all gone – they had not been in the upper half of the championship, and were fifteenth, seventeenth and sixteenth immediately prior to his arrival. Next year *Wisden* was declaring: 'Dooland, more than anyone, transformed the Nottinghamshire side'.

While his countrymen were losing the Ashes, Dooland bowls for the (English) Players against the Gentlemen in 1953

While the Australian tourists were losing the Ashes in 1953, Dooland captured more wickets than anyone else in the country, 172 at 16, and he lifted his county to eighth. In 1954 he again took by far the most wickets (196 at 15), set a new county record for the most in a season, and raised them to fifth. He was almost as influential in his next three years before returning to live in Australia. Then the county came bottom for three seasons out of four, and sixteenth in the other.

Dooland was a native of Adelaide, which meant that he was able to learn from another resident of that spacious and gracious city, Clarrie Grimmett. They did not quite overlap – when Dooland was chosen for the South Australian side at 17 he was refused leave by his employers – but Grimmett still aided him in refining his leg-break and googly, and taught him the flipper that skids through low. The ball that Grimmett had patented had quite in impact in Dooland's hands. Against Essex in 1954 he took 16 wickets for 83 runs, nine of them bowled. He didn't employ his googly frequently. He preferred control in English conditions (he was a league pro before joining Notts), and was brisk through the air while as steady as Hollies. He was more accurate than Walsh, who was a bigger tweaker.

Why was Dooland not a regular for Australia, especially as he did well on his début? Bradman, it seems, was a modern captain: he wanted to expose his opposition to the certain effects of pace rather than the hazards of leg-spin, especially as a new ball was to hand every 55 or 65 overs. So this great trier was neglected by his country. Nonetheless history should bracket Dooland with Gupte, Benaud and Qadir among the pick of post-war leg-spinners.

FIRST-CLASS CAREER (1945/6–57)

326 innings	33 not outs	7141 runs	average 24.37	4 hundreds
	1016 wickets	22332 runs	average 21.98	8–20 best

TEST RECORD (3 MATCHES)

5 innings	1 not out	76 runs	average 19.00	—
	9 wickets	419 runs	average 46.55	4–69 best

Series	Tests	O	M	R	W	Av
1946/7 v E	2	98 (8-ball)	9	351	8	43.75
1947/8 v I	1	12 (8-ball)	0	68	1	68.00

133

FRANK TYSON

Frank Holmes Tyson
(1930–   )
Northamptonshire and
England

One person saw Patrick Patterson bowling flat out on his Test début on a Kingston flier in 1985/6 against England, *and* Frank Tyson at full blast in Australia in 1954/5. That was John Woodcock, the correspondent of *The Times*, and it is his belief that they were equally quick, with one vital difference: that Tyson pitched the ball up as repeatedly as Patterson pitched short.

When the fast bowlers of the 1970s and 1980s have been timed, their top speed has been measured at around or just under 90mph, with their stock ball about 80mph. Just supposing Tyson wasn't quite so fast, any deficiency was made up for by the back foot no-ball rule. Tyson had a long drag, so he was delivering the ball a yard in front of the popping crease. If he was slower than Patterson, he was $\frac{1}{20}$th part closer to his target.

Tyson's aim was to drive the batsman back onto his stumps, to bowl him or trap him LBW. Of the 28 wickets in the series of his triumph, 12 occurred in these two ways – more than one with a low full toss, so hesitant were some batsmen. No helmets or chest-protectors were used against Tyson, or needed, as the short ball merely acted as a reminder every few overs. Even thigh-pads were uncommon in the 1950s, though Tyson rapidly brought into vogue the towel stuffed down the trousers.

Tyson was all explosive speed, generated by enormous shoulders, with a pair of legs and a back to match. He was no technician, which partly explains why Lancashire were not interested in him as an immature youth. He had to qualify by residence for Northamptonshire – not a good choice for him as Northampton's ground tended to draw his teeth. Meanwhile he studied at Durham University and impressed onlookers when allowed to play against the tourists of 1952 and 1953, in spite of being all chest and arm. Alf Gover taught him how to get more side-on, but even then his action involved a tremendous effort and heave.

If Tyson ever moved the ball it was into the right-hander. His arm was, to our eyes, low. Yet none of this technical unorthodoxy mattered so long as the human propeller of the ball could make it emit a fizzing sound as it passed the batsman, particularly an Australian batsman. 'The Typhoon' is alone with Larwood among English fast bowlers for having blitzed the Australians on their own pitches, although at various times Richardson, Trueman, Statham and Snow have administered a fair barrage.

By the end of his triumphal tour Tyson had 39 Test wickets, half his total tally. At the end of his first year in Test cricket he had taken 58 wickets in ten games, including a spell of five for five against South Africa in 1955 (four of them bowled). The pace and accuracy were diminishing by the 1956/7 tour of South Africa. Still, having selected

OPPOSITE: *When the*
Typhoon had moderated:
Tyson to the 1960 South
African tourists

him again for the 1958/9 tour of Australia, England could have made better use of him if they had played on Australian fears and past failures, instead of leaving him out to grass until the last two Tests.

Tyson, with the same sense of the appropriate as Larwood, settled in the country which had raised him to greatness.

FIRST-CLASS CAREER (1952–60)

316 innings	76 not outs	4103 runs	average 17.09	0 hundred
	767 wickets	16030 runs	average 20.89	8–60 best

TEST RECORD (17 MATCHES)

24 innings	3 not outs	230 runs	average 10.95	—
	76 wickets	1411 runs	average 18.56	7–27 best

Series	Tests	O		M	R	W	Av
1954 v P	1	22.4		5	57	5	11.40
1954/5 v A	5	151	(8-ball)	16	583	28	20.82
1954/5 v NZ	2	49		17	90	11	8.18
1955 v SA	2	103		19	258	14	18.42
1956 v A	1	14		5	34	1	34.00
1956/7 v SA	2	49	(8-ball)	14	100	8	12.50
1958/9 v A	2	54	(8-ball)	2	193	3	64.33
1958/9 v NZ	2	48		19	96	6	16.00

BRIAN STATHAM

To take his sweater off at the start of a spell, Brian Statham would put out his right hand and extend it to the bottom of his back, before pulling the sweater over his head. He was, in other words, as double-jointed as his pre-war predecessor as Lancashire's fast bowler, Ted McDonald. In addition, he hit the seam with such unremitting accuracy that he was the leading Test wicket-taker by the time he ripped out his last off-stump; and no one has taken more wickets for Lancashire than his 1816 at a mere 15 runs each.

John Brian Statham CBE
(1930–   )
Lancashire and England

Statham's early career was to be paralleled a generation later by Neil Foster. Both were picked prematurely in a time of dearth. Statham had to fly out to Australia at the age of 20, as the first of England's post-war bowling crop. At 24 he had been on four tours (Foster on five, thanks partly to the ban on English 'rebels' for visiting South Africa). Although both were burdened with this added task of learning their trade in the Test arena, they turned in creditable performances in India on their second tours.

Statham, or 'the Greyhound' or 'the Whippet', was not a swinger of the ball at all. He hit the seam unerringly, after which nine balls out of ten would dart into the right-hander. On odd days, without explanation, the ball would start seaming away and Statham was too natural a bowler to worry about why (for much the same reason he was not the best of captains when his turn at Lancashire came). He just bowled, and on a length that was never full enough to be driven or short enough to be forced. His bail-trimmers were especially adept at knocking over 'nine, ten, jack', so much so that once when he had to undergo a fitness test in Australia, he hit a single stump with 18 balls out of 24.

His unrelenting steadiness was sometimes held to be a defect, but it worked to the benefit of Tyson or Trueman at the other end if not to his own. A more serious lack was that of outright aggression, as in the case of Garth McKenzie or Wayne Daniel. It's said that he nearly hit a couple of batsmen when young and the experience helped to turn him into Gentleman George. Not that he couldn't produce a bouncer. He did – and it was a skidding one which came at the throat, and which therefore deserved to be aired more often. In the same easy-going fashion, he was content to let Tyson or Trueman have the advantage of the wind. Statham's Test record is infinitely more praiseworthy when you consider that he was at the wrong end for most of his England career.

Seldom did he bowl for England like the spearhead that he might have been in an age of less embarrassing riches. In the West Indies in 1953/4 he was given his head, and the new ball, and dismissed Worrell, Stollmeyer and Walcott in his opening spell. In 1955 at Lord's, when South Africa wanted 183 to win, Statham's 29 match-winning overs –

unchanged, though with a break for rain – brought seven for 39 and victory.

At Lancashire, on the other hand, where he appeared uncoached yet complete, he was entitled to a choice of ends and so his average for them is a truer reflection of his worth. His average in all first-class cricket is the lowest of any major pace bowler since the Great War. No pure bowler has been more highly decorated than Brian Statham, CBE.

OPPOSITE: *After a break of two years Statham returned for the 1965 Oval Test and seven South African wickets*

FIRST-CLASS CAREER (1950–68)

647 innings	145 not outs	5424 runs	average 10.80	0 hundred
	2260 wickets	36995 runs	average 16.36	8 34 best

TEST RECORD (70 MATCHES)

87 innings	28 not outs	675 runs	average 11.44	—
	252 wickets	6261 runs	average 24.84	7–39 best

Series	Tests	O	M	R	W	Av
1950/51 in NZ	1	20	5	47	1	47.00
1951 v SA	2	48	14	78	4	19.50
1951/2 in I	5	126	36	293	8	36.62
1953 v A	1	43	10	88	2	44.00
1953/4 in WI	4	153	24	460	16	28.75
1954 v P	4	89	26	213	11	19.36
1954/5 in A	5	143.3 (8-ball)	16	499	18	27.72
1954/5 in NZ	2	58.4	23	91	12	7.58
1955 v SA	4	177.2	54	363	17	21.35
1956 v A	3	106	35	184	7	26.28
1956/7 in SA	4	130.1 (8-ball)	20	349	14	24.93
1957 v WI	3	158.1	37	433	13	33.30
1958 v NZ	2	67	20	130	7	18.57
1958/9 in A	4	104 (8-ball)	12	286	12	23.83
1959 v I	3	112.2	44	223	17	13.12
1959/60 in WI	3	130.4	42	286	10	28.60
1960 v SA	5	203	54	491	27	18.18
1961 v A	4	201.4	41	501	17	29.47
1962 v P	3	120.1	40	278	16	17.37
1962/3 in A	5	165.2 (8-ball)	16	580	13	44.61
1963 v WI	2	81	10	243	3	81.00
1965 v SA	1	53.2	12	145	7	20.71

FRED TRUEMAN

Frederick Sewards Trueman
(1931–   )
Yorkshire and England

Those who know Fred Trueman only from his radio commentaries and lamentations about the modern game may be sceptical about his prowess, yet there can be no question that he possessed one of the most handsome of bowling actions. His black-haired gallop to the wicket, and the cartwheel of latent energy he formed before delivery, were so exciting that while others have and will overtake his record of 307 Test wickets, none will better him in this regard.

So fine indeed was his action that it was both a strength and a limitation. Trueman in his cartwheel turned himself as side-on as it was possible to go, making the outswinger his to command. He would start it, too, on middle-and-leg so that the batsman had no option but to grope. Yet this made it impossible for Trueman to produce the inswinger without a tell-tale change of action. He would have had to be more chest-on – as Marshall, say, became – to produce both swings.

Of course, as the man himself will no doubt tell you, he was able to go wide of the crease and push the ball into the right-hander for some variety. And, at much-reduced pace, there was that legendary off-cutter which won the Headingley Test of 1961 and featured a spell of five for nought. With his index finger he would cut the ball in slightly – and no kidding. For proof, he had another field day with it once at Swansea for Yorkshire.

This expertise was backed by aggression, confidence and a propaganda campaign of such artfulness that Trueman was perceived to be even more dangerous than he was. He wasn't actually the beer drinker that legend and the advertisers portrayed him to be, but the rest was true. He did spend his time in the opposition dressing-room sizing up young prey – 'Can you hook, son? You'll get the chance today' – and on the field he was the Spofforth or Lillee of his time, the master of sharp comments and gestures. Not that he was all talk: at the end of the longest day he could raise a gallop and let everyone know Fred Trueman was around.

He was always quick. When Yorkshire Second XI brought in a young colt who worked underground at Maltby Main colliery handling the tubs, Trueman immediately turned Jack Firth from wicket- to goal-keeper. Control, of mind and body, arrived in the due course of time and was completely achieved in the end. Along the road he had a pronounced drag of the back foot which had to be corrected, while the fiery temperament led to uproar on the 1953/4 tour of the West Indies and cost him his place to Australia the following winter (in all, he spent only four winters on tour). The promising start in 1952, when he scattered 29 Indians like a dog among sheep, was not fulfilled until the late 1950s.

His best series happened in 1963 when he was not fast at all, and had

The perfect cartwheel, 1953

almost given up the bouncer, which he always telegraphed too obviously in his run-up. But he certainly swung the ball a long way, as 34 West Indians found, 11 of them in one Test, 12 in another. Watching the film of that series, it is hard to think that he had been fast by the standards of today. There is, however, more than one way to skin a cat.

Trueman liked to call himself 'the finest bloody fast bowler that ever drew breath'. At the time of his retirement the statement was quite possibly true. Subsequently it has been overtaken by inevitable human progress.

FIRST-CLASS CAREER (1949–69)

713 innings	120 not outs	9231 runs	average 15.56	3 hundreds
	2304 wickets	42154 runs	average 18.29	8–28 best

TEST RECORD (67 MATCHES)

85 innings	14 not outs	981 runs	average 13.81	—
	307 wickets	6625 runs	average 21.57	8–31 best

Series	Tests	O	M	R	W	Av
1952 v I	4	119.4	25	386	29	13.31
1953 v A	1	26.3	4	90	4	22.50
1953/4 in WI	3	133.2	27	420	9	46.66
1955 v SA	1	35	4	112	2	56.00
1956 v A	2	75	13	184	9	20.44
1957 v WI	5	173.3	34	455	22	20.68
1958 v NZ	5	131.5	44	256	15	17.06
1958/9 in A	3	87 (8-ball)	11	276	9	30.66
1958/9 in NZ	2	44.5	17	105	5	21.00
1959 v I	5	177.4	53	401	24	16.70
1959/60 in WI	5	220.3	62	549	21	26.14
1960 v SA	5	180.3	31	508	25	20.32
1961 v A	4	164.4	21	529	20	26.45
1962 v P	4	164.5	37	439	22	19.69
1962/3 in A	5	158.3 (8-ball)	9	521	20	26.05
1962/3 in NZ	2	88	29	164	14	11.71
1963 v WI	5	236.4	53	594	34	17.47
1964 v A	4	133.3	25	399	17	23.47
1965 v NZ	2	96.3	23	237	6	39.50

LES JACKSON

The thigh-pad was not a common item of attire until the 1960s; Donald Carr, for instance, never wore one in his entire career which ran until 1962. But he, as captain of Derbyshire, had one great advantage: he never had to bat against Les Jackson on a cold morning at Derby when the wind was blasting across the bleak old Racecourse ground. This mean old fast–medium slinger, who made the ball hit the deck and dart around sharply, must have done more than anyone to make the thigh-pad part of standard equipment.

Jackson could be more of a handful still at Chesterfield where the trees around Queen's Park made the ball swing further. Some talk of Trueman and Tyson, and some of Statham and Loader, but of all the pace bowlers of the 1950s, none was dreaded more than Jackson in his element. He took his first-class wickets at 17 runs a time, and more of them than any other Derbyshire bowler (1670). In 1958 Jackson recorded the lowest average (10.99) for any bowler achieving a hundred wickets in a season since 1894.

Herbert Leslie Jackson (1921–   )
Derbyshire and England

Recalled after 12 years, and effective in the Headingley Test of 1961, Jackson still doesn't seem to impress the Establishment

143

Jackson was the youngest of 13 children born to a coal miner in Whitwell. He was tough all right, and he was hungry when he finally made his Derbyshire début at 26. He was a natural bowler, too, for he went straight into the Bassetlaw League without having had the chance to play cricket even at the village school.

The lack of coaching was evident in his rustic batting, and in his low bowling arm, but the latter scarcely mattered because he had a great body action. He placed his front foot close to the line of the stumps and turned right round. The delivery had a suggestion of the Jeff Thomson-style sling, and held the same sort of threat to the unprotected thigh. You might be able to play forward a couple of times in Jackson's first over but that was it for the day.

The question why such a bowler was only twice chosen for England cannot be satisfactorily answered. In 1949, when Alec Bedser was not fully fit, Jackson bowled 39 overs at New Zealand and took three for 72. Twelve years later he bowled 44 overs against Australia at Headingley, took four for 83, and was replaced for the next Test by Statham and Jack Flavell. True, he was 40 by then, but there is nothing in these performances to justify the fact that he had to spend his winters in the colliery. The only tour for which he was selected was one by a Commonwealth team to India in 1950/51, and then he had to return home for an elbow operation shortly after the start.

History is usually made and written by the Establishment. To it, a hard-boiled old customer like Jackson cannot have been a friend. Along the line he must have offended somebody. For in county cricket he was one of the very best; one who left an impression in many places.

FIRST-CLASS CAREER (1947–63)

489 innings	153 not outs	2083 runs	average 6.19	0 hundred
	1733 wickets	30101 runs	average 17.36	9–17 best

TEST RECORD (2 MATCHES)

2 innings	1 not out	15 runs	average 15.00	—
	7 wickets	155 runs	average 22.14	2–26 best

Series	Tests	O	M	R	W	Av
1949 v NZ	1	39	14	72	3	24.00
1961 v A	1	44	16	83	4	20.75

FERGIE GUPTE

During the 1950s batsmen around the world were more likely to pronounce Gupte's full name correctly than they were to read his wrist-spin consistently. His names however could be abbreviated to the nickname of 'Fergie'. There was little likelihood of deciphering his bowling unless a batsman dared to attack, for Fergie was rated the best wrist-spinner in Test cricket in the decade after the war.

Without long fingers but with the strong supple wrists which the subcontinent seems to nurture in its bowlers, Gupte could really spin his leg-break and googly and impart a nice loop initially. His pace was like that of Abdul Qadir when not pushing the ball through – that is, quick enough to deter all but the most adventurous from attempting the charge.

In his first series abroad Gupte was pitted against Weekes, Worrell and Walcott at the height of their powers, and he conceded well under two-and-a-half runs per over while taking 27 wickets at 29 runs each. In his eight first-class games on that tour he took 50 wickets for an Indian team that was making its first visit to the Caribbean, was poor at catching and had only Mankad to keep the other end going. No one since the First World War has fared better on a tour of the West Indies.

Gupte learned his bowling (he never picked up much about batting) at Shivaji Park, one of the few cricket nurseries that overcrowded Bombay has. He went on to Bombay University and made his début for Bombay when, with one wicket, he was only marginally more successful than he was to be on his Test début against England in 1951/2. His quality, however, was never in doubt, although he did lose something of his loop when he went into the Lancashire League after the West Indian tour and began pushing the ball through at sloggers careless of reputation.

He became the first Indian to take all ten wickets in a first-class innings, and the first to take nine in a Test innings. He was unlucky too: Lance Gibbs was the only West Indian batsman at Kanpur in 1958/9 whom he did not dismiss. And by then Mankad had faded away so that Gupte was no more supported than the left-hander had been before his advent. Gupte had 22 wickets in that series against West Indies; India's next highest had five.

These circumstances did nothing to remedy the Indian's one weakness which was not technical but temperamental. If a batsman got after him – as Neil Harvey once did – he could be too readily discouraged. He was a Maratha, a member of a warrior race, but without quite the resilience every spinner must have. The tactical withdrawal, by firing a few in at leg-stump, has to be followed by a later spell of renewed heart.

His career ended abruptly when he was banned from Test cricket – he should have gone to the West Indies again in 1961/2 – for disciplinary

Subhashchandra Pandhrinath Gupte (1929–   ) Bombay, Bengal, Rajasthan, Trinidad and India

A leg-break in the Nursery, 1959. It is vital for that left elbow to be dragged down and in, as Gupte does, to achieve the bounce

reasons. He was found guilty of partaking in a players' romp, but it was found out later that he had been framed. Too late, for he returned to Trinidad, married and settled there.

FIRST-CLASS CAREER (1948/9–63/4)

125 innings	32 not outs	761 runs	average	8.18	0 hundred
	530 wickets	12567 runs	average	23.71	10–78 best

TEST RECORD (36 MATCHES)

42 innings	13 not outs	183 runs	average	6.31	—
	149 wickets	4403 runs	average	29.55	9–102 best

Series	Tests	O	M	R	W	Av
1951/2 v E	1	18	0	57	0	—
1952/3 v P	2	47.2	13	133	5	26.60
1952/3 in WI	5	329.3	87	789	27	29.22
1954/5 in P	5	276.5	107	475	21	22.61
1955/6 v NZ	5	356.4	152	669	34	19.67
1956/7 v A	3	96.3	31	263	8	32.87
1958/9 v WI	5	312.3	71	927	22	42.13
1959 in E	5	199.4	51	589	17	34.64
1960/61 v P	3	134.4	52	243	8	30.37
1961/2 v E	2	109	34	257	7	36.71

HUGH TAYFIELD

As an off-spinner Hugh Tayfield was remarkably similar to John Emburey. Equally remarkable was the difference in their effect. While Emburey has had to be content with a couple of wickets per Test in recent years, Tayfield averaged nearer five than four. He was the first South African to take a hundred Test wickets, and he remains their leading wicket-taker by a lane if not a street.

Tayfield, like Emburey, placed his leading left foot in line with off-stump and came as close as possible to it without brushing off the bails. In consequence, when this type of bowler bowls a ball on off-stump, it will often pass outside it if straight. In other words, the angle is almost that of a bowler operating round the wicket.

This set Tayfield apart. He was treated like an off-spinner, yet it was only when his slower ball gripped and turned that he bowled like a conventional one. For the most part, batsmen were hitting against the tide when they aimed to leg; and there in waiting would be his famous 'gate' of two short mid-ons. Perhaps the best way to tackle Tayfield was to hit him with the prevailing tide through mid-off and over extra-cover; an inside-out batsman like Jim Parks was best suited to this counter-attack.

Tayfield – or 'Toey', from his habit of tapping his boot before each ball – had a longer arm-swing than Emburey and generally bowled a fuller length, tempting the batsman to mis-hit his drive. He could – and had to – bowl long spells, especially in Australia in 1952/3 when South Africa created a sensation. By fielding out of their skins, especially to Tayfield while he took 30 wickets, they squared the series.

Like Emburey again, Tayfield couldn't bowl round the wicket without going to the edge of the crease; this, combined with his lack of spin, made him relatively less of a performer on helpful pitches. His best work was done in adversity, when South Africa had batted no more than moderately, when Adcock was resting and no one else stood between his country and a trouncing. Only a slow bowler knows how much he depends on his fielders in those circumstances.

Tayfield entered first-class cricket under the wing of his uncle Sidney Martin, who had done the double for Worcestershire before the Second World War. A leg-spinner as a boy, Hugh acclimatised to off-spin so that he was playing for Natal at 17. His path into the Test side was then barred by Athol Rowan, a bigger off-spinner, said by some to have been superior to Tayfield in spite of his 54 Test wickets costing 38 each. When Rowan retired with knee trouble shortly before the tour to Australia, Tayfield got his break. He followed this up with 13 wickets in one Test, and 70 on the tour, both records for a South African in Australia.

The absence of the 3lb bat was a factor in Tayfield's favour and the

Hugh Joseph Tayfield
(1928–   )
Natal, Rhodesia, Transvaal and South Africa

1950s was the most defensive decade in Test cricket, so that Tayfield was often allowed to stay on top by supine batsmen. Few were more lethargic than England's on their 1956/7 tour when Tayfield was allowed to send down 137 balls without conceding a run – a statistic that shouldn't be broken. Further South African records fell to Tayfield with nine wickets in one innings and 37 in the series. He did well not to play a generation later.

FIRST-CLASS CAREER (1945/6–62/3)

259 innings	47 not outs	3668 runs	average 17.30	0 hundred
	864 wickets	18890 runs	average 21.86	9–113 best

TEST RECORD (37 MATCHES)

60 innings	9 not outs	862 runs	average 16.90	—
	170 wickets	4405 runs	average 25.91	9–113 best

Series	Tests	O	M	R	W	Av
1949/50 v A	5	198.4 (8-ball)	21	726	17	42.70
1952/3 in A	5	278.4 (8-ball)	58	843	30	28.10
1952/3 in NZ	2	118.5	46	162	10	16.20
1953/4 v NZ	5	192.6 (8-ball)	80	377	21	17.95
1955 in E	5	313.3	124	568	26	21.84
1956/7 v E	5	285 (8-ball)	105	636	37	17.18
1957/8 v A	5	276.3 (8-ball)	100	639	17	37.58
1960 in E	5	187.3	68	454	12	37.83

The two best off-spinners of the time, Tayfield and Titmus

ROY GILCHRIST

In January 1958 the modern era of West Indian fast bowling dawned. West Indies had just scored 579 in their first innings of the First Test against Pakistan. In front of a capacity Bridgetown crowd the new West Indian fast bowler measured out his run. He was a slightly built fellow with exceptionally long arms, no bigger than Constantine before him and smaller than Marshall was to be. But when Roy Gilchrist ran in, his first ball lifted and soared over the batsman's head, and the wicket-keeper's head, then after one more bounce hit the sightscreen and ricocheted back to the middle. The crowd roared its approval.

Gilchrist was soon to pass on the torch to Hall and Griffith and others. But while he held it, he illuminated the path for them to follow – and another path for them not to follow. He was raw in everything he did. He was intent on bowling as fast as he could with scant regard for length, swing or anything else. It was his successors who learnt that speed had to be combined with control, and self-control. Gilchrist was therefore not an unqualified great, yet he may be reckoned so for the fear he caused among batsmen, and the inspiration he became to youngsters.

He was born in the most rural backwaters of Jamaica on the south-east coast, in a family as large as it was impoverished. Apart from his long arms, there was little flesh on him until adulthood, but he was always bent on destruction with a ball in his hand. He actually made his Test début on the 1957 tour of England, before his opening ball in a Test in the Caribbean, but the pitches were too slow for him, the climate too cold. He was warming up in the series against Pakistan, without any attempt at the 'beamer', that ball with which he was to be infamously associated.

Gilchrist's career rose quickly to its climax on the 1958/9 tour of India and Pakistan. No fast bowler has ever wreaked such havoc on the subcontinent as Gilchrist, who scared, startled or petrified 71 batsmen out at an average of 13 – unless it was Wes Hall who took 87 at 15 each at the other end. The Indian batsmen then were unused to high speed (and thought that they were immune from it on baked-mud pitches), and to balls which did not hit the earth at all. In particular, Gilchrist made immoderate use of the beamer against a turbaned Cambridge blue who riled him and brought out the rebel in him. Gerry Alexander, West Indian captain and fellow blue, had already dropped Gilchrist from one Test and this latest display led to Roy being sent home in mid-tour and disgrace. Only Lala Amarnath in 1936 had been sentenced to a similar fate.

In the 1950s the beamer was not the taboo ball it has since become; Derek Shackleton, for example, would slip the odd one in early in his career. It was Gilchrist's high-speed use of it that served to make the delivery unethical; it was effectively outlawed when Tony Greig hit the

Roy Gilchrist
(1934–   )
Jamaica, Hyderabad and
West Indies

Mercifully, this ball from Gilchrist, when confined to the leagues, seems to have bounced

Australian all-rounder Graeme Watson flush on the nose and caused him to have 14 blood transfusions.

'Gilly' resorted to the Lancashire League, without ceasing to be controversial, and never played for West Indies again, although he was not formally banned. Aged 24 when he bowled his last for them, he was on the threshold of creating some real damage.

FIRST-CLASS CAREER (1956/7–62/3)

43 innings	10 not outs	258 runs	average 7.81	0 hundred
	167 wickets	4342 runs	average 26.00	6–16 best

TEST RECORD (13 MATCHES)

14 innings	3 not outs	60 runs	average 5.45	—
	57 wickets	1521 runs	average 26.68	6–55 best

Series	Tests	O	M	R	W	Av
1957 in E	4	152.3	19	466	10	46.60
1957/8 v P	5	187.1	32	636	21	30.28
1958/9 in I	4	198.1	73	419	26	16.11

ALAN DAVIDSON

Nobody has come closer to being the ideal left–arm fast–medium bowler than Alan Davidson. He was, for a start, blessed with the ideal physique. He was six feet tall and his torso tapered down from broad shoulders. Another of those athletic New South Welshmen who excelled at rugby league and cricket, he would have been as impressive in a life saver's swimming costume as in flannels.

If there was a drawback, it was that this superb specimen was a bit of a hypochondriac. His contemporaries say that it was fatal to ask 'how are you?' on seeing him in the morning, for an unending list of ailments would flow forth. When leading the Australian attack in his prime years of the late 1950s and early 1960s, he would often limp back to his mark – and limp so badly that batsmen who did not know their Davidson must have thought that he had bowled his last. But on reaching his mark he would be encouraged by a word from Richie Benaud, scent success again and come powering in off 15 paces to swing his shoulders and bowl some 'magic balls'.

*Alan Keith Davidson
(1929–   )
New South Wales and
Australia*

*Compare this with
Johnston's action.
Davidson's suggests the more
power. Ten out of ten, in fact*

Normally he would swing the ball into the right-hander, or run it across him. Occasionally, as in India where he once had 12 wickets in a Test, he would go round the wicket to bowl cutters with the keeper standing back. Otherwise the tactic of bowling round was to lose the wonderful advantages he had in being so well-constructed and left-handed.

His apprenticeship was lengthy before he broke through to the front rank. After 12 Tests he had taken 16 wickets. Lindwall and Miller, and more briefly Archer and Crawford, all took the new ball ahead of him until 1957/8 when Australia visited South Africa. Davidson hadn't been expensive; he had simply been given scant opportunity. Until then success had come unfailingly to him for he had been a star schoolboy all-rounder in Gosford, to the north of Sydney, where he initially bowled wrist-spin. Having moved to Sydney and picked up pace, he took a wicket with his first ball for New South Wales Second XI, and a wicket with his second ball for the first team.

In 1957/8, with only Meckiff now to challenge him for the new ball, Davidson took 25 wickets in the series, and that remained a typical return for the rest of his Test career. In his last 32 Tests he took 170 wickets. His average, too, was astonishing: at 20.58 it was not touched by a regular, post-war pace bowler until Marshall came along. He was a match-winning batsman as well at Old Trafford in 1961, and a match-tying one at Brisbane in 1960/61. On the latter occasion he was the first to do the match double in Tests of a hundred runs and ten wickets.

FIRST-CLASS CAREER (1949/50–62/3)

| 246 innings | 39 not outs | 6804 runs | average 32.86 | 9 hundreds |
| | 672 wickets | 14048 runs | average 20.90 | 7–31 best |

TEST RECORD (44 MATCHES)

| 61 innings | 7 not outs | 1328 runs | average 24.59 | — |
| | 186 wickets | 3819 runs | average 20.53 | 7–93 best |

Series	Tests	O		M	R	W	Av
1953 in E	5	125		42	212	8	26.50
1954/5 v E	3	71	(8-ball)	16	220	3	73.33
1956 in E	2	19.4		2	56	2	28.00
1956/7 in P	1	15		9	15	2	7.50
1956/7 in I	1	23		10	42	1	42.00
1957/8 in SA	5	201.5	(8-ball)	47	425	25	17.00
1958/9 v E	5	183.5	(8-ball)	45	456	24	19.00
1959/60 in P	3	148.5		34	298	12	24.83
1959/60 in I	5	244.5		85	431	29	14.86
1960/61 v WI	4	173.7	(8-ball)	25	612	33	18.54
1961 in E	5	280.2		86	572	23	24.86
1962/3 v E	5	175.6	(8-ball)	30	480	24	20.00

RICHIE BENAUD

There has not been a more famous spell of spin bowling than Richie Benaud's at Old Trafford. Yet it has to an extent distorted the image of his bowling, for otherwise he was never at his best in England. He was a wrist-spinner whose forte was bounce, and he was therefore better suited to overseas pitches.

England players and supporters of today may not understand how a Test match and a series could be lost to leg-spin from round the wicket. But there are two keys to the events on the last afternoon of the Fourth Test of 1961. The first is that those infamous footmarks were created by Fred Trueman under the back foot no-ball rule. Thus Trueman, who 'dragged' a fair distance, had roughened up the pitch in an area significantly close to a good length − whereas it has to be virtually a half-volley to land in modern footmarks. The second key is that England were going for a win. If they had not been tempted to chase 256 in 230 minutes (the series then stood at one-all), England should have been able to pad out Benaud and survive.

Benaud finished with six for 70. At the zenith of his spell he took five wickets − Subba Row, Dexter, May, Close and Murray − in 25 balls. His switch to round the wicket was not only a match-winning move but also dramatically sudden in its effect. Yet it would be a mistake to conclude, on the basis of Old Trafford in 1961, that Benaud was an exception to the rule which has seen all Australian leg-spinners as expensive luxuries in England since the Second World War. Benaud, on three tours of England, totalled 19 wickets outside that historic spell. While accurate, he wasn't particularly penetrative.

Some allowance should be made, though, for the shoulder damage he was suffering in 1961. At the start of the tour he inflamed a tendon in his right shoulder and could seldom bowl a leg-spinner, let alone a googly. This developed into the bursitis which caused his retirement, although not all batsmen by then had discovered that the googly had itself long since retired. In 1962/3 Benaud's seven for 18 helped New South Wales to administer the first innings defeat of an English touring team in 80 years by a state side.

In the New South Wales side at 18 and the Australian team at 21, Benaud needed plenty of time and practice before making his mark as a Test spinner. His apprenticeship ran almost parallel to Davidson's, and it was not until the 1957/8 tour of South Africa, when the Lindwall–Miller generation had passed on, that the pair of them came right to the fore.

Benaud then took the astonishing number of 106 wickets − the most in a South African season − including 30 in the series. (He was then employing the flipper which he had learnt from Grimmett via Dooland.) When he inherited the Australian captaincy the following year from Ian

Richard Benaud, OBE
(1930–)
New South Wales and
Australia

Craig who had hepatitis, Benaud if anything increased his performance. There haven't been better captains. To that must be added Benaud's gully fielding, forceful driving, and 248 Test wickets, the Australian record when he called it a day. As a cricketer, Benaud was even more influential than as a commentator.

OPPOSITE: *Benaud to Cowdrey in the Adelaide Test of 1958/9. Australia won by ten wickets*

FIRST-CLASS CAREER (1948/9–67/8)

| 365 innings | 44 not outs | 11719 runs | average 36.50 | 23 hundreds |
| | 945 wickets | 23370 runs | average 24.73 | 7–18 best |

TEST RECORD (63 MATCHES)

| 97 innings | 7 not outs | 2201 runs | average 24.45 | 3 hundreds |
| | 248 wickets | 6704 runs | average 27.03 | 7–72 best |

Series	Tests	O	M	R	W	Av
1951/2 v WI	1	4.3 (8-ball)	0	14	1	14.00
1952/3 v SA	4	105.6 (8-ball)	23	306	10	30.60
1953 in E	3	68	19	174	2	87.00
1954/5 v E	5	116.7 (8-ball)	23	377	10	37.70
1954/5 in WI	5	184.5	47	485	18	26.94
1956 in E	5	154	48	330	8	41.25
1956/7 in P	1	17	5	36	1	36.00
1956/7 in I	3	169.5	52	388	23	16.86
1957/8 in SA	5	242.1 (8-ball)	56	658	30	21.93
1958/9 v E	5	233.2 (8-ball)	65	584	31	18.83
1959/60 in P	3	224	94	380	18	21.11
1959/60 in I	5	322.2	146	568	29	19.58
1960/61 v WI	5	268.1 (8-ball)	56	779	23	33.86
1961 in E	4	214.3	76	488	15	32.53
1962/3 v E	5	233 (8-ball)	58	688	17	40.47
1963/4 v SA	4	169.1 (8-ball)	37	449	12	37.41

DEREK SHACKLETON

Derek Shackleton
(1924–   )
Hampshire and England

Nobody else has clocked up a hundred wickets in 20 consecutive seasons as Derek Shackleton did without fail from 1949 to 1968. Indeed, only Rhodes has reached that landmark more often (23 times). All this work Shackleton undertook with the utmost composure. If he ever turned a hair during his career, at least it never fell out of place; his hair was as immaculate as his length.

Those who have only seen Shackleton on the video of England's 1963 series against West Indies must have wondered how he played Test cricket at all: a few easy lopes, a ball of almost slow-medium pace and this guy was England's opening bowler! By then, however, Shackleton was verging on 39 and had cut down a lot on his speed. In the 1950s he had been brisk, so that Hampshire's keeper Leo Harrison had to stand back, and the ball would carry. By slowing down, Shackleton prolonged his career until he was 44. Everything was done with a view to economy.

He was a northerner, it may be deduced, by origin. Born in Todmorden, he played for its league team for a couple of seasons, mostly as a batsman; yet whenever he had a go at medium-pace he was naturally good. He moved south during his National Service in the army. He joined Hampshire as a batsman, and was also persuaded to take up leg-breaks. It was an interruption he could have done without: he was 25 at the end of 1949, the season he established himself with his first haul of a hundred wickets – at medium-pace – and 914 runs (he never approached the double again).

Shackleton was a swing bowler if the ball would swing, and a seamer if it would not. His principal ball was the outswinger. While the in-swinger was infrequent, the odd ball would nip back, and like even the greatest of pace bowlers he could not be sure when. One ball 'Shack' did not bowl was the half-volley – except possibly in his opening spell of the season, after a winter's lay-off, if the wind suddenly blew a sharp gust behind him.

He was consequently a bowler best suited to conditions in England, not least at Weston-super-Mare where, against Somerset in 1955, he achieved the most remarkable analysis in county cricket this century: eight wickets for four runs, and 14 for 29 in the match. On the other hand, when the assistance from the pitch was minimal, his penetration could be found wanting.

On his Test début he ran into Weekes and Worrell at Trent Bridge and emerged rather scathed, although he did top-score in England's reply with 42. He was selected for only two tours, one for England, the other for a Commonwealth team, and both to India in the early 1950s. He did well in the minor matches – indeed he had a hundred wickets on the two tours combined – but laboured against the best batsmen once the shine had gone.

Shackleton, immaculate, at Southampton in 1965. No wonder Hampshire captains have been able to set challenging targets, with Shackleton and Marshall to defend them

In county cricket he was unmastered – save, curiously and occasionally, by Fred Trueman who might put his foot down the pitch and mow him to mid-wicket. If any further proof of his economy were desired it arrived in 1969, the first year of the Sunday League. Admittedly, batting tactics were still naïve and Shack was allowed to bowl out his opening spell without having to return for the slog. Nevertheless, it was wondrous that he should have bowled 80 overs – at the age of 44 going on 45 – for only 168 runs.

FIRST-CLASS CAREER (1948–69)

852 innings	197 not outs	9574 runs	average 14.61	0 hundred
	2857 wickets	53303 runs	average 18.65	9–30 best

TEST RECORD (7 MATCHES)

13 innings	7 not outs	113 runs	average 18.83	—
	18 wickets	768 runs	average 42.66	4–72 best

Series	Tests	O	M	R	W	Av
1950 v WI	1	49	9	135	1	135.00
1951 v SA	1	25	7	39	1	39.00
1951/2 in I	1	29	7	76	1	76.00
1963 v WI	4	243.2	73	518	15	34.53

GARY SOBERS

In the Headingley Test of 1963 Gary, or Garry, Sobers decided he fancied a go with the new ball in England's second innings. And with his fourth ball he knocked Micky Stewart's off-stump back with an inswinger. Sobers had, of course, already hit a century and a half-century earlier in the match. He then finished England off with spinners which turned as much as Gibbs's off-breaks did at the other end.

Sobers is the most complete bowler, let alone cricketer, there has ever been. Alan Davidson could bowl fast–medium swing, even more consistently than Sobers, but the Australian had orthodox spin alone for variation. Sobers could bowl wrist-spin as well: chinaman, googly, finger-spinner, inswinger, bouncer, the lot. If he had a deficiency, it was that he failed to bowl right-handed as well.

He began in Barbados as a left-arm orthodox spinner, for which

Sir Garfield St Aubrun Sobers (1936–   ) Barbados, South Australia, Nottinghamshire and West Indies

Not a bad second, third or, in Sobers' case, fourth string to have to one's bow

159

Sobers has Dexter, England's captain, caught behind during the Oval Test of 1963

purpose the fifth finger he had on his hand before surgery (in addition to a thumb) may not have been a handicap. He made his début for West Indies at 17 when Valentine was injured and, being blessed by fortune, Sobers picked up three English tail-enders and four wickets in all. He did not turn much but had a nice arm-ball which drifted in.

By 1957 Sobers knew which way up a bat was to be held, and thereafter batting was the most important branch of his game. But in the nets meanwhile he was bowling pace, without being allowed to try his hand in the middle, even when Ramadhin had shot his bolt in the series against England. It was during Gary's subsequent period as a league professional that he brought his pace bowling and wrist-spin up to international scratch, so that Worrell had quite a useful all-rounder at his disposal by the 1960/61 tour of Australia.

For the occasions when he had to bowl slow, Sobers favoured his wrist-spin thenceforth until 1966, when he discovered that the tendons in his left shoulder had worked loose and that he would need an operation if he were to bowl the googly again. He kept to orthodoxy thereafter for his slower style, but mostly to pace. In 1970 at Lord's, in the first of the matches between England and the Rest of the World, Sobers came on to bowl after McKenzie and Procter, and demonstrated how to make best use of a humid morning. He ran through England with six for 21, and picked up 21 wickets in the series for the same average.

His Test bowling figures would have been more impressive if that series had been considered official – as it would have been if Sobers had not viewed cricket as a game of chivalry. But then he could afford to be generous, since the gods had been so generous with him.

FIRST-CLASS CAREER (1952/3–74)

| 609 innings | 93 not outs | 28315 runs | average 54.87 | 86 hundreds |
| | 1043 wickets | 28941 runs | average 27.74 | 9–49 best |

TEST RECORD (93 MATCHES)

| 160 innings | 21 not outs | 8032 runs | average 57.78 | 26 hundreds |
| | 235 wickets | 7999 runs | average 34.03 | 6–73 best |

Series	Tests	O	M	R	W	Av
1953/4 v E	1	29.5	9	81	4	20.25
1954/5 v A	4	93.5	36	213	6	35.50
1955/6 in NZ	4	46.5	26	49	2	24.50
1957 in E	5	134	24	355	5	71.00
1957/8 v P	5	171.3	53	377	4	94.25
1958/9 in I	5	119.1	33	292	10	29.20
1958/9 in P	3	66	36	77	0	—
1959/60 v E	5	114	14	355	9	39.44
1960/61 in A	5	191 (8-ball)	27	588	15	39.20
1961/2 v I	5	223.3	61	473	23	20.56
1963 in E	5	231	50	571	20	28.55
1964/5 v A	5	192.3	53	490	12	40.83
1966 in E	5	269.4	78	545	20	27.25
1966/7 in I	3	155.1	51	350	14	25.00
1967/8 v E	5	232.5	72	508	13	39.07
1968/9 in A	5	206.1 (8-ball)	37	733	18	40.72
1968/9 in NZ	3	105 (8-ball)	23	301	7	43.00
1969 in E	3	145	47	318	11	28.90
1970/71 v I	5	219	71	401	12	33.41
1971/2 v NZ	5	181	56	332	10	33.20
1973 in E	3	82.1	24	169	6	28.16
1973/4 v E	4	223.2	92	421	14	30.07

NEIL ADCOCK

Neil Amwin Treharne
Adcock
(1931–   )
Transvaal, Natal and South
Africa

After their googly bowlers in the period around the First World War, South Africa did not produce a great bowler until Neil Adcock appeared on the scene in the 1950s. It may have been partly a question of stimulus: for the 40 years from 1911, South Africa did not go on overseas tours except to England, and once to Australasia. There was no ban on their touring, as the apartheid system was not installed until the end of that period. The original constitution of India's Board of Control, for example, specifically enjoined the promotion of cricketing relations with – among others – South Africa.

In the 1950s, with the growth of air travel, the touring scene became more active. When the New Zealanders were visiting South Africa in 1953/4, a young fast bowler of English ancestry made an instant impact, not least on Bert Sutcliffe's skull so that he was never the same batsman again. Adcock then was 6′ 2″, genuinely fast if not in the highest Tyson–Thomson category, and never harboured the slightest qualm about pitching short. Indeed, allowing for a relatively limited career, he may have done more physical damage than any other bowler in the pre-helmet era.

On the 1955 tour of England, Adcock pitched too short when his foot was not in plaster with a broken bone. He remained prone to injury until he decided to build up his body with weight-lifting exercises before the 1960 tour. He then took 26 Test wickets, equalling Tayfield's record for a South African in a series in England; and 108 first-class wickets in all (at 14.03 runs each), the most by a South African pace bowler on a tour of England.

By then he was a burlier version of Statham, persistent in his stamina and forever nipping the ball back (he swung it little). That summer was a wet one, and Test pitches were not covered during the day's play, so that often a sharp shower would freshen up the pitch and the bowler. Some of the resulting fliers were unpleasant: Geoff Pullar had his left wrist broken by Adcock, who lacked nothing that summer except a partner.

Peter Heine had earlier done that job – taller, even more aggressive in character, but not quite so quick. In 1960 Geoff Griffin was to have been Adcock's partner, only he became the first bowler to be no-balled for throwing on a tour of England. It is easy to forget that in the late 1950s and early 1960s – no aspersion on Adcock who retired shortly afterwards – that throwing was all the rage.

FIRST-CLASS CAREER (1952/3–62/3)

117 innings	35 not outs	451 runs	average 5.50	0 hundred
	405 wickets	6989 runs	average 17.25	8–39 best

TEST RECORD (26 MATCHES)

| 39 innings | 12 not outs | 146 runs | average 5.40 | — |
| 104 wickets | 2195 runs | average 21.10 | 6–43 best |

Series	Tests	O		M	R	W	Av
1953/4 v NZ	5	170.3	(8-ball)	27	485	24	20.20
1955 in E	4	129		37	252	10	25.20
1956/7 v E	5	142	(8-ball)	32	313	21	14.90
1957/8 v A	5	131	(8-ball)	15	410	14	29.28
1960 in E	5	263		69	587	26	22.57
1961/2 v NZ	2	82		38	148	9	16.44

GARTH McKENZIE

*Graham Douglas McKenzie
(1941–   )
Western Australia,
Leicestershire and Australia*

'Garth' McKenzie was the youngest bowler to take a hundred, 150 and two hundred Test wickets at the time he set his records in the 1960s. He finished up with 246 Test wickets, two short of the Australian record set by Benaud. He then undertook a career with Leicestershire which helped the county to its first honours. Yet McKenzie is not celebrated today as much as he should be. Perhaps, at fast-medium off a nine-stride run, he wasn't quite fast enough to capture popular imagination; perhaps he falls into that gap between the historical and the topical; perhaps he was simply too nice a person to be lethal.

He might not have been an Aussie at all, so gentle was his nature, yet he came from the same city as Dennis Lillee: Perth. He was both the son and the nephew of Western Australian cricketers, and at first was a batsman and off-spinner. Only in his mid-teens did he take up pace bowling, and with such aptitude that he made his state début at 18 and a year later was included in the Australian party for the 1961 tour of England.

Not a bad action for someone who had virtually ended his Test career: McKenzie in 1970

Omitted from the First Test, McKenzie in the Second scored 34 on his twentieth birthday (his batting was not to progress), while in England's second innings he bowled 29 overs for five wickets and 37 runs. Both

efforts were match-winning performances. It was the first time in five years that England had lost at home.

For all his youth McKenzie was ready to take over immediately Davidson retired, and by the age of 23 he had clocked his first one hundred Test wickets. His secret, a superb physique apart, was to get so far round in delivery that he turned his body side-on to the batsman like a high-class off-spinner. This gave him an outswinger as his standard delivery, and not just with a new ball. At five o'clock on a slow pitch, with the batsmen ensconced and the ball a rag, McKenzie's action was capable of producing a partnership breaker.

He couldn't manage an inswinger with his action, like Trueman, but the odd ball would by chance nip into the right-hander after hitting the seam. These were armaments enough. In 1964 he equalled Grimmett's series record for an Australian in England (evidence of his stamina: 60 overs and seven wickets for 153 in England's total of 611 at Old Trafford). For the rest of the decade he continued his long, fruitful spells around the world until, straight after a productive experience in India, the energy ran out during an extraordinary series in South Africa when in three Tests he took a single wicket for 333.

It may be impossible for anyone to be too pleasant, but if only Garth had been able to lose his temper. . . .

FIRST-CLASS CAREER (1959/60–75)

471 innings	109 not outs	5662 runs	average 15.64	0 hundred
	1219 wickets	32868 runs	average 26.96	8–71 best

TEST RECORD (60 MATCHES)

89 innings	12 not outs	945 runs	average 12.27	—
	246 wickets	7328 runs	average 29.78	8–71 best

Series	Tests	O	M	R	W	Av
1961 in E	3	129	36	323	11	29.36
1962/3 v E	5	205.3 (8-ball)	25	619	20	30.95
1963/4 v SA	5	178.4 (8-ball)	14	689	16	43.06
1964 in E	5	256	61	654	29	22.55
1964/5 in I	3	108.3	26	214	13	16.46
1964/5 in P	1	55	14	131	8	16.37
1964/5 in WI	5	256	56	677	17	39.82
1964/5 v P	1	46.4 (8-ball)	6	140	7	20.00
1965/6 v E	4	133.1 (8-ball)	20	467	16	29.18
1966/7 in SA	5	275.2	70	624	24	26.00
1967/8 v I	2	72.4 (8-ball)	7	312	13	24.00
1968 in E	5	264	77	595	13	45.76
1968/9 v WI	5	206.1 (8-ball)	27	758	30	25.26
1969/70 in I	5	222	73	441	21	21.00
1969/70 in SA	3	110.5	21	333	1	333.00
1970/71 v E	3	110.4 (8-ball)	14	351	7	50.14

WES HALL

Wesley Winfield Hall
(1937–   )
Barbados, Trinidad,
Queensland and West Indies

Whatever the doubts surrounding some of his opening partners, Wes Hall was universally recognised as one of the great fast bowlers, without any qualification. He had a magnificent action following a 26-yard run during which, remarkably, his strides became ever shorter in defiance of the general rule. But the rest was orthodoxy; indeed he was as classical as Michael Holding.

After a quiet learning tour of England in 1957, aged 19, Hall let rip in India and Pakistan where he captured 48 wickets in his first eight Tests, including 11 on the matting in Kanpur and a hat trick on grass in Lahore. A year later he had been deprived of Gilchrist and was in the middle of various partners until Griffith matured; yet he still bowled like the wind at England, if not a hurricane. His stock ball rose at the ribs, before the time of Snow and Lillee and his own West Indian successors. Colin Cowdrey adapted a thigh-pad for use as a chest protector when he had the pleasure of opening against Hall.

Trueman and Statham, Lindwall and Miller, Larwood and Voce, Gregory and McDonald: to that list Hall and Griffith added themselves in 1963, although their first association had been in youth cricket in Barbados when Hall had kept wicket to Griffith's off-breaks! Hall had bowled admirably in Australia in the 1960/61 series which revitalised the sport, and had earned himself a two-year contract with Queensland. But he needed someone at the other end who was quicker than Worrell or Sobers; once he had Griffith, his tenth partner, there was no escape.

We should not forget that in 1963 the no-ball rule was still based on the back foot in the Test series, while county cricket saw the introduction of the present front foot law. Hall, therefore, was still able to land his front foot well in front of the popping crease while his back foot dragged over the line which mattered. Several batsmen found big Wes grinning at their doorstep, gold cross flapping around his neck (he set a fashion), wreathed in smiles and perspiration. Sightscreens were still not compulsory on English Test grounds.

His 40 brave overs in the epic at Lord's constituted his finest hour and his most gruelling day, from which he may have never fully recovered. Then, as ever, he was prepared to defy blisters for his captain's sake. We will probably not see his whole-hearted like again. A West Indian fast bowler now would not be asked to bowl for so long or, if he were, he would use his Sunday League run. He would do the same job no less efficiently, perhaps more so, but in an entirely different spirit. To Hall, cricket was still a game, not work.

It's strange, at least in retrospect, that Hall was a keeper and opening batsman until he left school. It was only when the Bridgetown Cable Office, for whom he worked and played, were short of an opening bowler that Hall took the ball – and, immediately, six wickets. Thus his career

OPPOSITE: *Big Wes traps*
Dennis Amiss, back and
across, in the Oval Test of
1966

was launched, and when it ended, after a tour too many to Australasia, so had the career of the last heroic fast bowler.

FIRST-CLASS CAREER (1955/6–70/71)

| 215 innings | 38 not outs | 2673 runs | average 15.10 | 1 hundred |
| | 546 wickets | 14273 runs | average 26.14 | 7–51 best |

TEST RECORD (48 MATCHES)

| 66 innings | 14 not outs | 818 runs | average 15.73 | — |
| | 192 wickets | 5066 runs | average 26.38 | 7–69 best |

Series	Tests	O	M	R	W	Av
1958/9 in I	5	221.4	65	530	30	17.66
1958/9 in P	3	100.5	18	287	16	17.93
1959/60 v E	5	236.2	49	679	22	30.86
1960/61 in A	5	144.6 (8-ball)	14	616	21	29.33
1961/2 v I	5	167.4	37	425	27	15.74
1963 in E	5	178	26	534	16	33.37
1964/5 v A	5	146	19	454	16	28.37
1966 in E	5	175.3	35	555	18	30.83
1966/7 in I	3	73	10	266	8	33.25
1967/8 v E	4	122	29	353	9	39.22
1968/9 in A	2	75.7 (8-ball)	5	325	8	40.62
1968/9 in NZ	1	16.2 (8-ball)	5	42	1	42.00

CHARLIE GRIFFITH

On the last day of 1959 the MCC touring party in the West Indies came across a new bowler who was to become great, albeit partly in notoriety. Charlie Griffith was making his début for Barbados at the age of 21 and bowling inswingers. In fact for a big-boned man, built on the same formidable lines as Wayne Daniel was to be, he was remarkably slow – about military–medium in pace. Then out of the blue would come a quicker ball, either a 90mph yorker or a bouncer that skimmed towards the batsman. In this match between MCC and Barbados, and with extreme variation in speed, the shy debutant dismissed Cowdrey, Mike Smith (twice), May, Barrington and Dexter.

Griffith made his international entry in the last Test match of that tour, but had no significant effect. The next time he made any impression was in 1961/2 when Barbados were playing host to the Indians. Nari

Charles Christopher Griffith (1938–   )
Barbados and West Indies

An exceedingly – shall we say? – difficult proposition for any batsman

Contractor, India's left-handed opening batsman and captain, went back to a ball from Griffith which rose and hit Contractor over the right ear as he bent back. In the second innings of the match, while the Indian was undergoing an emergency brain operation, Griffith was called for throwing by Cortez Jordan of Barbados.

By 1963 and his arrival in England, Griffith had given up the little inswingers and was bowling off a long run. He took 119 wickets at 12.83, the lowest average for a visiting bowler with a hundred wickets since the First World War. In the Test matches he was devastating: 32 wickets at 16. During the summer he was not no-balled for throwing, but was given a direct warning about short-pitching.

Griffith always bowled from wide of the crease with his left toes pointing towards third man, and he would fall away even further after delivery. He was, therefore, very chest-on and this unorthodoxy made him more dangerous, not less. While his partner Wes Hall was bowling, the batsman could see the ball all the way from the start of his arm-swing.

When West Indies met Australia, Norman O'Neill was unhappy about Griffith's action, especially when he was hit. On Griffith's return to England in 1966, Ken Barrington and Ted Dexter added to the chorus of public doubts. Umpire Charlie Elliott warned him for one ball during a Test. Under the weight of publicity Griffith retreated into his shell, taking the lethal yorkers and bouncers and the remarkable changes of pace with him. The Griffith affair, following upon the Griffin and Meckiff affairs, became the *cause célèbre* of the mid-1960s and brought the issue of throwing to a head. By then, happily, the television camera and action replays were coming into their own.

FIRST-CLASS CAREER (1959/60–68/9)

| 119 innings | 32 not outs | 1502 runs | average 17.26 | 0 hundred |
| | 332 wickets | 7172 runs | average 21.60 | 8–23 best |

TEST RECORD (28 MATCHES)

| 42 innings | 10 not outs | 530 runs | average 16.56 | — |
| | 94 wickets | 2683 runs | average 28.54 | 6–36 best |

Series	Tests	O	M	R	W	Av
1959/60 v E	1	24	3	102	1	102.00
1963 in E	5	223.5	54	519	32	16.21
1964/5 v A	5	155	22	480	15	32.00
1966 in E	5	144.3	27	438	14	31.28
1966/7 in I	3	80	23	291	9	32.33
1967/8 v E	4	93.1	29	232	10	23.20
1968/9 in A	3	104 (8-ball)	8	430	8	53.75
1968/9 in NZ	2	59.4 (8-ball)	11	191	5	38.20

FRED TITMUS

The three off-spinners employed by England during the 1960s finished with remarkably similar records. David Allen, Ray Illingworth and Fred Titmus each had their successes and strengths, although it was too much of a good thing to send all of them to Australia in 1962/3. On that occasion Titmus was the one to shine. Indeed his 21 wickets constituted the best return by an English off-spinner down under in modern times, until Geoff Miller beat it against a weakened Australia in 1978/9. It was a remarkable feat considering that Titmus's type was held to be useless there.

The norm for English off-spinners in Australia was established by Ted Wainwright when he toured at the end of the last century and never turned a ball on the iron pitches. When the Yorkshireman got home, he went straight to the nets without taking his coat off and wept with relief when he found that he could still achieve spin on more responsive surfaces. Tom Goddard, later, was never taken to Australia. But while quickish off-break bowlers have seen their deliveries do nothing there except skid away from the right-handed bat, Titmus found his slower off-spin would grip and turn.

And Titmus was slow. When he responded to the odd Middlesex emergency in the early 1980s, everyone was amazed at the comparison with John Emburey. Just a few slow paces from Titmus, a cocking of all the required mechanisms in the crease, and this drifting off-break hovering down the pitch. As he had made his Middlesex début in 1949, aged 16, he became one of the few to play first-class cricket in five decades.

By the early 1950s he was bowling seamers in the RAF, as Illingworth did during his National Service. In 1955 Titmus had his largest haul of 191 wickets (with off-spin), did the double for the first of eight times, and was selected for England. Like Ken Barrington, who made his début the same season, he was then dropped for a long time – an exile which prompted him to acquire an even more thorough grounding in the game. When a second opportunity came in 1962 he made himself an England regular, and remained so until he parted company with four of his toes in the boating accident which he suffered in the West Indies.

His most valuable work for England was done abroad as he was not quite so suited to wet wickets. A breeze from fine-leg, say at Sydney, was made for Titmus since it would assist him to drift the ball away and have right-handers caught at slip. His success in Australia was the more commendable considering the umpires' reluctance to give batsmen LBW when they missed a sweep.

At Lord's, from the pavilion end, he could make the ball drift so much that it would frequently scuttle away past off-stump for four byes. This was spin-swerve incidentally; it was not until the late 1960s that

Frederick John Titmus
MBE
(1932–   )
Middlesex, Surrey, Orange Free State and England

he developed his arm-ball. And while he wheeled away and captured more wickets for Middlesex than anyone in their history, he formed a commentary in himself on the nature of our game. Rhodes took wickets from 1898 to 1930 with barely diminishing facility. Titmus took wickets over no less a span, albeit at slightly increasing cost. Over the decades spin bowling, and the playing of it, cannot have changed vastly – until lately.

OPPOSITE: *Bowling well in the Melbourne Test of 1974/5 with a lot of forward momentum and, perhaps surprisingly after his injury, balance. See again the sheer physical effort required in bowling slow*

FIRST-CLASS CAREER (1949–82)

1142 innings	208 not outs	21588 runs	average 23.11	6 hundreds
	2830 wickets	63313 runs	average 22.37	9–52 best

TEST RECORD (53 MATCHES)

76 innings	11 not outs	1449 runs	average 22.29	—
	153 wickets	4931 runs	average 32.22	7–79 best

Series	Tests	O	M	R	W	Av
1955 v SA	2	33	10	101	1	101.00
1962 v P	2	44	12	74	3	24.66
1962/3 in A	5	236.3 (8-ball)	54	616	21	29.33
1962/3 in NZ	3	132	54	227	13	17.46
1963 v WI	4	101	23	256	6	42.66
1963/4 in I	5	398.5	156	747	27	27.66
1964 v A	5	202	92	301	10	30.10
1964/5 in SA	5	309.1	87	694	18	38.55
1965 v NZ	3	171	85	234	15	15.60
1965 v SA	3	149.4	51	316	8	39.50
1965/6 in A	5	210.3 (8-ball)	52	517	9	57.44
1966 v WI	3	81	20	190	5	38.00
1967 v P	2	72.1	28	133	6	22.16
1967/8 in WI	2	68	24	165	4	41.25
1974/5 in A	4	122.3 (8-ball)	30	360	7	51.42

PETER POLLOCK

*Peter Maclean Pollock
(1941–   )
Eastern Province and South
Africa*

On South Africa's last tour of England in 1965 Peter Pollock was no less outstanding than Neil Adcock had been on their previous tour, perhaps more so since he took 20 wickets in only three Tests. Whereas Adcock had nipped the ball in, Pollock swung the ball away from the right hander if he did anything. Above all, though, Pollock was an 'effort bowler' who kept going and overwhelmed the opposition with sheer perseverance.

By 1965 South African cricket had entered on its aggressive modern phase and Pollock, with his speed and his comments directed at the batsman, played a full part in supplying this new edge. Surprising as it may now seem, the South Africans in the 1950s had been as defensively-

A big effort in 1965 – the seam not quite vertical but still pretty steady

minded as everyone else: Jackie McGlew blocked all day, Tayfield bowled his maidens, and their crowds flocked away from the cricket. The change from caution to confidence was sparked by Roy McLean, who alone had borne the torch of attack.

Pollock perhaps was over-aggressive when he entered first-class cricket, banging the ball in as consistently short as Adcock had done in his youth. But on hard pitches this was sufficient to give him 17 cheap wickets in his first three Tests against New Zealand when he was but 20, and 40 wickets in an eight-Test tour of Australasia in 1963/4.

He still had a deal to learn when he arrived in England aged 24, and he learnt it. While he preserved his long, time-consuming run-up (it helped Pollock to reduce the over-rate to 14 an hour to save the Oval Test and give South Africa the series), he reduced his pace for the stock ball and pitched it further up, naturally retaining the bouncer. In the Trent Bridge Test which South Africa narrowly won, Pollock took ten for 87 and his younger brother scored 184 runs in the best sibling double-act in Test cricket to that point.

Owing to politics, Pollock's Test career did not have long to go. He and his countrymen had only two more series left at home to Australia, in the first of which he fared moderately, and in the second devastated the tourists with Mike Procter's inswing as a complement. In what was unwittingly his final over in Test cricket, Pollock pulled a hamstring and was unable to complete it.

Originally an opening batsman in school cricket in Port Elizabeth, Pollock had good reason to take up fast bowling. In order to get a bat in back-yard cricket at home – his father, who hailed from Scotland, had played as a wicket-keeper for Orange Free State – he had first to get his younger brother out. Since the brother was Graeme Pollock, considerable effort and skill were necessarily involved.

FIRST-CLASS CAREER (1958/9–71/2)

| 177 innings | 43 not outs | 3028 runs | average 22.59 | 0 hundred |
| | 485 wickets | 10620 runs | average 21.89 | 7–19 best |

TEST RECORD (28 MATCHES)

| 41 innings | 13 not outs | 607 runs | average 21.67 | — |
| | 116 wickets | 2806 runs | average 24.18 | 6–38 best |

Series	Tests	O	M	R	W	Av
1961/2 v NZ	3	128.4	35	299	17	17.58
1963/4 in A	5	159.3 (8-ball)	11	710	25	28.40
1963/4 in NZ	3	130.1	44	258	15	17.20
1964/5 v E	5	169.1	51	445	12	37.08
1965 in E	3	164.2	55	366	20	18.30
1966/7 v A	5	167.1	35	470	12	39.16
1969/70 v A	4	115	39	258	15	17.20

TOM CARTWRIGHT

Thomas William Cartwright
(1935–   )
Warwickshire, Somerset,
Glamorgan and England

If you walked out to the middle after a game involving Warwickshire in the 1960s, or Somerset in the early 1970s, you would see – especially if the pitch had been damp – an area two feet long and six inches wide on a good length. This was the patch which Tom Cartwright had been consistently hitting with his medium-pace and gradually wearing away. He was a neglected bowler, underrated by people who watched and selected, but not by those who had to bat against him.

His name was often linked with Derek Shackleton's, especially when leading county bowlers were being dismissed from Test consideration for being too dependent on English-style conditions. In fact, Cartwright's methods were the reverse of Shackleton's. Whereas the Hampshire man would try to swing the new ball, and only after failing to find movement there fall back on seam, Cartwright as a first-change bowler tried seam for preference. He reasoned that the ball would change course later that way, and would therefore be more difficult to counter. So he would amble in from a few paces and bang out this patch, only resorting to swing if the pitch did not respond to his initial advances.

Nor was it ordinary seam bowling. The tautness of his action and high arm injected the ball with bounce, so that the joys of a Monday morning at Edgbaston or Nuneaton not only included a ball nipping back sharply but one that hit your glove as well and lobbed up to short-leg. This was enough to alarm certain wicket-keepers into standing back; Cartwright would have been far better served if his custodians had stood up all the time, to prevent batsmen standing outside the crease. A few worked out that this was the way to disturb the automaton's length, and it led to one mother and father of a hiding in the Sunday League.

Cartwright was once a batsman himself, pure and simple. After making his début in 1952, he had by the start of the 1958 season taken exactly two wickets for Warwickshire. And he became not merely a damp-wicket seamer: on a dry pitch, when his county was short of spinners, he could fill in, not with cutters but by pegging the batsmen down until either he strangled them out, or they gave themselves up to suicide at the other end. Yet the public perception continued to label Cartwright 'a typical English seamer'. So he was given no overseas tour, except to South Africa in 1964/5, when he aggravated an old football injury.

There weren't many Test appearances at home either. He didn't fit into the England pattern of the day. For their third seamer England wanted someone who could bat, then bowl a short incisive spell before the two spinners came on. To get the best out of Cartwright, he had to be given one end and allowed to get on with it; and that happened only in the Trent Bridge Test of 1965, when Cartwright took six South African wickets for 94 in one innings – and broke his thumb. He worked

by the drip–drip effect: take him off after ten overs, when he was about to get a stranglehold, and the effect was lost.

Perhaps he should have played in the nineteenth century when long-spell medium-pacers were welcome (there is even an echo of David Harris in that Cartwright was always 'up about the hands'). That he wasn't accommodated in the England side of his day was the fault of the system, not his own.

Against Notts at Trent Bridge in 1970 Cartwright sings a song of sixpence for Somerset – or at least lands the ball on one

FIRST-CLASS CAREER (1952–77)

737 innings	94 not outs	13710 runs	average 21.32	7 hundreds
	1536 wickets	29357 runs	average 19.11	8–39 best

TEST RECORD (5 MATCHES)

7 innings	2 not outs	26 runs	average 5.20	—
	15 wickets	544 runs	average 36.26	6–94 best

Series	Tests	O	M	R	W	Av
1964 v A	2	139	55	228	5	45.60
1964/5 in SA	1	79	24	196	2	98.00
1965 v NZ	1	19	9	26	2	13.00
1965 v SA	1	31.3	9	94	6	15.66

LANCE GIBBS

Lancelot Richard Gibbs
(1934–   )
British Guiana or Guyana,
Warwickshire, South
Australia and West Indies

In his last Test match Lance Gibbs broke Fred Trueman's record of 307 Test wickets. Long before he had set the record for the most balls bowled in Test cricket (27115). Though Lillee was to overtake his number of wickets within a decade, these distinctions were fitting rewards for a career of loyalty and real devotion to West Indian cricket. Given the same chance as Clive Lloyd, his cousin, Gibbs might well have shown the same qualities of leadership.

As an off-spinner his characteristics were long, banana-like fingers which put a lot of work on the ball so that it dipped in its flight and spun off the truest pitch, and (less of a blessing), a chest-on action. This made the arm-ball impossible in the first part of his career and always difficult thereafter. Gibbs therefore took his wickets more by way of the inside than outside edge. Happily for him, Sobers was around the corner at short-leg to take 39 catches off him, the most effective combination in Test history between a bowler and non-keeper. Being left-handed, Sobers could stand quite fine, without a helmet, at backward short-leg.

The lack of body in his action did not matter so much on dry pitches. In the Old Trafford Tests of 1963 and 1966 Gibbs did all that was expected of him, picking up ten or 11 wickets to win both matches for West Indies by an innings. In 1961/2 he was even more effective when West Indies won their first-ever clean sweep at home to India. Gibbs at Bridgetown had a spell that read: 15.3 overs, 14 maidens, six runs and eight wickets. At other times he would have the advantage of bowling into the footmarks outside off-stump which Sobers had created by bowling his over-the-wicket pace at the other end.

Gibbs' bowling hand became somewhat distorted

On wet pitches the lack of body action and bounce was more important, as was his deeply-held reluctance to bowl round the wicket. These combined to make Gibbs a moderate force in county cricket with Warwickshire until 1971. By then he had overcome a lot of his reluctance to bowl round, developed an adequate arm-ball and finished with 131 wickets, the most that anyone bar Marshall has managed since the size of the championship was reduced in 1969.

For a great bowler Gibbs's average in first-class cricket is high; in Test cricket it is highly creditable, but it increased as time wore on. In his early years, when he displaced Ramadhin, he was coming on after Hall, Griffith and Sobers: batsmen were not too keen to hang around until their return. When West Indies were short of penetrative pace in the late 1960s and early 1970s – incredible though that may seem now – Gibbs tried as hard as ever without quite making good the deficiency. Around the world, of course, off-spinners found their costs increasing as conditions changed. It was as well that Gibbs set his world record when he did, for no slow bowler could achieve the same under the present scheme of things.

By the 1973 series, after his experiences with Warwickshire, Gibbs had learnt to bowl round the wicket

FIRST-CLASS CAREER (1953/4–75/6)

| 352 innings | 150 not outs | 1729 runs | average 8.55 | 0 hundred |
| | 1024 wickets | 27878 runs | average 27.22 | 8–37 best |

TEST RECORD (79 MATCHES)

| 109 innings | 39 not outs | 488 runs | average 6.97 | — |
| | 309 wickets | 8989 runs | average 29.09 | 8–38 best |

Series	Tests	O	M	R	W	Av
1957/8 v P	4	166.5	47	392	17	23.05
1958/9 in I	1	30	12	61	0	—
1958/9 in P	3	94.1	33	180	8	22.50
1960/61 in A	3	192.2 (8-ball)	65	395	19	20.78
1961/2 v I	5	264.5	93	490	24	20.41
1963 in E	5	249.3	74	554	26	21.30
1964/5 v A	5	278.3	87	556	18	30.88
1966 in E	5	273.4	103	520	21	24.76
1966/7 v I	3	204.1	59	397	18	22.05
1967/8 v E	5	318.3	114	610	20	30.50
1968/9 in A	5	292.2 (8-ball)	52	923	24	38.45
1968/9 in NZ	3	132.4 (8-ball)	28	362	8	45.25
1969 in E	3	168.4	57	317	6	52.83
1970/71 v I	1	40	17	65	0	—
1971/2 v NZ	2	130	37	267	3	89.00
1972/3 v A	5	325	108	696	26	26.76
1973 in E	3	135.1	46	227	9	25.22
1973/4 v E	5	328	103	661	18	36.72
1974/5 in I	5	259.5	103	454	21	21.61
1974/5 in P	2	89.5 (8-ball)	27	210	7	30.00
1975/6 in A	6	232.5 (8-ball)	48	652	16	40.75

RAY ILLINGWORTH

Ray Illingworth was the foxiest of English off-spinners and the most mindful of economy. He was in his special element on the last afternoon of a match at Bradford or Bramall Lane, hustling Yorkshire towards another championship title on a damp or dusty pitch. With Jimmy Binks behind the wicket, Phil Sharpe at slip, the unhelmeted Close at silly point and Fred Trueman at short-leg, Illingworth helped to fashion county cricket's last era of consummate professionalism before the one-day game intruded.

When there was something in the wicket, and batsmen under pressure had to be forced to play at every ball, Illingworth was perhaps the pick of the many English off-spinners of the 1960s. In Test cricket, on covered pitches, he never ran amok but he was always tidy, abroad and at home. Of course, when he was the England captain, he would not bowl when conditions appeared to be unfavourable for him, but this was in part the result of a shrewd calculation that others would be more effective. His Test bowling average was 27 before he was captain and 35 while he was, which suggests he did not do himself too many favours.

Not so big a spinner as the Gloucestershire pair of Allen and Morti-more, Illingworth had the best of arm-balls. This ability was born in his early years when he bowled outswing off a 12-pace run and had to force his left shoulder side on. With this action he was capable of an arm-ball that would have the batsman missing his sweep or caught by Sharpe. One season Illingworth reckoned – in the way Yorkshire crick-eters used to do – that 44 of his 135 wickets were captured with this delivery.

He turned to off-spin in the nets at Farsley and by 1953 was bowling a bit of both for Yorkshire. On Appleyard's retirement he was able to fill the off-spinning rôle full-time for his county and intermittently for England. In 1959/60, while he was utterly ineffectual in the West Indies in terms of wickets, he did a fine stock job by bowling outside off-stump with a packed field to Hunte, Kanhai and Sobers. Even in the era of heavy bats and of stroke-play developed by limited-overs cricket, he still held his own when he returned to Yorkshire's fold and led them to the Sunday League title in 1983.

Throughout the 1960s Illingworth was more often out of the England side than in, for it was not as if he made runs initially at Test level: he did not score his first 50 until he was appointed England captain in 1969, at the age of 37. By then Titmus had lost four of his toes, Allen had retired and Cowdrey had snapped an Achilles' tendon. Illingworth, fully matured and the captain of Leicestershire, was now without rivals and for four years he made England's little talent go a long way.

His immortal triumph will be his winning of the Ashes in 1970/71, but even then the issue was in doubt on the last morning of the series.

Raymond Illingworth CBE (1932–   )
Yorkshire, Leicestershire and England

Australia still had five wickets left to score the one hundred runs they wanted to draw the series and keep the urn. Greg Chappell then moved down the Sydney pitch to Illingworth and failed to see that the ball wasn't an off-break at all. Alan Knott stumped him. The years of patient craftsmanship had reached fulfilment.

OPPOSITE: *In his Leicestershire years, as with Yorkshire, Illingworth gets cannily close to the stumps and concentrates. However the ball is wedged remarkably deeply into his palm*

FIRST-CLASS CAREER (1951–83)

1073 innings	213 not outs	24134 runs	average 28.06	22 hundreds
	2072 wickets	42023 runs	average 20.28	9–42 best

TEST RECORD (61 MATCHES)

90 innings	11 not outs	1836 runs	average 23.24	2 hundreds
	122 wickets	3807 runs	average 31.20	6–29 best

Series	Tests	O		M	R	W	Av
1958 v NZ	1	45		18	59	3	19.66
1959 v I	2	85		33	124	4	31.00
1959/60 in WI	5	196		61	383	4	95.75
1960 v SA	4	77		32	146	6	24.33
1961 v A	2	55.3		17	126	3	42.00
1962 v P	1	34		14	81	1	81.00
1962/3 in A	2	40	(8-ball)	10	131	1	131.00
1962/3 in NZ	3	46		20	73	5	14.60
1965 v NZ	1	35		14	70	4	17.50
1966 v WI	2	63		24	165	4	41.25
1967 v I	3	154.3		68	266	20	13.30
1967 v P	1	46		25	58	3	19.33
1968 v A	3	183.2		82	291	13	22.39
1969 v NZ	3	101.3		43	154	10	15.40
1969 v WI	3	93		32	218	5	43.60
1970/71 in A	6	132	(8-ball)	43	349	10	34.90
1970/71 in NZ	2	41	(8-ball)	12	102	0	—
1971 v I	3	118.3		43	202	7	28.85
1971 v P	3	87		36	162	6	27.00
1972 v A	5	88		28	197	7	28.14
1973 v NZ	3	68		20	139	0	—
1973 v WI	3	128.4		39	311	6	51.83

JOHN SNOW

John Augustine Snow
(1941–   )
Sussex and England

There were two John Snows. One usually purveyed medium-pace for Sussex whenever, that is, he could be persuaded to bowl. It would be a Monday afternoon at Hove or Leicester, when Sussex had fallen behind on first innings. Why bother to bust a gut? Common sense said that the struggle would naught availeth. Snow would wander off to fine-leg and spend the rest of his day in contemplation, possibly composing a few verses.

In Bridgetown or Brisbane another John Snow was on view, the best fast bowler in the half-dozen years before Dennis Lillee. The blood would course, the ball lift around the batsman's chest or head. For no apparent reason the mood would be on him. His England captains never found out what spurred him into action; his Sussex captains, in his later years, seldom got that far and dropped him for lack of effort. Spectators said he didn't care, but the explanation is not so simple, as you only have to read his poem 'On being dropped' to know he didn't like it.

When the cylinders were firing from the late 1960s onwards, Snow led fast bowling into the present era. Statham had focussed the odd short ball at a batsman's throat, Hall and Lindwall too, but Snow set out to explore the whole upper part of the Australian anatomy in 1970/71. He hit Terry Jenner on the back of the head and was warned for bowling bouncers, but he argued that this short-of-a-length lifter was something different. It was an innovation which few Englishmen, but plenty of others, have chosen to copy.

Snow could move the ball either way, his high action keeping the seam upright until it hit the grass and developed a mind of its own. But what did turn him on or off? Egotism and the predatory instinct are relevant here. Any cricketer must have a high opinion of himself in order to perform in public. Any fast bowler must also have that primitive, animal urge to hunt and kill, in a civilised fashion of course. Lillee is the finest example of one who possessed it.

Snow could be aggressive in a Test match – enough to push Sunil Gavaskar out of his path when he attempted a single in the 1971 Lord's Test – but simply to feel the ball in his hand was not an automatic cue. Perhaps he was too sensible to flog himself out for the meagre rewards which cricket then offered (£120 a Test in 1968). It is certain that he found no pride or pleasure in hard work for its own sake, for example in the five for 60 at Derby which is the county cricketer's bread and butter. In this reluctance to bend his back on the county grind he was to find some willing disciples.

His background may have been influential, for he wasn't a Trueman or Larwood fighting his way out of the mines. Snow came out of a rectory – the family's only boy – and was educated at Christ's Hospital where he excelled at batting. It was primarily on this account that he

was accepted on the Sussex staff, for not until almost 16 did he develop a physique or taste for pace bowling.

Working his way up through a line of other England candidates like Jeff Jones, David Brown, Ken Higgs and Geoff Arnold, Snow went to the fore with his 27 wickets on the tour of the West Indies in 1967/8. In 1970/71 he had 31 wickets – top-order ones mainly – and would have fared better still but for tiring under the strain of five Tests in seven weeks (one abandoned), and breaking his hand on a Sydney fence. He was a controversial fellow, but in retrospect and at the time his exclusion from the next Ashes tour to Australia was one of the great sins of omission.

FIRST-CLASS CAREER (1961–77)

| 451 innings | 110 not outs | 4832 runs | average 14.17 | 0 hundred |
| | 1174 wickets | 26675 runs | average 22.72 | 8–87 best |

TEST RECORD (49 MATCHES)

| 71 innings | 14 not outs | 772 runs | average 13.54 | — |
| | 202 wickets | 5387 runs | average 26.66 | 7–40 best |

Series	Tests	O	M	R	W	Av
1965 v NZ	1	35	6	80	4	20.00
1965 v SA	1	55	12	146	4	36.50
1966 v WI	3	138.5	29	451	12	37.58
1967 v I	3	112.4	30	264	10	26.40
1967 v P	1	49.1	13	126	3	42.00
1967/8 in WI	4	165	29	504	27	18.66
1968 v A	5	203	44	508	17	29.29
1968/9 in P	2	37	12	85	4	21.25
1969 v WI	3	139.3	26	406	15	27.06
1969 v NZ	2	61	14	154	3	51.33
1970/71 in A	6	225.5 (8-ball)	47	708	31	22.83
1971 v I	2	74	21	169	6	28.16
1972 v A	5	205.5	46	555	24	23.12
1973 v NZ	3	135.1	27	320	13	24.61
1973 v WI	1	49	12	133	3	44.33
1975 v A	4	135.5	31	355	11	32.27
1976 v WI	3	106.4	16	423	15	28.20

BRUCE TAYLOR

The windiness and dampness of New Zealand have served to give seamers preferential treatment over the years. After Jack Cowie there was a robust line of medium and fast-medium bowlers: John Hayes and Tony MacGibbon, Frank Cameron, Dick Motz, the left-handed Dick Collinge, and later Lance Cairns and Ewen Chatfield. None was glamorous and all of them were stalwarts when New Zealand was at its pre-professional and pre-Hadlee poorest. But the pick of them was Bruce Taylor, from the country town of Timaru in the South Island, a man built to carry a sheep around under each arm.

Had Taylor been the third seamer in a strong side, not the opening bowler in a weak one, what might he not have done! If he could have been Bill Johnston, following on after the depredations of Lindwall and Miller, or Trevor Bailey sweeping up after Trueman and Statham. . . . Yet Taylor's record is still pretty creditable – the more so because his bowling abroad was even more effective than in New Zealand, where conditions supply all too much assistance to the seamer. In ten Tests at home he took only 31 wickets, in 20 Tests abroad 80.

*Bruce Richard Taylor
(1943–   )
Canterbury, Wellington and
New Zealand*

*Not much orthodoxy here –
the hand is between his legs –
but that doesn't make batting
any easier*

As a big, gangling, shoulder-heaving bowler Taylor was often more difficult to counter than a man of smoother, more predictable method. His opponent was never completely set, for a ball of exceptional bounce could be detonated by that high and vigorous action. He could swing the ball away; if it seamed, it was usually in. And not only did he have a lot of heart but a touch of panache as well – as revealed in an 86-minute century against West Indies – which set him apart from team-mates of habitual caution.

On his Test début Taylor hit a century and took five wickets in an innings, the only person to have done so. In his first three Tests, in India, he had 15 wickets, and thus was set the pattern of his career: penetrating abroad on harder wickets which had some bounce, not consistently accurate enough to 'put the ball there' on the responsive pitches at home. His peak came in the West Indies in 1971/2 when his 27 wickets in four Tests matched Snow's incisiveness. The highlight occurred when West Indies chose to bat on a moist Bridgetown strip and Taylor demolished them with seven for 74. If only a slip catch had been held off Taylor in the second innings, New Zealand might have won their first Test and series in the Caribbean.

Taylor on that tour became the first New Zealander to take as many as 25 wickets in a rubber, as they used to be called. For someone who didn't play cricket for a living or have the attitude of a professional, and who had the stimulus of playing in a winning team only twice in his Test career, that was pretty good going.

FIRST-CLASS CAREER (1964/5–79/80)

210 innings	25 not outs	4579 runs	average 24.75	4 hundreds
	422 wickets	10605 runs	average 25.13	7–74 best

TEST RECORD (30 MATCHES)

50 innings	6 not outs	898 runs	average 20.40	2 hundreds
	111 wickets	2953 runs	average 26.60	7–74 best

Series	Tests	O	M	R	W	Av
1964/5 in I	3	82.2	13	276	15	18.40
1964/5 in P	3	79	20	211	6	35.15
1965 in E	2	75	12	259	4	64.75
1965/6 v E	1	33	10	66	5	13.20
1967/8 v I	3	109.1	23	285	8	35.62
1968/9 v WI	3	62.3 (8-ball)	4	268	5	53.60
1969 in E	2	63.5	17	155	10	15.50
1969/70 in I	2	48.2	14	105	6	17.50
1969/70 in P	1	28.5	10	39	3	13.00
1971/2 in WI	4	172.2	39	478	27	17.70
1972/3 v P	3	108.4 (8-ball)	20	416	13	32.00
1973 in E	3	136	24	395	9	43.88

ERAPALLI PRASANNA

Throughout the 1960s and 1970s India's bowling was in the hands of their spinners. Bedi, Chandrasekhar, Venkataraghavan and Prasanna made up the most famous quartet of bowlers between the South African googly bowlers and the first West Indian quartet of Roberts, Holding, Garner and Croft. The difference was that since India's four were all specialist spinners, their selectors were not disposed to pick all of them in the same Test team (they did however play together in the Edgbaston Test of 1967, when Prasanna was the most effective of them).

For the most part, therefore, the two off-spinners had to cut in and out. Venkat was a fine bowler in his early years: he took 21 cheap wickets against New Zealand at the age of 20, but he then grew a few more inches, which can make all the difference to a bowler's flight. Venkat subsequently pushed the ball through in a defensive, English style. On hard pitches Prasanna was preferred as a more flighty bowler.

His career was a curious one. He played his first Test against England in 1961/2, and a second in the West Indies shortly afterwards. He then disappeared from Test cricket for four years. Cricketers outside England in those days were amateurs with few exceptions. Prasanna, from a South Indian middle-class family, was forced to complete his engineering degree before returning to cricket again. In financial terms this was a sensible move as he secured a good job in Sydney when he moved to Australia after his Test career, before returning to India.

In those four years however, as Prasanna pursued his sedentary studies, his body was not being trained to concert pitch. The result was a certain portliness and any number of strained muscles when he did play Test cricket. The trimmer Venkat could bowl untiringly, field at slip and score a few runs, even if he was not such a bowler (his 156 wickets in 57 Tests cost 36 each). Prasanna, more amply built, was an artist and like many an artist was none too careful about his health and fitness.

Still, he shot to prominence in 1967/8 when India made their second tour of Australia, after a gap of 20 years, and their first to New Zealand. In the two four-Test series Prasanna took 25 wickets in Australia, where he was rated the equal of any off-spinner since the war, and 24 in New Zealand, where India won a Test and a series away from home for the first time. In the Antipodes Prasanna, like Titmus, enjoyed the wind from fine-leg that drifted the ball away and had the groping right-hander caught at slip.

Prasanna never quite touched the same heights again, although he went on to be the leading wicket-taker among Test off-spinners of his generation after Gibbs. He had a good series against England in 1972/3 whenever Bedi and Chandra did not take their fill; and three years later his eight for 76 in a New Zealand innings made his best Test figures.

Erapalli Anatharao Srinivas Prasanna (1940–   ) Mysore or Karnataka, and India

This ball is going to off-break a lot, even if it hails from a small hand, because the amount of spin on it is keeping the seam at right angles to the batsman

Otherwise, as the decade wore on, more and more batsmen 'padded out' off-breaks on ever slower pitches, instead of moving out to drive and being beaten by Prasanna's late dip and turn.

In the space of less than 20 years India's quartet of spinners dismissed 856 batsmen between them in Test cricket. It is dispiriting to know for certain that we will never see their like again.

FIRST-CLASS CAREER (1961/2–78/9)

275 innings	67 not outs	2476 runs	average 11.90	0 hundred
	957 wickets	22442 runs	average 23.45	8–50 best

TEST RECORD (49 MATCHES)

84 innings	20 not outs	735 runs	average 11.48	—
	189 wickets	5742 runs	average 30.38	8–76 best

Series	Tests	O	M	R	W	Av
1961/2 v E	1	20	5	39	1	39.00
1961/2 in WI	1	50	14	122	3	40.66
1966/7 v WI	1	78	20	224	5	44.80
1967 in E	3	156.3	32	430	9	47.77
1967/8 in A	4	197.5 (8-ball)	34	686	25	27.44
1967/8 in NZ	4	197.5	63	451	24	18.79
1969/70 v NZ	3	198.3	69	433	20	21.65
1969/70 v A	5	295	107	672	26	25.84
1970/71 in WI	3	159.5	40	407	11	37.00
1972/3 v E	3	84	16	202	10	20.20
1974 in E	2	86	10	267	3	89.00
1974/5 v WI	5	207.2	49	601	15	40.86
1975/6 in NZ	3	71 (8-ball)	13	223	11	20.27
1975/6 in WI	1	24	2	66	0	—
1976/7 v E	4	232.4	79	389	18	21.61
1977/8 in A	4	122.4 (8-ball)	32	279	6	46.50
1978/9 in P	2	81	17	251	2	125.50

BHAGWAT CHANDRASEKHAR

Chandra was perhaps, along with Underwood, the last original. The nearest anyone came to resembling him was Doug Wright who, however, bowled medium-paced leg-breaks whereas Chandra was all top-spinners and googlies with only an occasional leg-break. Tommy Greenhough of Lancashire was quite similar, but he was not deformed by polio in his right arm at the age of nine.

Bhagwat Subramanya Chandrasekhar (1945–) Mysore or Karnataka, and India

Chandra took over a thousand wickets without playing in county cricket; if he had, it would not have suited him. A grey morning at Edgbaston or Headingley, in front of a hundred people, was not his scene. He had to be inspired and warm and confident, to be on top psychologically, and this occurred when Eden Gardens in Calcutta was brimming over with 100,000 spectators and as many fire-crackers. Then he would bound in, the withered right arm would complete a full arc and the ball would spit as if from a snake-pit. Viv Richards always thought the mild-mannered South Indian was the most dangerous bowler he ever faced.

Confronted with a difficult spinner the usual ploy is to resort to the old maxim: when in doubt, push out. As moving forward was always Richards' first movement, this led him into trouble against Chandra. Against him it was wiser to hold back in the crease and wait for the ball to bounce, before playing it down past Solkar at short-leg. If you invariably pushed forward, you would get the ball on the rise or risk a short one up the nose.

It was those who stood and waited who were the only ones to prosper when Chandra was on song. Colin Cowdrey, born in the same city of Bangalore, was one such; so was Tony Greig when he initiated the standing-up stance which Gooch and others have copied. Even then a magical ball might come along: a surprise off-break, a quick seamer, a slower leg-break that did just enough ... anything that bounced abnormally thanks to, or in spite of, that withered whiplash arm.

His finest hour in England was at the Oval in 1971 when he led a rout with six for 38. In a way it's a measure of how irresistible he could be when the spirit moved him that one of his wickets then came from a full toss and two more from half-volleys. On that tour, as in 1967, the Indians visited England in the second half of the summer and Chandra, appreciating the warmer weather, took 50 or more wickets on both occasions. He did not enjoy the first half of 1974, and by 1979 he had gone.

He arrived more suddenly than he left. He was playing club cricket in Mysore when selected for his state side, and after four games for them was selected for South Zone, whence it was a short step to making his Test début against England in 1963/4. (A brilliant wrist-spinning contemporary was V. V. Kumar, a real artist, but he had no stomach for

Colin Croft: hostility incarnate

Balderstone bowled by Holding at the Oval in 1976 during, arguably, the single greatest display of fast bowling

Willis in Pakistan, 1977/8, when he was still running in wide

OPPOSITE *Lion hunting: Imran attacking Gower, 1982*

A rare moment on England's 1987/8 tour of Pakistan: this LBW decision against Broad seems to be right

Garner clears up in the World Cup final of 1979

OPPOSITE *Years of effort and planning are consummated when Hadlee goes ahead of Botham with his 374th Test wicket in Bangalore*

When England found batting impossible and terrifying: the Old Trafford Test of 1976

Incredible self-belief as Botham breaks the world record with his 356th Test wicket

OPPOSITE *Kapil Dev models cricket's latest fashion*

*Marshall, looking 'inside' his
arm, in the Port-of-Spain Test
against England, 1985/6*

the big occasion.) As inconsistency was inherent in Chandra's style, lean months or years naturally followed the fat ones. But it was an unexpectedly long trough that he went through at the end of the 1960s.

On the 1967 tour of England he was over-bowled, and Chandra was not a stock bowler to be flogged into the ground – when he was tired, he would commit his cardinal sin of dropping short. In fact he only re-emerged just in time for the 1971 tour to England; then it was on to 35 wickets against them in the 1972/3 series. When he was buoyant, as then, he had a touch of genius never seen in the county game.

OPPOSITE: *Chandra brings animation and energy to the Lahore Test of 1978/9; and litheness as well as slenderness of limb*

FIRST-CLASS CAREER (1963/4–79/80)

244 innings	114 not outs	600 runs	average 4.61	0 hundred
	1063 wickets	25547 runs	average 24.03	9–72 best

TEST RECORD (58 MATCHES)

80 innings	39 not outs	167 runs	average 4.07	—
	242 wickets	7199 runs	average 29.74	8–79 best

Series	Tests	O	M	R	W	Av
1963/4 v E	4	161.3	46	339	10	33.90
1964/5 v NZ	2	108	41	292	8	36.50
1964/5 v A	2	92.5	39	189	9	21.00
1966/7 v WI	3	196.5	52	513	18	28.50
1967 in E	3	169.5	40	435	16	27.18
1967/8 in A	2	47.1 (8-ball)	4	174	1	174.00
1971 in E	3	146.1	32	379	13	29.15
1972/3 v E	5	291.1	83	662	35	18.91
1974 in E	2	41.3	7	126	2	63.00
1974/5 v WI	4	157.2	27	579	14	41.35
1975/6 in NZ	3	89.7 (8-ball)	12	294	11	26.72
1975/6 in WI	4	201.2	43	656	21	31.23
1976/7 v NZ	3	169.1	47	391	17	23.00
1976/7 v E	5	194	40	537	19	28.26
1977/8 in A	5	197.3 (8-ball)	25	704	28	25.14
1978/9 in P	3	96	13	385	8	48.12
1978/9 v WI	4	160	33	431	12	35.91
1979 in E	1	29	1	113	0	—

BISHEN BEDI

Bishen Singh Bedi
(1946–   )
Northern Punjab, Delhi,
Northamptonshire and
India

Bishen Bedi is a Sikh, and while religion does not normally affect the way a man bowls, it may have in his case. By upbringing Sikhs are more aggressive than other Indians, and they are dressed for the part with a dagger always on their person as well as a patka or turban. Bedi was an aggressive bowler, not only the most effective slow left-hander of modern times with 267 Test wickets, but also the most attacking.

India in the 1960s and 1970s had left-arm spinners every bit as good as Bedi on helpful pitches, although names like Goel and Shivalkar mean little to followers outside India. Where Bedi was superb was in this ability to attack and take wickets – four per Test on average – when everything was in the batsman's favour. Whereas the others would push the ball through to contain, Bedi would air his mystifying loop and raise doubts in the batsman's mind. Then, once the doubts had been sown – and this was Bedi's secret – the ball would come off the pitch so rapidly (so forceful was his body action) that the batsman had scant chance of recovering.

Bedi also concentrated on the stumps because it was not in his character to aim defensively wide of the wicket to one side or other (thus he was not at his best in limited-overs cricket in his Northamptonshire years). In addition to that line, he would make the ball drift in, or spin it past you, or undercut the ball so that it looked as though it would turn but skidded straight on instead. Everyone thought Bedi was a genial, sporting fellow – and so he was off the field – whenever he clapped the batsman for hitting a six. But Bedi was actually encouraging him to have another go and get himself caught off a swirling mis-hit.

The action was as beautiful as that of any slow bowler, yet here again it was not quite so natural as it seemed. Bedi had to work long hours in the nets to regain his rhythm after a break from cricket, and he did yoga exercises to achieve the suppleness he was not born with. Yet it is true that he did just pick up a ball in Amritsar about the age of 13 (by the official reckoning), and two years later was making his first-class début for Northern Punjab. That was in 1961. On New Year's Day in 1967 he made his début for India and was a regular fixture thereafter, even though Durani and Nadkarni were no mean left-armers, and Chandrasekhar, Prasanna and Venkataraghavan were all demanding inclusion in the same team.

OPPOSITE: *The personification of left-arm spin is bowling for Northamptonshire in 1973, the front leg braced, not too wide in the crease, and about to give the ball a 'rip'*

In Tests in England, Bedi was not especially successful (which can be the sole explanation for his never having been chosen as one of *Wisden's* Five Cricketers of the Year), but he twice took a hundred wickets in a season for Northamptonshire. In the West Indies in 1970/71, while India were in the middle of winning three successive series under Wadekar and were briefly the leading Test side, Bedi was almost too good to take wickets: everyone blocked him, and attacked Venkat at the

194

other end who was turning the ball in. But most of his best times were at home, when dynamic close fielders like Solkar or Yajuvendra would crowd the bat and 50,000 voices would appeal along with them. Curiously, in India and occasionally elsewhere, Bedi would employ a different method of delivery which made every ball turn quite sharply.

He was batted out of Test cricket at the end of the 1970s when he lost that vital nip and thus allowed batsmen a split second to recover. By then he had been the captain of India and been involved in several brushes with authority. More importantly, he had kept slow left-arm bowling alive and taken it to the modern heights.

FIRST-CLASS CAREER (1961/2–80/81)

426 innings	111 not outs	3584 runs	average 11.37	0 hundred
	1560 wickets	33843 runs	average 21.69	7–5 best

TEST RECORD (67 MATCHES)

101 innings	28 not outs	656 runs	average 8.98	—
	266 wickets	7637 runs	average 28.71	7–98 best

Series	Tests	O	M	R	W	Av
1966/7 v WI	2	83	21	228	7	32.57
1967 in E	3	97.2	36	236	7	33.71
1967/8 in A	2	79 (8-ball)	17	223	4	55.75
1967/8 in NZ	4	176.1	65	371	16	23.18
1969/70 v A	5	273.4	120	432	21	20.57
1969/70 v NZ	3	187.5	82	308	15	20.53
1970/71 in WI	5	310.4	95	656	15	43.73
1971 in E	3	151.3	46	325	11	29.54
1972/3 v E	5	372.5	134	632	25	25.28
1974 in E	3	172.2	28	523	10	52.30
1974/5 v WI	4	183.2	55	499	15	33.26
1975/6 in NZ	2	60 (8-ball)	13	122	4	30.50
1975/6 in WI	4	200.5	61	456	18	25.33
1976/7 v NZ	3	203.1	91	290	22	13.18
1976/7 v E	5	298	106	574	25	22.96
1977/8 in A	5	219.7 (8-ball)	39	740	31	23.87
1978/9 in P	3	138	24	449	6	74.83
1978/9 v WI	3	130	40	324	7	46.28
1979 in E	3	103.3	23	249	7	35.57

INTIKHAB ALAM

Intikhab's record may be one of the least distinguished of the world's one hundred best, but then he had to labour under the severest disadvantages. He had to purvey his leg-spin in a more sophisticated era of pad-play than Hollies or Dooland, Wright or O'Reilly. The heavier bat sent the attacking edge over cover's head instead of nestling in his hands, a dolly catch. He was given a shinier ball than his predecessors, one preserved by lusher outfields. And in the first innings of every county match he played for Surrey, his captain must have been tempted to keep proceedings tight with his seamers until the bonus points were settled and a second new ball available.

At the Oval in Intikhab's day, as in the rest of England, the tired old strips which had been piled high with dressings for a hundred years had not been re-laid, so the defensive edge would often drop short of short-leg or slip. In Pakistan his fate was no better; in the 1960s and early 1970s the objective was to maintain national honour by drawing every Test and series (it was after his time that the country determined to go for victory at all cost). Huge totals were the norm on cautiously prepared pitches. It was as well that 'Inti' was brought up a Muslim, but he did more than accept the will of Allah: he twirled bat or ball in his hand enthusiastically and so relished cricket that he could never play it too often.

He was born on the 'wrong' (for him) side of the border, in Hoshiarpur in the Indian Punjab, where his father was an important engineering contractor. The father was a big man in the physical sense too and played his cricket as a fast bowler, as did Intikhab initially. When he switched to leg-spin in his teens he already had the build to keep going – commentators called him the burly, if not the wily Intikhab – in addition to an indefatigable heart.

One has to be sceptical about certain official ages – would Intikhab's family have remembered to save their birth certificates in the uproar of Partition? – but officially he was 17 when he bowled his first ball in Test cricket to Australia's Colin McDonald. It wasn't his leg-break or googly but one resembling a leg-spinner from the front of the hand that skidded through and bowled McDonald as he went to cut. In the subsequent 30 years nobody else has taken a wicket with his first Test ball.

Wickets did not tumble so quickly afterwards, for those varied reasons. So Inti concluded he would have to be a stock bowler and concentrated on his accuracy accordingly. In his desire to improve and to play cricket for a year-round living, he spent three years with the West of Scotland club where his cheerfulness made him immensely popular, before he was registered by Surrey. (This is the perpetual problem for English leg-spinners: how are they ever going to bowl the thousands of overs they need before entering county cricket?)

Intikhab Alam
(1941–   )
Karachi, Pakistan
International Airlines,
Public Works Department,
Sind, Punjab, Surrey and
Pakistan

More of a front-of-the-hand roller than Qadir, Intikhab bowls another leg-break during the 1974 tour of England when his Pakistanis were undefeated

Intikhab took 589 wickets for Surrey. In 1971 he took 72 wickets for the Pakistanis, the most on a short tour of England; he was the first of his countrymen to take a thousand wickets. He captained Pakistan honourably, and batted aggressively in spite of defective eyesight. The least he deserved was a chance to bowl for Surrey on a re-laid bouncy pitch at the Oval, after Sylvester Clarke had made an early breakthrough.

FIRST-CLASS CAREER (1957/8 82)

| 725 innings | 78 not outs | 14331 runs | average 22.14 | 9 hundreds |
| | 1571 wickets | 43472 runs | average 27.67 | 8–54 best |

TEST RECORD (47 MATCHES)

| 77 innings | 10 not outs | 1493 runs | average 22.28 | 1 hundred |
| | 125 wickets | 4494 runs | average 35.95 | 7–52 best |

Series	Tests	O	M	R	W	Av
1959/60 v A	1	25	5	62	3	20.66
1960/61 in I	3	90	24	184	5	36.80
1961/2 v E	2	78	9	214	3	71.33
1962 in E	3	77	10	275	3	91.66
1964/5 v A	1	44	8	131	2	65.50
1964/5 in A	1	10 (8-ball)	0	51	0	—
1964/5 in NZ	3	94	30	188	2	94.00
1964/5 v NZ	3	88.3	23	191	9	21.33
1967 in E	3	94	15	268	4	67.00
1968/9 v E	3	133.1	24	359	8	44.87
1969/70 v NZ	3	123.4	46	282	10	28.20
1971 in E	3	143.1	46	366	8	45.75
1972/3 in A	3	55.6 (8-ball)	7	308	4	77.00
1972/3 in NZ	3	85.4 (8-ball)	10	323	18	17.94
1972/3 v E	3	190	53	428	15	28.53
1974 in E	3	98.4	25	235	8	29.37
1974/5 v WI	2	55 (8-ball)	6	200	6	33.33
1976/7 v NZ	3	120.4 (8-ball)	35	331	15	22.06
1976/7 in WI	1	31	7	96	2	48.00

DEREK UNDERWOOD

Derek Leslie Underwood
(1945–   )
Kent and England

As a left-arm cutter of slow-medium pace Derek Underwood was the most original bowler in English cricket after Doug Wright, of the same county and much the same speed. He was 'Deadly' on good wickets in his unceasing accuracy, so that the man at bat-pad was as safe as could be; on helpful pitches he was Deadly in his penetration. Even at the end of his 25 seasons, this courteous old-fashioned figure was regarded by young players with respect amounting to awe.

If he had a limitation it was in the definition of that word helpful. He wanted a pitch which had either begun the match wet or had been rained on in the course of it – and there were plenty of these for him to savour in the early stage of his career when he raced to a thousand wickets by the age of 25, the third youngest to that number. His most famous wet-wicket bowling was in 1968 when he ran through Australia in the nick of time after the Oval pitch had been flooded and mopped up, thus levelling the series with six minutes to spare. In the first innings, on the other hand, on a dry pitch, Underwood had bowled 54.3 overs for his two wickets.

So long as pitches were damp he was happy, but they were drier in the 1970s until, in 1979, full covering began (it has lasted ever since with the exception of the 1987 season). His second consignment of a thousand wickets took ten years to arrive, against eight for the first. At the Oval in 1971, and in the decider at Sydney the winter before, England were slightly disappointed in Underwood, as the man was himself. He thought of slowing down and acquiring more spin, in other words of changing from cutter to spinner. But he was born with a slow arm not the quick one that spinners need (his throw-in was evidence of that). Wisely he decided to remain what he was.

Norman Gifford, who turned the ball more, was so frequently brought in during Illingworth's captaincy that Deadly rarely completed a full series. But he never failed for want of trying: however unsympathetic the pitch, like the one at the Oval in 1976 when Viv Richards hit 291, Underwood always thought of a towel as something to wipe his brow on, not to be tossed in. He would vary his pace, try over-spin to make the ball dip, or introduce the quicker one with the arm. If nothing else, he could rely on Alan Knott for a stumping if the batsman was over-adventurous.

He learned his cricket at home, on matting spread over concrete. On this quick surface he tried to bowl as fast as he could, which when combined with his accuracy helped him to overwhelm all his young contemporaries. It was not until he joined in adult cricket at Beckenham that he realised he wouldn't be able to bowl flat out at every level. So he moderated his splay-footed run-up and cut the ball.

It is well known that in his début season of 1963 he became the

youngest person to take a hundred wickets (he was 17 at the start of it). Less famed but equally notable was his performance in one of those new-fangled one-day games in the Gillette Cup, then in its inaugural year. Underwood's 11 overs were actually hit by Sussex for 87 runs! Nothing similar was permitted to happen again, not even at Lord's in 1980 when Richards went after him to hit him out of the series.

How could anybody have possibly thought that a fellow with such a run to the wicket could ever be turned into a spinner?

201

As a keen student of figures Underwood will forever be aware that he finished three short of three hundred Test wickets. But he profited enough financially from the years with World Series Cricket and the English rebel team in South Africa not to be too full of regrets. As late as 1988 he could have reached his landmark, if only he had continued for one more season with Kent. England were searching for a left-armer for the Old Trafford Test against West Indies: a 44-year-old Underwood would have been as deadly as anyone.

FIRST-CLASS CAREER (1963–87)

710 innings	200 not outs	5165 runs	average 10.12	1 hundred
	2465 wickets	49993 runs	average 20.28	9–28 best

TEST RECORD (86 MATCHES)

116 innings	35 not outs	937 runs	average 11.56	—
	297 wickets	7674 runs	average 25.83	8–51 best

Series	Tests	O	M	R	W	Av
1966 v WI	2	69	25	172	1	172.00
1967 v P	2	66	27	129	8	16.12
1968 v A	4	209.5	103	302	20	15.10
1968/9 in P	3	106	40	204	8	25.50
1969 v WI	2	53	29	101	6	16.83
1969 v NZ	3	150	70	220	24	9.16
1970/71 in A	5	194.6 (8-ball)	50	520	16	32.50
1970/71 in NZ	2	84.1 (8-ball)	28	205	17	12.05
1971 v P	1	41	13	102	0	—
1971 v I	1	63	20	121	4	30.25
1972 v A	2	125	49	266	16	16.62
1972/3 in I	4	214.4	82	457	15	30.46
1972/3 in P	2	96	35	215	3	71.66
1973 v NZ	1	18	6	41	0	—
1973 v WI	3	133	38	330	8	41.25
1973/4 in WI	4	137.5	45	314	5	62.80
1974 v I	3	67	25	146	4	36.50
1974 v P	3	113.5	48	218	17	12.82
1974/5 in A	5	185 (8-ball)	42	595	17	35.00
1974/5 in NZ	2	54.5 (8-ball)	18	120	7	17.14
1975 v A	4	131	15	266	6	44.43
1976 v WI	5	224	59	631	17	37.11
1976/7 in I	5	252.5	95	509	29	17.55
1976/7 in A	1	23.6 (8-ball)	4	54	4	13.50
1977 v A	5	169.1	61	362	13	27.84
1979/80 in A	3	160.2	48	405	13	31.15
1979/80 in I	1	7	1	28	0	—
1980 v WI	1	29.2	7	108	1	108.00
1981/2 in I	6	228	99	438	10	43.80
1981/2 in SL	1	55.5	21	95	8	11.87

DENNIS LILLEE

Geoff Boycott was batting for MCC against Western Australia on the 1970/71 tour. The game was at Perth, on a pacey wicket, and a dark-haired young man was striving to create the impression that he was the pace bowler to succeed McKenzie as the head of Australia's attack. Boycott was batting in his cap when Dennis Lillee ran in, banged a ball short and hit the peak of the cap so that it turned round and pointed backwards on Boycott's head. Australia had their new fast bowler at last.

During the 1970s Lillee reigned as the fast bowler supreme. In that decade he took 209 wickets in 41 Tests. In addition he took 24 wickets in four games between Australia and the Rest of the World in 1971/2, including eight for 29 at Perth with the quickest bowling many (like Sobers) had seen. He then took 79 wickets for WSC Australia in 15 international games every bit as demanding as Test matches. If all those wickets had been taken in official Tests for Australia, and he had avoided the back injury which kept him out altogether from early 1973 to late 1974, he would surely have set insuperable records.

As a pure fast bowler Lillee had almost everything: outswing and an occasional inswinger, a nip-backer and a bouncer, and above all a ferocious determination to get his man even if it killed him. Lillee aimed to capture two wickets per Test innings, and he so far exceeded his target that in spite of a series on Pakistan's deadest pitches he averaged over five per game, as only Grimmett and O'Reilly had done before him since the First World War. Even after suffering four stress fractures at the base of his spine, Lillee was no less of a terror than Thomson at the other end. But he did have one minor, non-physical weakness: when it came to 'nine, ten, jack', he could not pitch a full length at them, so he kept beating their bats and stumps. When Lillee joined the two hundred Test-wicket club he was the only pace bowler to have bowled less than 20 per cent of his victims (Lindwall, at the opposite extreme, bowled 43 per cent).

Yet what Lillee achieved in the 1980s was not less than what had gone before. He transformed himself into a fast-medium, or even medium-fast, bowler every whit as fine. In his last 29 Tests he took 146 wickets, still at the rate of five per game. Furthermore, Lillee was an innovator in that time. He pioneered a new form of attack, based on the off- and leg-cutters he had occasionally employed before then, and he was paid the sincerest compliment of being quickly imitated by Roberts, Hadlee and others.

If confronted with steady batting on a plumb pitch, Lindwall had only to wait until a second new ball was available after 55 or 65 overs. In earlier periods a fast bowler might not be used at all if the pitch was too good: then it was the turn of the spinners. Lillee, competitor that

*Dennis Keith Lillee (1949–   )
Western Australia, Tasmania, Northamptonshire and Australia*

Tony Crafter watches the man who developed the craft of fast bowling more than any other. Even in the 1982/3 series there was still devilry in Lillee's eyes

he was, assumed this role from them. He wanted to do the stock bowling, perhaps with Bruce Yardley's off-breaks at the other end. Fast bowlers had slowed down before to move the ball around – Fred Trueman at Headingley in 1961, for example – but that was in order to exploit helpful conditions.

Lillee therefore reduced his run and evolved a form of attack for days when no help existed. He had bowled his cutters at England in 1979/80, taking 11 wickets on a slow Melbourne pitch, and these he used more and more. He would keep the batsman contained by bowling steadily on and outside off-stump, until the batsman fished for that leg-cutter delivered from wide in the crease and Rod Marsh took the catch, adding one more victim to the bag of the most prolific combination in Test history.

The memory of unworthy incidents involving aluminium bats and the kicking of Javed Miandad will fade away. Lillee will be recalled as the pace bowler who never gave up until the day's play was over, whereupon he would be as friendly as anyone in the bar and most encouraging to youngsters. For many, the man who would flick with a finger the sweat from his brow as he stalked back to his mark, then turn and plunge towards the batsman with unyielding determination, has to be called the greatest of fast bowlers.

FIRST-CLASS CAREER (1969/70–88)

| 241 innings | 70 not outs | 2377 runs | average 13.90 | 0 hundred |
| | 882 wickets | 20695 runs | average 23.46 | 8–29 best |

TEST RECORD (70 MATCHES)

| 90 innings | 24 not outs | 905 runs | average 13.71 | — |
| | 355 wickets | 8493 runs | average 23.92 | 7–83 best |

Series	Tests	O	M	R	W	Av
1970/71 v E	2	62.3 (8-ball)	5	199	8	24.87
1972 in E	5	249.5	83	548	31	17.67
1972/3 v P	3	96.1 (8-ball)	19	353	12	29.42
1972/3 in WI	1	32	5	132	0	—
1974/5 v E	6	182.6 (8-ball)	36	596	25	23.84
1975 in E	4	207	72	460	21	21.90
1975/6 v WI	5	129.3 (8-ball)	7	712	27	26.37
1976/7 v P	3	130.2 (8-ball)	16	540	21	25.71
1976/7 in NZ	2	82.4 (8-ball)	13	312	15	20.80
1976/7 v E	1	47.7 (8-ball)	9	165	11	15.00
1979/80 v WI	3	120.1	24	365	12	30.41
1979/80 v E	3	155.1	41	388	23	16.86
1979/80 in P	3	102	19	303	3	101.00
1980 in E	1	34	9	96	5	19.20
1980/81 v I	3	148.3	33	452	21	21.52
1980/81 v NZ	3	106	27	245	16	15.31
1981 in E	6	311.4	81	870	39	22.30
1981/2 v P	3	104.3	22	332	15	22.13
1981/2 v WI	3	121.3	26	317	16	19.81
1981/2 in NZ	3	79	23	183	7	26.14
1982/3 v E	1	71	25	185	4	46.25
1982/3 in SL	1	30	6	107	3	35.66
1983/4 v P	5	230.3	51	633	20	31.65

JEFF THOMSON

Jeffrey Robert Thomson
(1950–   )
New South Wales,
Queensland, Middlesex and
Australia

Who has been the fastest bowler? It may be a question worth asking but there can be no precise answer. Since Charlie 'the Terror' Turner was timed at 55mph in 1888, the methods for testing have varied. The only valid test therefore must be the relative one, when everybody is measured by the same equipment on the same pitch and in the same atmospheric conditions. In 1974/5 Jeff Thomson was measured to be bowling at 99.6mph. But it is more relevant that during World Series Cricket, when all the fastest bowlers of the time were tested on one day in Perth, Thomson was the winner.

His rate of hospitalisation would also tend to confirm that he was consistently – for every top bowler has the odd day when everything clicks – the fastest ever. In 1974/5, when he took 33 English wickets in four and a half Tests, he was claiming scalps almost literally and turning grey the remaining hair of old pros who thought they had seen it all. Before he entered first-class cricket, when he was playing for Bankstown and fighting his way out of a disadvantaged background in suburban Sydney, 'Thommo' put a grade batsman in intensive care for a week, and the ball wasn't short enough to have been a bouncer.

The danger was a result of his javelin-style method as well as his speed. After his quick-stepping run, wonderfully certain in its footwork, he would brace himself for delivery with the ball tucked behind his backside. Slow bowlers through the ages have benefited from 'hiding' as it adds to the element of surprise; in Thommo's case it was shock. He was the opposite of classical fast bowlers like Lillee and Holding in this respect: they held the ball up beside their heads, plainly visible to the batsman, before beginning the arm-swing.

If the ball came from nowhere at England in 1974/5, so did Thomson himself. He had played one previous Test match some two years before, and it had proved a 'shocker' as he had a broken bone in his foot and didn't want to tell the selectors. The ensuing exile had the effect of putting a lid on a boiling saucepan. When he was let loose against England he took nine wickets in the First Test at Brisbane, where he had moved after seven games for New South Wales. For the Australian slip and gully fielders Thomson was a dream since opportunities to make the greatest catch in history kept on coming. For England the sole consolation was that he and Lillee did exactly the same to West Indies the following year: heads were jerked back, hair parted, ribs clutched and brave men cowered.

The next year he collided with another Australian fieldsman when going for a catch, and damaged his right shoulder so severely that a steel pin had to be inserted. He could still be awesomely quick but he wasn't quite the same Thommo again. He kept the official Australian side going, until he couldn't afford not to join WSC. After it he was often

kept out of the Test side by Lenny Pascoe, who came from the same Punchbowl High School as Thomson and had the same explosive drive to bowl himself into the big time. Thommo therefore signed to play a season with Middlesex in 1981, until a hernia operation interrupted him half-way. He couldn't have been more mild-mannered off the field or more gentlemanly on it, contrary to legend.

He surprised people again by working hard enough to come back strongly and to be as fast as anyone in Australia in 1982/3. His 1985 tour of England however was a mistake (although he clocked up two hundred Test wickets, half against England) as he did not have the technical virtuosity to compensate for advancing years. Never mind; the cricket world will long remember that quick-stepping run, the flowing mane, the raised left leg, and the end-product that was as fast as anything we have seen.

FIRST CLASS CAREER (1972–85/6)

| 216 innings | 64 not outs | 2065 runs | average 13.58 | 0 hundred |
| | 675 wickets | 17864 runs | average 26.46 | 7–27 best |

TEST RECORD (51 matches)

| 73 innings | 20 not outs | 679 runs | average 12.81 | — |
| | 200 wickets | 5601 runs | average 28.00 | 6–46 |

Series	Tests	O	M	R	W	Av
1972/3 v P	1	19 (8-ball)	1	110	0	—
1974/5 v E	5	175.1 (8-ball)	34	592	33	17.93
1975 in E	4	175.1	56	457	16	28.56
1975/6 v WI	6	150.5 (8-ball)	15	831	29	28.65
1976/7 v P	1	8.5 (8-ball)	2	34	2	17.00
1977 in E	5	200.5	44	583	23	25.34
1977/8 v I	5	145.7 (8-ball)	21	516	22	23.45
1977/8 in WI	5	151.2	25	576	20	28.85
1979/80 v E	1	32	6	100	3	33.33
1979/80 v WI	1	27	6	93	4	23.25
1981/2 v P	3	69	12	219	5	43.80
1981/2 v WI	2	83.1	9	317	9	35.22
1981/2 in NZ	3	89	31	192	6	32.00
1982/3 in P	3	79	12	295	3	98.33
1982/3 v E	4	127.4	22	411	22	18.68
1985 in E	2	56	4	275	3	91.66

MIKE PROCTER

Mike Procter, Imran Khan and Sylvester Clarke have been the finest inswing bowlers of recent years. What the first-named would have achieved in Test cricket is unknowable, but we can have a guess on the basis of the seven Test matches he played against Australia before the curtain came down on South Africa. To judge by them, Procter would have achieved a Test record on the lines of Miller, Botham or Imran, if not of Sobers.

In three Tests against Australia in 1966/7, aged 20 and before he had played county cricket, Procter took seven, six and two wickets. Three years later he captured in successive Tests six, five, six and nine wickets. And that was it: Procter had stampeded to the wicket like a springbok, wound himself up, and delivered – impervious to tendon and sinew – for the last time in Test cricket. His Test average of 15 is the lowest of any proper bowler this century, and only bettered by Lohmann and Ferris (both of whom played 'Tests' of uncertain quality against South Africa in the nineteenth century), and by Albert Trott of passing fame. Procter's striking rate of one wicket every six overs has not been surpassed except by Lohmann and Trott.

Thereafter, denied an international stage, Procter was confined to domestic competitions in England and South Africa. Far from embittered, he devoted himself so whole-heartedly to Gloucestershire that no overseas player can have given more to any county since 1968, when the two-year qualifying rule was ended and instant registration allowed. Gloucestershire, who had never had an outright fast bowler before, suddenly had in Procter one of the greatest triers of all time.

The effort he expended on the county's behalf is the more amazing when his action is taken into account. Procter hurtled in not only to deliver the ball but, as it appeared, himself too. The wrong-footed action puts an immense strain on the bowling shoulder – just try it – yet Procter never seized up there. The only complaint came from his knees, which had to be operated on and finished his county career.

He used to bowl at first from a position as wide in the crease as Croft; he had to start his inswinger well outside off-stump if he was to be effective. (From 1966 more than five fielders were allowed on the leg-side but still only two behind the wicket, so Procter could not attack with an array of short-legs like Bedser or Gladwin had.) Later he learnt to get closer to the stumps and make the odd ball go straight on, or to bowl around the wicket. While not an express, he could make the ball bounce in the batsman's half so that he had many 'fending off'. And when his knees were wobbly or he was simply exhausted he would still grab the ball and bowl big off-breaks, accompanied by exhortations to the batsman to have a go and hole out to his boundary fielders.

Procter's schoolboy feats were so outstanding that the Gloucestershire

Michael John Procter (1946–   ) Gloucestershire, Natal, Western Province and South Africa

Just try it – Procter's action – for one ball, and see if you don't wrench a muscle. But you don't have to bowl off the wrong foot, simply be open-chested

coach asked David Allen, who was touring South Africa in 1964/5, to make acquaintance and invite him to Bristol. The boy arrived with a contemporary, Barry Richards, and both would have probably qualified by residence for the county had not the rule been altered, allowing Richards to sign instantly for Hampshire. While Richards was scoring prolifically in his early seasons, Gloucestershire must have had their doubts. Procter however not only took wickets but came to score as many runs as Richards, including six centuries in a row (for Rhodesia) as only Fry and Bradman have done.

Twice Procter scored a century and took a hat trick in the same match; nobody else has done that more than once. Four times he achieved a hat trick, two of them all LBW. Had he played Test cricket after the age of 23, what might he not have done?

FIRST-CLASS CAREER (1965–88/9)

667 innings	58 not outs	21936 runs	average 36.01	48 hundreds
	1417 wickets	27679 runs	average 19.53	9–71 best

TEST RECORD (7 MATCHES)

10 innings	1 not out	226 runs	average 25.11	—
	41 wickets	616 runs	average 15.02	6–73 best

Series	Tests	O	M	R	W	Av
1966/7 v A	3	109.2	30	263	15	17.53
1969/70 v A	4	143	50	353	26	13.57

ANDY ROBERTS

Andy Roberts entered Test cricket no more than six years after Wes Hall had left it, yet between the two was the gulf of a generation. The phrase 'calypso cricketer', if pejorative in its overtones, was not inappropriate to Hall: he found the game exciting, enjoyed himself and did not play too much. Roberts was a professional through and through and, as the current line of West Indian fast bowlers began with him, his approach was crucial in shaping theirs.

At first Roberts bowled flat out, both for Hampshire (such an impact in 1973 – 119 wickets at 13) and for West Indies. Like his fellow Antiguan Viv Richards (they were the first regular Test cricketers from outside the main islands), he had plenty to prove in a hurry. But while Richards proclaimed himself like a messiah, Roberts went about his business with the minimum of fuss. Like Hall, he was devastating in his first series in India, with 32 wickets including 12 at Madras, the first time a West Indian had reaped so many in a Test. Roberts routed Australia with seven for 54 at Perth, his best Test figures, and had 28 wickets in his first series in England. After 20 Tests of all-out speed he had taken 103 wickets at 22 runs each.

Hereafter the changes became apparent. Whereas Hall was happy to keep pounding himself into an early retirement, Roberts calculated that he would be better off cutting down his run and prolonging his career. He gave up Hampshire, and later played only part-time for Leicestershire. He learnt to move the ball away from the bat, to augment his natural inslant. World Series Cricket was a turning-point in helping cricketers to realise their own value. And it worked: whereas Hall was burnt out well before he played his last Test at 31, Roberts remained in Test cricket until he was 33, in spite of the intense demand for fast-bowling places.

So by the 1980s Roberts was another proposition altogether. More than anything he was unhittably accurate, whereas once in his raw youth he was taken apart in a Second XI game by Nigel Ross, Middlesex's reserve keeper–batsman. His run-up was little longer than a Sunday League 15-yarder and his pace fast-medium but he could always delve into his locker for a quicker ball. Helped by not taking too long a delivery stride he could produce at least two sorts of bouncer, the first tempting you to hook, the second making you bitterly regret even toying with the idea. There was a leg-cutter, to compensate for the infrequency of his yorker. Above all he had a wide range of armaments and of thought, and perhaps more than any other post-Statham fast bowler he made the batsman play.

Clive Lloyd appointed him his fast bowler-in-chief in succession to Keith Boyce and Vanburn Holder. This was an almost formal rôle of bringing on the young fast bowlers, which other countries would do

Anderson Montgomery Everton Roberts (1951–) Combined Islands, Leeward Islands, Hampshire, New South Wales, Leicestershire and West Indies

OPPOSITE: *Great fast bowling – and what is required to combat it*

well to emulate. On retirement Roberts set himself up as a fisherman in Antigua, with his own motor-boat; but he had long been a fisher of batsmen.

And so the nature of the West Indian fast bowler changed, at least in its image, from being calypso to more English than English in its professionalism. Roberts may have appeared moody, sullen and colourless: he was actually, beneath his small-islander reserve, a deep thinker about the game, which his acute radio commentaries on the Antigua Test of 1985/6 served to confirm. Excitable and carefree? Roberts and his colleagues developed into some of the coolest heads in the game. If his later years of controlled fast-medium bowling were not so prolific on paper, his influence was immense and everlasting.

FIRST-CLASS CAREER (1970–84)

291 innings	67 not outs	3516 runs	average 15.69	0 hundred
	889 wickets	18679 runs	average 21.01	8–47 best

TEST RECORD (47 matches)

| 62 innings | 11 not outs | 762 runs | average 14.94 | — |
| | 202 wickets | 5174 runs | average 25.61 | 7–54 best |

Series	Tests	O	M	R	W	Av
1973/4 v E	1	50	12	124	3	41.33
1974/5 in I	5	208.3	51	585	32	18.28
1974/5 in P	2	90 (8-ball)	12	322	12	26.83
1975/6 in A	5	141.6 (8-ball)	15	580	22	26.36
1975/6 v I	2	53	12	176	6	29.33
1976 in E	5	221.4	69	537	28	19.17
1976/7 v P	5	236.3	37	763	19	40.15
1977/8 v A	2	64.2	14	211	12	17.58
1979/80 in A	3	112	20	296	11	26.90
1979/80 in NZ	2	72	14	196	3	65.33
1980 in E	3	105.2	24	262	11	23.81
1980/81 v E	3	104	28	251	8	31.37
1981/2 in A	2	76	24	178	6	29.66
1982/3 v I	5	187.5	36	545	24	22.70
1983/4 in I	2	55.4	14	148	5	29.60

SARFRAZ NAWAZ

Malik Sarfraz Nawaz
(1948–   )
Lahore, Punjab University,
Punjab Railways, United
Bank, Northamptonshire
and Pakistan

Sarfraz could once claim the best innings figures by any pace bowler in Test cricket: nine for 86, and if they were recorded against Australia when they lacked their World Series cricketers, and have since been surpassed, the achievement was no fluke. Sarfraz may not have been in the very highest rank of quality and pace, but he was in the next highest, and a seriously underrated bowler.

It was the same with Imran Khan before Pakistan's 1982 tour of England. However well either of them performed in other surroundings, neither was going to win the label of world-class cricketer until he starred in Tests in England. Imran took his chance. Sarfraz didn't, largely because he was frequently injured on that and his three other tours of England, when only three-Test series were held.

At first, when Roger Prideaux signed him for Northamptonshire on Mushtaq's recommendation, Sarfraz was a bit wild and woolly, and the county were right to release him after a brief apprenticeship. But 'Sarf' was a thoughtful man in an unorthodox way. He decided to acquire more control of what he did on the field (if not off it) and began making the ball move around, and not just on green-tops in England. Given an old rag of a ball at the Qaddafi Stadium in his native Lahore, he could still move it when an English seamer would have gone straight through.

Sarf developed the habit of soaking the old ball with sweat on its less polished side, and could thereby swing the ball at any time of day, or cut it back very nastily. Sarfraz did much to popularise the second thigh-pad on the back leg. And he kept going for long hard spells, as Pakistan have tended to pack their batting and work their three main bowlers into the ground. He had guts all right, this pugilistic Punjabi, for he was ready to give a fellow fast bowler a bouncer and accept one in return, no quarter asked or spared.

His Test bowling average has to be assessed in the light of all the unsympathetic pitches he was given. As with his reputation it would have been substantially better if he had played more Tests in England. In the event, he was injured in 1971, topped Pakistan's averages in 1974, broke down at the start of the 1978 series before returning with five for 33 at Headingley, and managed one Test in 1982 – six in England in all. However well Sarfraz did for Northamptonshire – and he took 101 wickets at 20 in 1975 – county performances didn't have the same cachet as international ones.

Nor did it do much for Sarfraz's reputation that he kept being banned by the Pakistan Board. He had so many interminable disputes over pay and airfares and the captaincy and other issues, not always without reason in an outsider's view, that he was probably given more life-bans in his career than hot lunches. Like Barnes he combined a strong temperament with a knowledge of his own worth.

OPPOSITE: *Sarfraz ready to give and take with Willis during the Karachi Test of 1983/4*

FIRST-CLASS CAREER (1967/8–84/5)

366 innings	72 not outs	5705 runs	average 19.41	0 hundred
	1003 wickets	24664 runs	average 24.59	9–86 best

TEST RECORD (55 MATCHES)

72 innings	13 not outs	1045 runs	average 17.71	—
	177 wickets	5798 runs	average 32.75	9–86 best

Series	Tests	O	M	R	W	Av
1968/9 v E	1	34	6	78	0	—
1972/3 in A	2	84.5 (8-ball)	16	308	12	25.67
1972/3 in NZ	3	63 (8-ball)	7	275	5	55.00
1972/3 v E	2	74	26	156	1	156.00
1974 in E	3	121	34	259	9	28.77
1974/5 v WI	2	68 (8-ball)	5	266	8	33.25
1976/7 v NZ	3	79.2 (8-ball)	12	283	13	21.76
1976/7 in A	2	63 (8-ball)	11	218	8	27.25
1976/7 in WI	4	197.3	54	579	16	36.18
1977/8 v E	2	77 (8-ball)	24	152	5	30.40
1978 in E	2	26	7	51	5	10.20
1978/9 v I	3	148.2	27	425	17	25.00
1978/9 in NZ	3	101.2 (8-ball)	27	296	8	37.00
1978/9 in A	2	111.3 (8-ball)	21	322	13	24.76
1979/80 v A	3	111	30	256	2	128.00
1980/81 v WI	2	33.2	10	79	2	39.50
1981/2 in A	3	118	32	306	9	34.00
1982 in E	1	37	9	78	3	26.00
1982/3 v I	6	241.1	62	633	19	33.31
1983/4 in A	3	137.2	26	359	14	25.64
1983/4 v E	3	179	41	419	8	52.37

MICHAEL HOLDING

Those who attended the Oval Test of 1976, and more especially those England batsmen who were dismissed 14 times by Michael Holding on a featherbed, did not have a lot of time to think while the ball was in the air. But after the game many must have reflected on the fast bowlers through history and concluded: 'the word of the coaching manual has been made flesh and dwells amongst us'.

Never had any type of West Indian bowler taken over 12 wickets in a Test. Holding dismissed 12 Englishmen in that match on his own, either bowled or LBW (nobody was stumped). The pitch, which had yet to be dug up and re-laid, would not let a ball bounce above stump-high even at Holding's extreme pace. The outfield in that parched summer shredded all the shine off the ball. It is scarcely conceivable that there has been a finer display of straight, fast bowling.

Holding on that occasion performed with all the enthusiasm of youth for he had not yet entered county cricket – if he had, he would no doubt have throttled down to contain with line and length. He had done the same at Old Trafford but had got carried away at seeing the ball fly against Close and Edrich, sometimes against their bodies. At the Oval he pitched the ball up, and although he was but 22 it is hard to think he was not at the height of his powers.

A fool could see that something special was imminent when Holding walked back to the start of his full-length run. He had a hurdler's legs, and had been through enough athletic training in his early teens to make him keep his head still in the vertical plane as he ran. But a slight shaking movement of the head remained, as if he were expressing his personal doubt about the batsman's prospects for survival. When delivery-time arrived he cocked his wrist in the shape of a cobra's head, a trait his fellow Jamaican Courtney Walsh was to copy. The one consolation that a batsman had was that Holding would do his work quicker than snake poison.

In 1976 Holding was taking time out from university in Jamaica, where he was doing a course in computer science. He had decided to give cricket a go when, out of the Caribbean blue, he was invited on the tour of Australia the previous winter, but he was going to return to qualify. World Series Cricket changed his attitude: he was going to make softening up batsmen, not software, his profession. Thereafter he cut his pace and run, in order to play the year round, and while gaining in sagacity he was never quite the same great, flat-out fast bowler.

Roberts influenced him and made him streetwise: he had advised Holding from the outset, when he had suggested that a short ball at Max Walker might do the trick and Holding secured his first Test wicket. Holding became quite happy, perhaps overly so, to let others take the new ball ahead of him. He made a fine captain of Jamaica, like

Michael Anthony Holding
(1954–)
Jamaica, Lancashire,
Derbyshire, Tasmania,
Canterbury and West Indies

Joel Garner of Barbados – quite the reverse of the old thick-as-a-short-plank, beer-swilling image of fast bowlers.

Holding assessed his career prospects so intelligently that he was still able to make a living out of county cricket 16 years after his first-class début. But he could have been meteoric, like Tyson, and majestic, as he was at his beginning.

OPPOSITE: *The stuff of which bad dreams are made: imagine facing Holding just before bedtime in a day/night international*

FIRST-CLASS CAREER (1972–)

263 innings	38 not outs	3439 runs	average 15.28	0 hundred
	740 wickets	17102 runs	average 23.11	8–92 best

TEST RECORD (60 MATCHES)

76 innings	10 not outs	910 runs	average 13.78	—
	249 wickets	5898 runs	average 23.68	8–92 best

Series	Tests	O	M	R	W	Av
1975/6 in A	5	140.5 (8-ball)	15	614	10	61.40
1975/6 v I	4	138	35	378	19	19.89
1976 in E	4	159.3	54	356	28	12.71
1979/80 in A	3	111	24	319	14	22.78
1979/80 in NZ	3	94	21	236	7	33.71
1980 in E	5	230.5	56	632	20	31.60
1980/81 v E	4	132.2	38	315	17	18.52
1981/2 in A	3	140.3	37	344	24	14.33
1982/3 v I	5	162	23	500	12	41.66
1983/4 in I	6	223.4	43	663	30	22.10
1983/4 v A	3	101.5	20	245	13	18.84
1984 in E	4	122.2	24	343	15	22.86
1984/5 in A	3	88.1	20	249	15	16.60
1984/5 v NZ	3	82	24	220	9	24.22
1985/6 v E	4	102.4	16	385	16	24.06
1986/7 in NZ	1	37	8	99	0	—

BOB WILLIS

Robert George Dylan Willis
MBE
(1949–   )
Surrey, Warwickshire,
Northern Transvaal and
England

Bob Willis was as undisputed in his leadership of England's attack as John Snow before him. From 1977, when Willis's seven-year apprenticeship ended, until his retirement in 1984, he rushed in on wobbly knees, whirled arms even longer than his hair, and placed an immense strain on an unathletic body. It was not so much part of the natural order as in defiance of it that Willis finished as England's highest wicket-taker, until Ian Botham superseded him.

There was no economic imperative driving Willis to bowl fast as he came from a comfortable middle-class background like Snow. The spur for a beanpole of a boy at Guildford Royal Grammar was the chance to get his own back on contemporaries who singled him out at rugby, which he loathed, and to get his own back on 'the system' too. These were the rebellious years of the 1960s, and the young Robert was spending his spare moments listening to Bob Dylan.

From the age of 14, Willis raced in and wrought havoc among all schoolboy opposition. When Alan Ward broke down in 1970/71, he made a rapid leap from Surrey Schools to an England cap. His county performances were nothing special for Surrey, and from 1972 they weren't special for Warwickshire either. Like Snow he didn't enjoy bowling on a dark May morning, nor was he a sufficiently natural bowler to move the ball around at medium-pace. The number of wickets he took outside international cricket is astonishingly low: in his best English season he took 65 wickets, and 25 of those were for England.

His years of intermittent Test appearances were marked by an angled approach to the crease which he had to remedy. The run from wide mid-off led him to be so chest-on at the crease that the ball would only move into the right-handed batsman, rendering him liable to be bowled or LBW but little else. It was not till the end of the 1970s that Willis changed to running straight, so that the ball itself could go straight or lift away from the batsman.

Another early trait was acute insomnia. Willis would often spend a night without sleeping, which when allied with the strain of a Test match did not do him much good. On England's 1974/5 tour of Australia he happened to be invited to the home of a Sydney hypnotist, Dr Jackson, who gave him tapes to help him sleep at night and keep the pressure in perspective by day. The glazed look came into his eyes; he would never have been in a fit state to be considered as England captain in 1982 if he hadn't developed the ability to switch off to some degree.

By the 1980s Willis was not outright fast, but he was an even better bowler for being so accurate in his off-stump line. The peak was reached one Tuesday at Headingley when Australia needed 131 to win. Willis – not for the first time – had been pencilled in for retirement by the time he switched to the Kirkstall Lane end and at last came down the slope

in full manic flight. A suspicion existed in the visitors' minds that there was a spot from which the ball would rear, and when Trevor Chappell was dismissed by one that took off almost vertically, a 'harrier', the other batsmen fell prey to doubts and to a rampant Willis. His eight for 43 were the figures of his Test life, and the finest by any English pace bowler against Australia.

Willis on the warpath, and close to the stumps, while bowling to Ray Bright at the climax of Headingley '81

FIRST-CLASS CAREER (1969–84)

333 innings	145 not outs	2690 runs	average 14.30	0 hundred
	899 wickets	22468 runs	average 24.99	8–32 best

TEST RECORD (90 MATCHES)

128 innings	55 not outs	840 runs	average 11.50	—
	325 wickets	8190 runs	average 25.20	8–43 best

Series	Tests	O		M	R	W	Av
1970/71 in A	4	88	(8-ball)	16	329	12	27.41
1970/71 in NZ	1	20	(8-ball)	3	69	2	34.50
1973 v WI	1	35		3	118	4	29.50
1973/4 in WI	3	73		15	255	5	51.00
1974 v I	1	36		8	97	5	19.40
1974 v P	1	35		4	129	2	64.50
1974/5 in A	5	140.4	(8-ball)	15	522	17	30.70
1976 v WI	2	57.3		11	234	9	26.00
1976/7 in I	5	135		25	335	20	16.75
1976/7 in A	1	30	(8-ball)	0	124	2	62.00
1977 v A	5	166.4		36	534	27	19.77
1977/8 in P	3	59	(8-ball)	8	190	7	27.14
1977/8 in NZ	3	103.6	(8-ball)	27	255	14	18.21
1978 v P	3	88.4		16	233	13	17.92
1978 v NZ	3	99.2		33	229	12	19.08
1978/9 in A	6	140.3	(8-ball)	23	461	20	23.05
1979 v I	3	102		23	298	10	29.80
1979/80 in A	3	98		26	224	3	74.66
1980 v WI	4	110.1		27	407	14	29.07
1981 v A	6	252.4		56	666	29	22.96
1981/2 in I	5	129.1		29	381	12	31.75
1981/2 in SL	1	28		10	70	3	23.33
1982 v I	3	88		11	330	15	22.00
1982 v P	2	74		4	222	10	22.20
1982/3 in A	5	166.3		28	486	18	27.00
1983 v NZ	4	123.3		38	273	20	13.65
1983/4 in NZ	3	115.1		28	306	12	25.50
1983/4 in P	1	19		6	46	2	23.00
1984 v WI	3	85		15	367	6	61.17

COLIN CROFT

Of the modern West Indian fast bowlers, Colin Croft was the least athletic and most temperamental. He could also be superlatively mean and difficult when he was worked up on a wicket of some pace, and the sweat was pouring from him, the veins standing out from a face that snarled hatred at the batsmen.

When England toured West Indies in 1985/6 Croft's ghost was still lingering in the background. On the previous tour, five years before, he had been the most formidable opponent, even more so than Garner, Holding, Roberts or Marshall. Then he was at his peak, whereas those who saw him in England usually saw a desultory version of Croft. He needed a pitch that would react to the immense force he put into his bowling; he needed hot or at least warm weather to become animated; and he had to be in the West Indian team. Only once by all accounts did he fully exert himself when playing for Lancashire, in a Roses match.

Croft's specialness, aside from his brute strength, lay in the angle from which he bowled. His right arm came over almost on the same line as mid-off – certainly wide of one or two sightscreens in the Caribbean which could not be shifted to behind his arm. The laws have a rather unfair loophole here: while the back foot has to be entirely within the return crease, the front can go as wide as it likes so long as it remains on or behind the popping crease. Croft's front foot was therefore allowed to splay way out so that he was entirely chest-on. Only a man as powerful as he could have stood the strain.

When his right hand came over in delivery, it was natural that he should drag his fingers across the seam. Often this would have no effect on the ball and it would keep coming into the right-hander after pitching. But the odd ball would grip, rear and cut away frighteningly from the tentative bat. Which was the nastier type of delivery depended on whether you preferred to get out or get hit.

These deliveries were not usually bouncers, although Croft would pitch in with his fair share or more. These balls, aided by a violent flick of the wrist, were lifting from barely short of a length. The advice of certain old-timers to hook them only emphasised the gap between the generations.

Croft was no sort of batsman, unlike the other West Indian fast bowlers, and had none of their litheness in the field. He was pure bowler, and according to Clive Lloyd never wanted to be taken off while bowling for West Indies. Like Roberts he may not have given the appearance of being clever but he was an air-traffic controller in Guyana and sub-sequently in America after emigrating, which most Guyanese who have the chance tend to do.

Hurled into Test cricket as if by a catapult, Croft bowled like one in his second Test to take eight for 29 against a strong Pakistan side. His

Colin Everton Hunte Croft (1953–   )
Guyana, Lancashire and West Indies

223

Had Muhammad Ali bowled quick in his prime, he might have resembled this

33 wickets in his début series equalled Valentine's record. His Test career might have continued for much longer on those lines had he not joined, firstly, World Series Cricket and, later, the rebel West Indian tour to South Africa. It is a pity that the last time Croft reached the headlines was for being ejected from a whites-only train compartment.

FIRST-CLASS CAREER (1971/2–82)

131 innings	50 not outs	853 runs	average 10.53	0 hundred
	419 wickets	10277 runs	average 24.52	8–29 best

TEST RECORD (27 MATCHES)

37 innings	22 not outs	158 runs	average 10.53	—
	125 wickets	2913 runs	average 23.30	8–29 best

Series	Tests	O	M	R	W	Av
1976/7 v P	5	217.5	45	676	33	20.48
1977/8 v A	2	55.1	13	170	9	18.88
1979/80 in A	3	121.3	20	378	16	23.62
1979/80 in NZ	3	103	18	265	10	26.50
1980 in E	3	104	25	306	9	34.00
1980/81 in P	4	130	32	302	17	17.76
1980/81 v E	4	157.5	34	455	24	18.95
1981/2 in A	3	138.1	25	361	7	51.57

IMRAN KHAN

Beyond dispute Imran Khan is the finest fast bowler produced by Pakistan, or by anywhere else in that part of the world for that matter. It is impossible to imagine that anyone has bowled a more devastating inswinger than Imran did around 1980, and he could move the ball away almost as viciously. Add to these abilities his inspiring captaincy, and his disciplined batting once he had become captain, and you have a highly desirable candidate for a World All-Time XI.

Imran Khan Niazi (1952–) Lahore, Worcestershire, Oxford University, Pakistan International Airlines, Sussex and Pakistan

Nobody, at least in modern times, has done more with an old ball on unresponsive surfaces. Lillee was utterly frustrated in Pakistan; Hadlee toured the country once in his novitiate; Trueman and Statham declined to visit. Imran took half his Test wickets there, at lower cost than his wickets abroad. At three o'clock on a dusty afternoon in Faisalabad, when not a blade of live grass was to be seen on the pitch, Imran could set the heart of a batsman a-flutter as if he were one of Khan's female admirers.

In addition to the age-old tricks of the fast bowler's trade, Imran pioneered a couple of new techniques. Along with Sarfraz, his scarcely inferior partner, he learnt to soak the ball on one side with sweat to make it heavier, and so to proceed more slowly through the air than the polished half. The other technique he picked up was 'reverse-swing'. In Pakistan and the Caribbean he discovered that the ball, if gripped for what would be an inswinger in England, would swing away in less temperate climes, in defiance of previous theory.

All this lay far ahead of Imran when he arrived in England in 1971 as a gawky 18 year old who had little more than his pedigree – two of his cousins, Javed Burki and Majid Khan, had captained Pakistan – to recommend him. As a bowler he filled out at Oxford and at Worcester and became decidedly hostile, blessed as he was with an inswinging bouncer which kept coming at a right-hander's head. But it was when he joined World Series Cricket that he began developing his talents to the full, which says a lot for the importance of the game's collective wisdom.

Whereas Pakistan had no tradition of fast bowling to speak of – Khan Mohammad was the one top-class practitioner around to coach – a wealth of experience was to be found and listened to in the Kerry Packer circus. John Snow advised Imran, as they played together in the Rest of the World team, to stop being so chest-on and to lift his left shoulder up. The outswinger resulted, although it was to recede again after Imran's long absence from Test cricket through 1983 and 1984. The stress fracture in his left foot led to a slightly less rigorous action and to a predominance of inswing again.

But what inswing! From the end of the 1970s when Imran acquired his final leap into the crease, here was an inswinger from wide out which

would demolish a batsman's toes or leg-stump. But no sooner had he got it all together than Pakistan embarked on a programme of very few Test matches – and only Tests would bring the best out of him. At his peak he took 40 wickets at an average of 13 in a six-Test series against India: a few more series like that and he would have secured the world Test wicket record.

One other feature of Imran's cricket is how long it took to mature. He used his years of county cricket to get all the excesses out of his system, to acquire patience as a batsman and to learn to pitch the ball up. His experience was the reverse of Botham's. So it was that when Imran was made captain of his country for the 1982 tour of England he was fully prepared to stake his claim to greatness.

OPPOSITE: *A wonderful leap, and fluency, even as late as the Lord's Bicentennial Match in 1987*

FIRST-CLASS CAREER (1969–   )

| 551 innings | 91 not outs | 16534 runs | average 35.94 | 27 hundreds |
| | 1255 wickets | 27444 runs | average 21.86 | 8–34 best |

TEST RECORD (75 MATCHES)

| 108 innings | 19 not outs | 3000 runs | average 33.71 | 4 hundreds |
| | 341 wickets | 7517 runs | average 22.04 | 8–58 best |

Series	Tests	O	M	R	W	Av
1971 in E	1	28	9	55	0	—
1974 in E	3	112	26	258	5	51.60
1976/7 v NZ	3	113.4 (8-ball)	15	421	14	30.21
1976/7 in A	3	120.4 (8-ball)	15	519	18	28.83
1976/7 in WI	5	236.1	54	790	25	31.60
1978/9 v I	3	162.1	42	441	14	31.50
1978/9 in A	2	94.1 (8-ball)	22	285	7	40.71
1978/9 in NZ	2	82 (8-ball)	17	255	10	25.50
1979/80 in I	5	152.2	38	365	19	19.21
1979/80 v A	2	56	14	144	6	24.00
1980/81 v WI	4	91	13	236	10	23.60
1981/2 in A	3	150.2	39	312	16	19.50
1981/2 v SL	1	52.2	11	116	14	7.28
1982 in E	3	178.1	48	390	21	18.57
1982/3 v A	3	103.2	35	171	13	13.15
1982/3 v I	6	223.1	69	558	40	13.95
1983/4 in A	2	did not bowl				
1985/6 v SL	3	120.4	37	271	17	15.94
1985/6 in SL	3	116	27	270	15	18.00
1986/7 v WI	3	106.2	23	199	18	11.05
1986/7 in I	5	123.1	21	392	8	49.00
1987 in E	5	168.2	33	455	21	21.66
1987/8 in WI	3	129.5	16	416	23	18.08
1988/9 in NZ	2	103.2	36	198	7	28.28

JOEL GARNER

Joel Garner
(1952–   )
*Barbados, Somerset, South
Australia and West Indies*

One of the innumerable difficulties for anyone attempting to play an innings against the West Indian fast bowlers of the late 1970s onwards was that each member of the prevailing quartet was distinct from the others. While commentators blithely said West Indies lacked variety in that they did not possess a medium-pacer or spinner, there was quite enough variation to exercise a batsman's mind.

Joel Garner's contributions were his exceptional accuracy, economy and height. These were constants, and they made him the hardest bowler of his period to hit. He was thus the ideal one-day bowler. In the 1979 World Cup final against England he had a spell of five wickets for four, and six for 29 in the same year for Somerset at Lord's when the Gillette Cup was their first prize in 104 years. Two years later in a Benson and Hedges final it was five for 14.

But these hauls were all too seldom emulated in Test cricket, or in the county championship. Once his reputation had been made, in the same 1976/7 series which launched Croft, Garner was ready to throttle back. After Roberts and Holding had opened up, Garner would keep it tight while Croft worked up a lather. He did the job with the utmost economy, but he was not making complete use of his talents.

It was when Garner really ran in that he fully earned the title of greatness. Those occasions were instantly recognisable: he would lean well forward from the waist, his legs kicking up high, until he rose up and his tremendous figure rocked back like a leaning tower of Pisa prior to delivery. Now he was not only economical but penetrative, too. When given the new ball and Marshall at the other end, along with the intention to bowl flat out, Garner was a colossus of a bowler.

He did this in 1983/4 when Australia visited the West Indies and Border alone defied the pace. He did it in 1984 when England's first 'blackwash' occurred: he and Marshall shared the new ball and 28 wickets apiece. Roberts had retired, Holding was ageing, Davis and Daniel were not accepted. Perforce Garner had to go all out, instead of graze and pasture.

Too often with Somerset, however, Garner wasn't inclined to pitch the ball well up with outswing to an attacking field. He preferred to post a mid-on and mid-off and aim that little bit shorter. He disliked being driven – or hit to any other point of the compass. The greatest of bowlers is prepared, if needs be, to give a few runs away in return for a wicket. Of course, Garner had to conserve his energy in county cricket to some extent as he had an enormous frame to look after. Nevertheless, while his average was always low, his striking rate was not what it might have been.

Set this thriftiness down to environment perhaps. He was brought up in Barbados by his grandmother, as so many children are there, in

Not leaning so far back as in his youth (this is 1984), but still reaching for the sky and aiming for a yorker

circumstances that taught him to husband resources. He joined Cable and Wireless as a telegraph operator, or rather to play alongside Wes Hall, who taught him how to use the width of the crease. In 1976 Garner became an overnight sensation as a professional with Littleborough. He eventually returned, after the Somerset crisis, to league cricket. One-day cricket suited him, almost too much.

FIRST-CLASS CAREER (1975–1987/8)

231 innings	54 not outs	2964 runs	average 16.74	1 hundred
	881 wickets	16333 runs	average 18.53	8–31 best

TEST RECORD (58 MATCHES)

68 innings	13 not outs	672 runs	average 12.21	—
	259 wickets	5433 runs	average 20.97	6–56 best

Series	Tests	O	M	R	W	Av
1976/7 v P	5	219.3	41	688	25	27.52
1977/8 v A	2	62.1	16	195	13	15.00
1979/80 in A	3	127.4	34	301	14	21.50
1979/80 in NZ	3	122.1	34	235	14	16.78
1980 in E	5	212.4	73	371	26	14.26
1980/81 in P	3	90.3	25	192	10	19.20
1980/81 v E	4	151.2	48	303	10	30.30
1981/2 in A	3	122	37	275	12	22.91
1982/3 v I	4	113	35	301	7	43.00
1983/4 v A	5	208.5	53	523	31	16.87
1984 in E	5	217.5	60	540	29	18.62
1984/5 in A	5	177.4	33	566	19	29.78
1984/5 v NZ	4	136.2	37	302	10	30.20
1986/7 v E	5	156.1	30	436	27	16.14
1987/8 in NZ	2	77	16	205	12	17.08

RICHARD HADLEE

In late 1988, Richard Hadlee took sole possession of the world record for Test wickets which he had shared for almost a year with his great rival Ian Botham. The delay in exceeding 373 Test wickets had been the one interruption to a career which since its start in 1973 had been increasingly triumphant. His one hundred Test wickets had arrived in 1979; his two hundred in 1983; his three hundred in 1986. Whereas it had been Dennis Lillee's signal achievement to be no less of a bowler after the age of 30 than he had been when young and quick, Hadlee's greatness lay in improving with age until he verged on the four hundred wicket barrier.

On a pitch of any dampness Hadlee became the finest operator of his time, though whether he was better than Brian Statham, say, or Les Jackson, can only be debated. Give him a greenish Trent Bridge when he was playing for Nottinghamshire, or a lively Brisbane pitch for a New Zealand Test, and he could be pencilled in for an analysis of six for 40 or five for 68. And the work would be done to the maximum effect with a minimum of effort. His father Walter Hadlee was not only a fine batsman and captain of New Zealand but also an accountant, and Richard calculated precisely what he required of himself for each day, each match and each series, and set about achieving it as economically as possible. He admitted quite freely that it was the fulfilment of these statistical ambitions which kept him going.

It was not necessarily a handicap for Hadlee, as some have said, that he had only the modest and essentially defensive support of Ewen Chatfield at the other end. Being pre-eminent he always enjoyed first choice of everything – end, wind, new ball – and he had any pickings to himself, unlike a West Indian fast bowler. New Zealand moreover nearly always play three-Test series at home and abroad. Thus Hadlee could always exert himself entirely, knowing the end was in sight.

Another advantage he had lay in the ball, of much thicker seams than the ones Statham or Jackson knew. Between the 1960s and the 1980s the number of threads in an English-made ball almost doubled, making the seams nearly twice as prominent. On almost every surface Hadlee was able to make this sort of ball nip back after hitting the seam. Nor did it do anything to hinder his outswinger, bang on off-stump, which was his stock delivery – unless Mike Gatting was batting, in which case he would switch to inswing. Then he had a slower ball which drew his keeper forward, and a quicker ball which knocked slip backwards after taking the edge. All this was allied to an unwavering length (so grooved that he might get slogged at the end of a one-day game) and to equally probing brainwork.

While effortlessly simple in its final appearance, his rhythmical method took him years to perfect: indeed only Imran of modern pace

Richard John Hadlee
(1951–   )
Canterbury,
Nottinghamshire, Tasmania
and New Zealand

231

No one has come closer to day-in, day-out mechanised perfection

bowlers has required so long to reach the highest plateau. Setting off with his Groucho Marx shuffle, Hadlee ran a long way at first and bowled pretty like his elder brother Dayle. He was faster and less accurate when he took seven for 23 against India in 1975/6, prompting New Zealand crowds to chant 'Hadlee, Hadlee!' and giving his country's cricket a self-confidence it had lacked. Not until 1980 did Richard cut down his run in order to prolong his career and attain those landmarks.

On a hard dry pitch, however, Hadlee could not quite be the equal of Lillee, strive though he did to emulate the master. At Lord's in MCC's Bicentenary Match, on the best of batting pitches, there was an ordinariness about Hadlee's bowling which Lillee would not have allowed, while Malcolm Marshall overcame the turf with high pace. Lillee, like Barnes of old, would fall back on his leg-cutter to obtain some movement where Hadlee could find little in the air or off the pitch. Moreover, Lillee had that insatiable desire. Hadlee, with his calculating mind, might decide it was more economical to conserve his energy for another day than expend it in possibly fruitless pursuit. A love of the chase drove Lillee onwards so long as he had breath in his body, while Hadlee would reason that he was better off cutting his losses.

Hadlee otherwise was as near mechanical perfection as it is possible for a human to be. Who could have done more than take nine for 52 against Australia as Hadlee once did at Brisbane, the best Test figures this century outside Laker 1956? In the match he had 15 wickets for 123 runs, one of his innumerable New Zealand records. For Nottinghamshire, his worst bowling average in ten seasons was 17. If figures are the record-breaker's ultimate source of satisfaction, he had plenty of which to be proud.

FIRST-CLASS CAREER (1971/2–   )

460 innings	92 not outs	11625 runs	average 31.59	14 hundreds
	1440 wickets	25750 runs	average 17.88	9–55 best

TEST RECORD (79 MATCHES)

127 innings	19 not outs	2884 runs	average 26.70	2 hundreds
	396 wickets	8800 runs	average 22.22	9–52 best

Series	Tests	O	M	R	W	Av
1972/3 v P	1	25 (8-ball)	0	112	2	56.00
1973 in E	1	45	8	143	1	143.00
1973/4 in A	3	66.7 (8-ball)	9	255	7	36.42
1973/4 v A	2	50.4 (8-ball)	7	225	10	22.50
1975/6 v I	2	48.3 (8-ball)	4	197	12	16.41
1976/7 in I	3	127	18	437	13	33.61
1976/7 in P	3	75.2 (8-ball)	2	447	10	44.70
1976/7 v A	2	72 (8-ball)	7	354	6	59.00
1977/8 v E	3	121.3 (8-ball)	26	371	15	24.73
1978 in E	3	121.1	31	270	13	20.76
1978/9 v P	3	117.6 (8-ball)	13	414	18	23.00
1979/80 v WI	3	161.3	50	361	19	19.00
1980/81 in A	3	147.3	35	364	19	19.15
1980/81 v I	3	119.3	36	288	10	28.80
1981/2 v A	3	91.5	25	226	14	16.14
1982/3 v SL	2	77.3	27	141	10	14.10
1983 in E	4	232	65	559	21	26.61
1983/4 v E	3	109.5	33	232	12	19.33
1983/4 in SL	3	117.5	48	230	23	10.00
1984/5 v P	3	118.5	29	306	16	19.12
1984/5 in WI	4	143	31	409	15	27.26
1985/6 in A	3	169.3	42	401	33	12.15
1985/6 v A	3	157.5	36	387	16	24.18
1986 in E	3	153.5	42	390	19	20.52
1986/7 v WI	3	113.1	20	354	17	20.82
1986/7 in SL	1	38.5	10	102	4	25.50
1987/8 in A	3	156	44	353	18	19.61
1987/8 v E	1	18	3	50	0	—
1988/9 in I	3	100.5	25	252	18	14.00
1988/9 v P	2	82	21	169	5	33.80

WAYNE DANIEL

Wayne Wendell Daniel (1956–)
Barbados, Middlesex, Western Australia and West Indies

At the end of 1976 Wayne Daniel had played five Tests and was on the verge of an outstanding Test career. He had been destined for greatness since his schooldays when he was legendarily quick even by Barbadian standards. All he wanted was a little more experience and rhythm.

Daniel turned out to be a great bowler all right, but for Middlesex in county cricket not for West Indies. His international career was already half over by the end of 1976; his remaining five Tests would come seven years later. It is almost but not quite inexplicable that a man of Daniel's strength and ability should have finished with as few as 36 Test wickets. At any other period, or in any other country, he would have been a recognised world-beater.

The competition was fierce of course, and this had a lot to do with his infrequent appearances, if not entirely in the way one would have expected. In 1976/7, when Daniel was injured, Colin Croft and Joel Garner emerged to join Roberts and Holding. Then it was World Series Cricket, and while Daniel was doing his bit in the circus to popularise

Fine concentration and balance, and a braced front leg, not so universal as the textbook demands

the helmet, Clarke and Marshall seized their chance. Later Winston Davis appeared, and Eldine Baptiste. Daniel was always one of many.

And this had its psychological effect on him. Far from being the cold-blooded slaughterer of schoolboy legend, Wayne was a highly sensitive man. He needed to be wanted – and in the West Indian team he was always an outsider, first change at best. In Test cricket he never felt secure, and a bowler has to be as confident and relaxed as a batsman in order to give of his best.

At Middlesex in the late 1970s and early 1980s it was the reverse. Daniel was leader of the attack, and everybody – not only he – knew it and told him so. He was surrounded by friends in the dressing-room, not rivals. When Vintcent van der Bijl played for a season, he made sure not to tread on Daniel's toes (although if he had, Daniel would have anointed them with acne cream, his panacea for everything including rheumatism). There are plenty of batsmen who can only perform in the security of their county side, and not when exposed to Test matches.

Pounding in from the pavilion end at Lord's, Daniel was guaranteed to take a couple of early wickets. If a partnership developed, he was certain to come back and break it. The ball would usually come into the right-hander down the slope, or sometimes hold its own. Only when he was tired would the wrist fall over and push the ball down the leg-side.

Daniel's sole deficiency in county cricket was psychological, springing from that same sensitivity. He would not bowl intimidating bouncers: he preferred to see a half-volley driven than hit a man. Exactly why this was so, he would never say; he'd just give a nebulous sort of answer. Only twice on the field did he become angry, once when Franklyn Stephenson, then playing for Gloucestershire, aimed bouncers at him and Daniel replied to his fellow Barbadian in kind. The second occasion was when he and Imran Khan had a similar exchange.

His best years ended in 1984. By then Norman Cowans was no longer the admiring pupil but had taken over at Middlesex. Daniel drifted away, gentle soul that he was, never one to relish the heat of rivalry.

FIRST-CLASS CAREER (1975/6–88)

| 241 innings | 106 not outs | 1551 runs | average 11.48 | 0 hundred |
| | 867 wickets | 19490 runs | average 22.47 | 9–61 best |

TEST RECORD (10 MATCHES)

| 11 innings | 4 not outs | 46 runs | average 6.57 | — |
| | 36 wickets | 910 runs | average 25.27 | 5–39 best |

Series	Tests	O	M	R	W	Av
1975/6 v I	1	23.2	7	64	2	32.00
1976 in E	4	108	28	317	13	24.38
1983/4 in I	3	98	12	332	14	23.71
1983/4 v A	2	63	13	197	7	28.14

IAN BOTHAM

Ian Terence Botham
(1955–   )
Somerset, Worcestershire,
Queensland and England

If Ian Botham had been one of those whom the gods loved, he would have stopped bowling at the age of 24, and then he would have been rated unequivocally as one of the greatest bowlers. His mistake was to go on bowling after April 1980 when he damaged his spine in such a way that he virtually lost his outswinger thereafter. The critics were thus able to look at his record, compare it with his later medium-pace, and assert that Botham was simply a lucky bowler.

These people utterly fail to appreciate the technical qualities that Botham had as a bowler in his young lion years. When his left arm was raised high and he turned side-on, he bowled as brilliant an outswinger as anyone has done at fast-medium pace. At Lord's in 1978 one Monday morning he took eight for 34 from the Nursery end. Again the detractors were ready to knock him down: it was a Pakistan Second XI not up to county standard. World Series had creamed off their best batsmen. Nevertheless, some of us playing in the game knew we had never seen a ball swing so far at high pace.

We are falsifying history if we call Botham's wicket-taking from 1977 until early 1980 lucky. In his 25 Tests in that period he took 139 wickets. Surely, some of the opposition was below the standard it is today; but if Botham was no good, why did he lead the mayhem with five-and-a-half wickets a game? And some of the opposition was at full strength. India for example had not lost any players to WSC when Botham became the first man in history to do the Test double of a century and not merely ten but 13 wickets in the match for 106 runs. It was his last game before injuring his back one April morning in the Oxford Parks.

The bouncer was always something Botham liberally sprinkled on a pitch, and it was sometimes a winner – as when Viv Richards was caught for nought in an Antigua Test – without directly costing England a game as Trueman's bouncers to Burge did in 1964. To the whole was added all the self-confidence which youth should have but which other players leave behind in the dressing-room. Botham was never afraid to experiment, to attempt his slower ball, to use the crease, to bowl at a batsman's strength in the hope he would fall to greediness. He could afford this adventurousness, for if he gave away 20 runs to get a wicket, he was going to score over 30 himself, on average.

OPPOSITE: *In 1977, in his
first Test series, Botham is
turning side-on, although he
is still looking past the
'wrong' side of his left arm.
Strangely, he will land on
the ball of his left foot, not
the heel*

Thereafter he had outstanding days – when Mike Brearley revived him and his outswinger in 1981, when he took eight West Indian wickets at Lord's in 1984 – but for the most part his later wickets represented a triumph of will rather than technique. The inswinger, which puts less strain on the back as it is bowled chest-on, replaced the outer as his stock ball. And the determination became a two-edged sword. It helped to drive him to all those five-wicket hauls he had at the outset, and to another at Edgbaston in 1981 when the smell of Australian blood

inflamed him. But it became mere obstinacy when his body was not responding. He needed a stronger captain than he was given.

A Brearley would have worked out a new rôle for him in the England side. On the 1982/3 tour of Australia he took the new ball all right but he was acting the part of opening bowler. He should have been encouraged to concentrate on his batting, to become a number five and to be not so much a third as fourth seamer, a faster version of d'Oliveira. But then the man's capacity to surprise is limitless. In 1985 he rolled back the years, lengthened his run and charged in to scatter Border's Australians with his pace and willpower.

Aside from all his other immense contributions as batsman and fielder, Botham reached two hundred wickets in his forty-first Test (or four years and 34 days, easily a record). He had still not doubled that figure when, after 94 Tests, he had his back operation, but he had set a new world and England record for the most wickets. His days of great bowling had gone, in short, but he remained a great wicket-taker.

FIRST-CLASS CAREER (1974–)

| 509 innings | 37 not outs | 16422 runs | average 34.79 | 33 hundreds |
| | 1005 wickets | 26980 runs | average 26.84 | 8–34 best |

TEST RECORD (94 MATCHES)

| 150 innings | 5 not outs | 5057 runs | average 34.87 | 14 hundreds |
| | 373 wickets | 10392 runs | average 27.86 | 8–34 best |

Series	Tests	O	M	R	W	Av
1977 v A	2	73	16	202	10	20.20
1977/8 in NZ	3	101 (8-ball)	17	311	17	18.29
1978 v P	3	75.5	19	209	13	16.07
1978 v NZ	3	142.1	42	337	24	14.04
1978/9 in A	6	158.4 (8-ball)	25	567	23	24.65
1979 v I	4	179	49	472	20	23.60
1979/80 in A	3	173.1	62	371	19	19.52
1979/80 in I	1	48.5	14	106	13	8.15
1980 v WI	5	131	41	385	13	29.61
1980 v A	1	31.2	3	132	1	132.00
1980/81 in WI	4	145.2	31	492	15	32.80
1981 v A	6	272.3	81	700	34	20.58
1981/2 in I	6	240.3	52	660	17	38.82
1981/2 in SL	1	24.5	2	65	3	21.66
1982 v I	3	93.3	16	320	9	35.55
1982 v P	3	150.5	33	478	18	26.55
1982/3 in A	5	213.5	35	729	18	40.50
1983 v NZ	4	112.5	27	340	10	34.00
1983/4 in NZ	3	109.4	25	354	7	50.57
1983/4 in P	1	30	5	90	2	45.00
1984 v WI	5	163.2	30	667	19	35.10
1984 v SL	1	56	12	204	7	29.14
1985 v A	6	251.4	36	855	31	27.58
1985/6 in WI	5	134.5	16	535	11	48.63
1986 v NZ	1	26	4	82	3	27.33
1986/7 in A	4	106.2	24	296	9	32.88
1987 v P	5	134.3	30	433	7	61.85

SYLVESTER CLARKE

As in the case of Wayne Daniel, the Test record of Sylvester Clarke is no illustration at all of his merits. In the right mood – and he was as much of a mood bowler as Croft or Qadir – 'Sylvers' could be as ferocious a proposition as any there has been. That he played so little Test cricket was due to circumstances – like the West Indian rebel tour of South Africa – not to lack of greatness.

With his barrel of a chest pointed down the wicket, his action was of a rare kind similar only to Mike Procter's among the best. But Clarke did not require the long run that Procter did: indeed he had the same facility as Marshall to bowl a fast ball off a couple of paces, so powerful

Sylvester Theophilus Clarke (1954–)
Barbados, Surrey,
Transvaal and West Indies

Not a braced front leg but an immensely strong back and arms. The batsman may also deduce from his view of the shiny side that an outswinger is coming, whereas a last-second turn of Clarke's wrist will result in the opposite

were his shoulders. To some county batsmen in Clarke's early years with Surrey the combination of open-chestedness and speed from nowhere was suspicious, but he has not been no-balled for throwing, unlike another Barbadian and rebel, Hartley Alleyne.

Clarke's stock ball swung into the right-hander – a slower one might hold its own – and if he was in the mood it would do a whole lot more besides. Only Imran can have produced as disturbing a bouncer as Clarke: it would pitch wide, so you thought of letting it pass harmlessly by, only it would abruptly decide to come at you. If you started to bend back, the ball would keep on coming, until time expired and you had to abandon yourself to fate. I remember this happening at the Oval on a re-laid pitch, and the ball went off my helmet, bounced once and crossed the ropes. Later – the highlight of the Edmonds batting career – I hooked Clarke for three sixes and immediately got out to a simple medium-pacer at the other end. That is the effect a great fast bowler has, and one which cannot be measured in figures.

Another time a good county batsman was facing up to Clarke at the Oval. He hooked a four, not a sensible move, for the next ball had whistled past his head before he knew what had happened – but he quickly went white when he did. That sort of speed is dangerous, when the ball has passed before the batsman has focussed or reacted.

West Indies gave Clarke his break when World Series signed up their established bowlers. With Holder and Norbert Phillip he was left to carry the West Indian attack round India on pitches designed to blunt their edge. Clarke was easily the most successful of them.

The only other series in which Clarke was allowed a full part was in Pakistan in 1980/81. Given the new ball he took 14 cheap wickets to head the Test bowling averages. He also provoked a riot when oranges were thrown at him while he was fielding in the deep at Multan, and he threw a loose brick into the crowd. A student leader failed to avoid the brick, not surprisingly: it probably swung in late and viciously before hitting him on the head.

FIRST-CLASS CAREER (1977–   )

258 innings	43 not outs	3203 runs	average 14.89	1 hundred
	922 wickets	17926 runs	average 19.44	8–62 best

TEST RECORD (11 MATCHES)

16 innings	5 not outs	172 runs	average 15.63	—
	42 wickets	1171 runs	average 27.88	5–126 best

Series	Tests	O	M	R	W	Av
1977/8 v A	1	49	8	141	6	23.50
1978/9 in I	5	233.5	39	711	21	33.85
1980/81 in P	4	98	21	243	14	17.35
1981/2 in A	1	32	13	76	1	76.00

KAPIL DEV

It is the strangest of cricket's coincidences that the four most prolific all-rounders in Test history – the only ones to have achieved three hundred wickets and two thousand runs – should have been contemporaries. Kapil Dev was the fourth of the quartet chronologically, joining Imran Khan, Ian Botham and Richard Hadlee. And if he has been the least of the four as a bowler in speed and quality, judging them all at their peak, he has still been India's finest pace bowler since Independence, not so much by the width of the Peshawar–Calcutta Grand Trunk Road as by its length.

Kapil Dev Nikhanj
(1959–   )
Haryana,
Northamptonshire,
Worcestershire and India

The sobriquet Kapil quickly earned in India, 'the Haryana Hurricane', would strike a cricket follower from any other country as sheer hyperbole. His bouncer had to be dropped fairly short for he was not one to get alarming lift from a length. Against that, Kapil learnt to move the ball appreciably and he reached fulfilment as a high-quality medium-pacer rather than some form of anticyclone.

His basic action, prefaced by a skip and leap, turned him as side-on as Trueman or McKenzie – when Kapil was fully fit, that is. From this position he could outswing the old ball, once he had learnt to hug the stumps; but he was too side-on to produce inswing, unlike his three contemporaries who could manage both forms. Still, he would cut the ball in and he developed a fine line and a yorker. And he bowled and he bowled, with whatever advantages of end or wind there were, as he had no other challenger, so that sooner or later the wickets had to come.

He beat Botham's record by reaching a hundred Test wickets at 21 years and 25 days officially, but dates of birth in northern India are not always strictly recorded. So much indeed did he have to bowl for India – even when the diminutive Chetan Sharma offered some support – that it was a transparently unwise move for all parties when he signed for Northamptonshire (later he played even more transiently for Worcestershire). The over-load – not forgetting more overs for Haryana in the Ranji Trophy and for North Zone in the Duleep Trophy – served only to rob him of his nip in the mid-1980s. Having averaged four wickets a Test for his first 50 Tests, he struggled to and beyond three hundred in ones, twos and threes.

His best Test figures were achieved at Ahmedabad in 1983/4 on a pitch which the visiting, and winning, captain Clive Lloyd described as atrocious. Aside from his nine for 83, he would often skid through and trap batsmen in front on ever slower and lower Indian pitches. At his best he was therefore doing the destructive work that Bedi and Chandra had done in the two previous decades but which no current Indian spinner was great enough to do. Thus it was that under Kapil Dev's influence, and sometimes captaincy, India's bowling attack came to resemble that of every other Test-playing nation.

As his bowling declined, and made his 1959 birthdate the more implausible, Kapil's batting developed so that he was not the least of the four all-rounders in that department. From a swashbuckling hitter he became a more reliable performer against pace. As a captain he was a cut above Botham or Hadlee, if one below Imran. As such he knew the happiest moment that cricket can offer, when he lifted up the World Cup of 1983.

OPPOSITE: *Ideal for the outswinger. In later years, when the litheness left, he managed an inswinger too*

FIRST-CLASS CAREER* (1975/6–   )

302 innings	34 not outs	8797 runs	average 32.82	13 hundreds
	658 wickets	17760 runs	average 26.99	9–83 best

TEST RECORD (95 MATCHES)

137 innings	12 not outs	3996 runs	average 31.97	6 hundreds
	329 wickets	9686 runs	average 29.44	9–83 best

* First-class career figures to the end of the 1988 English season.

Series	Tests	O	M	R	W	Av
1978/9 in P	3	117	18	426	7	60.85
1978/9 v WI	6	155.4	27	561	17	33.00
1979 in E	4	173.5	49	495	16	30.93
1979/80 v A	6	223	53	625	28	22.32
1979/80 v P	6	211.5	53	566	32	17.68
1979/80 v E	1	37	10	85	3	28.33
1980/81 in A	3	120.5	26	333	14	23.78
1980/81 in NZ	3	106	27	255	8	31.87
1981/2 v E	6	243.5	40	835	22	37.95
1982 in E	3	133	21	439	10	43.90
1982/3 v SL	1	47.2	5	207	8	41.40
1982/3 in P	6	205.2	22	831	24	34.62
1982/3 in WI	5	153.5	32	424	17	24.94
1983/4 v P	3	91	23	225	12	18.75
1983/4 v WI	6	203.5	39	537	29	18.51
1984/5 in P	2	35	4	126	1	126.00
1984/5 v E	4	161.5	33	436	10	43.60
1985/6 in SL	3	129.4	30	372	11	33.81
1985/6 in A	3	118	31	276	12	23.00
1986 in E	3	128.2	36	306	10	30.60
1986/7 v A	3	45	12	124	0	—
1986/7 v SL	3	88	22	231	9	25.66
1986/7 v P	5	162	37	430	11	39.09
1987/8 v WI	4	113	34	309	8	38.62
1988/9 v NZ	3	89	22	232	10	23.20

VINTCENT VAN DER BIJL

Vintcent Adriaan Pieter van der Bijl
(1948–   )
Natal, Transvaal and Middlesex

Vintcent van der Bijl captured the most wickets in Currie Cup history, after setting the record for most wickets in a domestic season with 65 then breaking it himself with 75. When he did eventually play outside South Africa, with Middlesex in 1980, he headed the national averages for regular bowlers and confirmed what had already been widely suspected: that he was the finest bowler of modern times never to have played Test cricket.

Fielding in the slips to van der Bijl's bowling, one had the impression that the ball was attached to a long piece of elastic held by the wicket-keeper. Once Vintcent had released the ball, it seemed to increase in velocity, even after hitting the pitch, until it reached the keeper's gloves. That was a measure of how hard he hit the deck.

Although he may look a bit ponderous at the moment, he is readying himself nicely and the final result will be fluent

Naturally enough he had a rather ponderous run-up as he was as massively constructed as a Springbok forward at 6′ 8″, but he had gathered himself together by the vital moment. His aim was at or outside off-stump when bowling from the Nursery end at Lord's, and thanks to his height he always achieved some lift. He did not bowl a particularly good bouncer though, as his natural length was well-up to the bat, which allowed the ball to swing if it wanted to.

Like most present-day South Africans he was well coached in the fundamentals. His father was Director of Coaching for Western Province, as well as a Rhodes scholar, a schoolmaster, and a steady opening bat who averaged 51 for South Africa and made a century in the Timeless Test of 1938/9. Vintcent's grandfather played first-class cricket too, while a great-uncle was picked for a tour of England but had to decline. The one tour Vintcent was chosen for was the one by South Africa to Australia in 1971/2, which had to be cancelled.

His one opportunity to play in the outside world therefore was in county cricket. He may have been 32 when it arrived but he bowled with the enthusiasm of youth and could not have fitted more harmoniously into the side. He fell into his rhythm immediately and took 85 wickets at 14 each to enable Middlesex to win the championship, not to mention the Gillette Cup. So direct was his bowling that 66 of his wickets were bowled, LBW or caught behind.

When he returned to South Africa and Natal, he followed his success with 54 wickets at an average of nine! He was one of the best fast-medium bowlers – like a burlier Statham – and of people. And had he played Test cricket, he could have been confidently inked in for a record pretty similar to Statham's.

FIRST-CLASS CAREER (1968/9–82/3)

| 188 innings | 48 not outs | 2269 runs | average 16.20 | 0 hundred |
| | 767 wickets | 12692 runs | average 16.54 | 8–35 best |

TEST RECORD: NO MATCHES

TERRY ALDERMAN

*Terence Michael Alderman
(1956–   )
Western Australia, Kent,
Gloucestershire and
Australia*

Terry Alderman has to rank among the pick of seam and swing bowlers, in the company of Jackson and van der Bijl. He was thus at his best in English conditions – first when representing Australia in England in 1981 and setting an Ashes record of 42 wickets in his début series, and subsequently when representing Kent or Gloucestershire in the county championship, although by then his pace had been reduced by a severe shoulder injury.

Conditions in Alderman's native city of Perth prepared him for these highlights, since they are as near to English-style as one may find in Australia. The pitch at the WACA (the Western Australia Cricket Association) is usually moist, and spin superfluous, while the wind coming off the Swan River can be an influence. Possessed of an action that led to outswing, Alderman rose rapidly through the schoolboy ranks and was in the State side at 18. He then spent several years as a rather wild and woolly performer with no great love of fitness-training or practice, until a fine talent was on the verge of being wasted.

Alderman dismisses Mike Brearley after lunch in the Old Trafford Test of 1981, having bowled throughout the morning

A summer spent in Scotland in 1980, and the tour of England the following year, saved him in time. He found British pitches responsive and dove-tailed his methods to them. He learnt about 'the corridor of uncertainty'. He appreciated the need to run in close to the stumps, aim at off-stump or a fraction outside, and swing the ball away – a quicker version of Emburey's arm-ball in effect. He and Lillee sustained the 1981 Australians like a pair of nineteenth-century stalwarts.

On returning to Australia Alderman found, like other English seamers, that he was effective in Perth but less so elsewhere on hard wickets. He then suffered shoulder damage during the Perth Test of 1982/3 when rowdy pitch invaders incensed the otherwise mild ex-primary school teacher to the point of his rugby-tackling one of them. After a long convalescence he recovered all his old accuracy and more but he had lost the sharp edge of his pace. Before then a nasty bouncer had been evidence that he had once aspired to fast bowling.

Still, even at reduced speed, Alderman would clock up 80 or 90 wickets in a county season. When he had served his three-year ban from Test cricket for touring South Africa with a rebel side under Kim Hughes, Australia made further use of him at the age of 32. The discipline had gone out of Australian bowling as younger hands had to be promoted before their time. The Western Australian was a most disciplined performer.

FIRST-CLASS CAREER (1974–   )

| 201 innings | 88 not outs | 1110 runs | average 9.82 | 0 hundred |
| | 755 wickets | 17750 runs | average 23.51 | 8–46 best |

TEST RECORD (24 MATCHES)

| 36 innings | 15 not outs | 125 runs | average 5.95 | – |
| | 86 wickets | 2766 runs | average 32.16 | 6–128 |

Series	Tests	O	M	R	W	Av
1981 in E	6	325	76	893	42	21.26
1981/2 v P	3	93.2	23	252	8	31.50
1981/2 v WI	2	69	17	196	5	39.20
1981/2 in NZ	3	117.5	33	311	8	38.87
1982/3 in P	1	37	4	154	2	77.00
1982/3 v E	1	43	15	84	1	84.00
1983/4 in WI	3	111.2	18	368	4	92.00
1984/5 v WI	3	99	31	339	9	37.66
1988/9 v WI	2	80.1	23	169	7	24.14

JOHN EMBUREY

John Ernest Emburey
(1952–   )
Middlesex, Western
Province and England

In John Emburey's time the rôle of England's off-spinner changed from what it was in Jim Laker's day. The task for Laker was to wrap up the opposition's second innings on a damp or dusty pitch. Emburey's main function has been to keep the game tight while England's pace bowlers have rested and recovered their breath. This stock-bowling brief he has fulfilled superbly.

Since 1977 he has kept one end tight for Middlesex, following a long apprenticeship to Fred Titmus. In 1980/81 and 1985/6 he accomplished for hours on end the hardest job in modern bowling – imposing some measure of control over West Indian stroke-makers while in the ascendancy on their own grounds, equipped as they are with short boundaries. If the West Indians got some of their own back in 1988, when 'Embers' had his brief taste of the England captaincy, he remained the best of non-pace bowlers in limited-overs cricket.

The straightness of his line – from wicket to wicket – and the accuracy of his length have been the exceptional features of Emburey's bowling. Possessed of them, he has been able to dictate through an innings, and has been especially lethal against the lower orders. If they miss when they take a heave, he hits their stumps, often with a yorker.

As the years have passed, the span between his index and middle fingers has contracted so that he has not been able to get so much purchase on the ball. His arm-ball, though, remains as fine as ever. By placing his first finger at 11 o'clock, so to speak, and the seam upright at noon, he has drifted the ball from leg-stump to middle-and-off; and in England at least the umpires are disposed to give a batsman leg-before if he misses his sweep against it.

For years batsmen allowed Emburey to get on top of them from the start of his spell, which was fatal. With half-a-dozen maidens to his name, Embers will work over a batsman until the latter loses his last shred of patience. It has been the bold batsman who has succeeded against him; none has been bolder than Viv Richards, who never permitted him to settle into that rigid length and line.

If Emburey's striking-rate dwindled during the 1980s, spinners struggled throughout the world except in Pakistan where certain local conditions aided their continued success. No self-respecting batsman was bowled in defence between bat and pad, whereas Laker hauled in many that way. Prominent seams, half as thick again as those on traditional or club balls, are welcomed by spinners too – but how can they get their hands on such a ball when any medium-pacer can make it deviate as much as Qadir, at higher speed and perhaps more accurately? Worst of all has been the heavy bat which sends even the mis-hit ball for four or six. These were handicaps unknown to the three leading wicket-takers in first-class history, Rhodes, Freeman and Parker, spinners all.

OPPOSITE: *About to go wide and already focussing on his target, Emburey clasps both hands together in preparation, like the majority of slow bowlers*

248

FIRST-CLASS CAREER (1973–   )

435 innings	90 not outs	7874 runs	average 22.82	3 hundreds
	1092 wickets	27551 runs	average 25.22	7–36 best

TEST RECORD (57 MATCHES)

84 innings	17 not outs	1409 runs	average 21.02	–
	130 wickets	4763 runs	average 36.63	7–78 best

Series	Tests	O	M	R	W	Av
1978 v NZ	1	29.1	14	40	2	20.00
1978/9 in A	4	144.4 (8-ball)	49	306	16	19.12
1979/80 in I	1	did not bowl				
1980 v WI	3	39.3	13	83	6	13.83
1980 v A	1	47	11	139	1	139.00
1980/81 in WI	4	185	62	419	7	59.85
1981 v A	4	193.5	58	399	12	33.25
1981/2 in I	3	99	31	222	6	37.00
1981/2 in SL	1	44	14	88	6	14.66
1985 v A	6	248.4	75	544	19	28.63
1985/6 in WI	4	153	34	448	14	32.00
1986 v I	3	76.5	28	141	4	35.25
1986 v NZ	2	79.5	33	141	4	35.25
1986/7 in A	5	315.5	86	663	18	36.83
1987 v P	4	107	21	222	0	—
1987/8 in P	3	124	48	251	7	35.85
1987/8 in A	1	68	15	155	1	155.00
1987/8 in NZ	3	133.5	48	236	3	78.66
1988 v WI	3	62	14	228	3	76.00
1988 v SL	1	20	10	38	1	38.00
1987/8 in NZ	3	133.5	48	236	3	78.66
1988 v WI	3	62	14	228	3	76.00
1988 v SL	1	20	10	38	1	38.00

ABDUL QADIR

Abdul Qadir has taken three-quarters of his Test wickets in Pakistan, to date, and they have come at half the cost of his wickets abroad. He has had a fair series in the West Indies, and he enjoyed the Oval Test of 1987 when he took ten wickets without winning the match. Nevertheless, the differences between what he has done at home and abroad are so vast as to be almost irreconcilable.

At least there is no question that Qadir is a great bowler in Pakistan. Give him the driest, barest and hardest strip of earth anywhere from Lahore to Karachi and he will make the ball talk when nobody else can get a squeak out of it. He can grip the ball as his fingers are warm and the outfield roughens up the ball as in a hot English summer before the invention of artificial fertilisers. Seam bowling is almost a waste of time, so after a few overs with the new ball, the limelight falls on the man who steps up to the crease with a bounce and slight scowl, the last prince of leg-spin.

In Pakistan the umpiring is – how shall we say? – more sympathetic to Qadir than it is abroad, especially when it comes to interpreting his flipper. Dragging the ball's seam back with his fingers to make it revolve backwards on its axis as it goes down the pitch, Qadir makes this ball hurry on to the right-hander pushing half-forward. What is out in Pakistan, to a passionate appeal, is often not out in England or India or the West Indies, while in Australia in 1983/4 Qadir came up against a phalanx of left-handers whom he hates like all his type.

There is also the question of his mood. Qadir is either on song or out of sorts – there is seldom a state in between. He is a prima donna, or at any rate a fast bowler in temperament (he tried to bowl quick when young in the back streets of Lahore). Like a tenor or soprano he wants the audience to be on his side, not hostile, as the Bridgetown crowd was when Qadir jumped a fence to confront a spectator who had abused him.

Perhaps Qadir, like Chianti, simply does not travel. He describes himself as a simple man who was born in the less affluent parts of Lahore to an 'imam' or preacher. He is a religious man and bowls with such a fundamentalist fervour that he seems to be waving the banner of Islam as well as the flag of Pakistan. He has, in short, the aggression of the very greatest bowlers like Barnes and O'Reilly and Lillee, but he cannot always channel it into defeating the opposition, especially away from home.

His first bowling of note was done in his second Test when he bowled into Bob Willis's footmarks at Hyderabad and took six for 44. He was a self-taught bowler who had experimented with wrist-spin until he had been noticed and employed by Habib Bank. Even then he had the late dip without which a spinner is ordinary, and some of the tennis-ball

Abdul Qadir Khan (1955–   )
Punjab, Lahore, Habib Bank and Pakistan

bounce which was to make him exceptional. But in a wet English summer a few months later he could do nothing, and not until 1982 did he play a Test match in England. Then he was effective against inexperienced batsmen, and expensive at other times as Imran demonstrated too much faith in him. At home that winter he dismissed more than a hundred batsmen, the first to do so in a Pakistani season.

Subsequently there were ups and downs, as there will be with any wrist-spinner, but Qadir had them off the field as well – with the Pakistan Board, like Sarfraz. (Among innumerable disputes he was sent home from a tour of New Zealand.) Better for him was a technical development: he left out the leap in his stride before delivery. Steadier on the ground as a result, he cut down on the short balls to which he was prone without losing his bounce, and set himself up for the Lahore Test when his nine for 56 against England was a Pakistani record. On his home pitch, and supported by everyone, Abdul was qualified to be a member of the Magic Circle, as fine as any bowler when in the mood.

OPPOSITE: *A back-of-the-hander – but which? – as Qadir takes ten wickets in the Oval Test of 1987*

FIRST-CLASS CAREER* (1975–   )

| 208 innings | 35 not outs | 3419 runs | average 19.76 | 2 hundreds |
| | 831 wickets | 18742 runs | average 22.55 | 9–49 best |

TEST RECORD (63 MATCHES)

| 70 innings | 8 not outs | 967 runs | average 15.60 | – |
| | 224 wickets | 7112 runs | average 31.75 | 9–56 best |

* First-class career figures to the end of the 1988 English season.

Series	Tests	O	M	R	W	AV
1977/8 v E	3	132 (8-ball)	31	305	12	25.41
1979/80 in I	3	60	17	173	2	86.50
1980/81 v WI	2	73.1	9	224	8	28.00
1982 in E	3	160.5	48	406	10	40.60
1982/3 v A	3	212.2	48	562	22	25.54
1982/3 v I	5	151.3	23	526	11	47.81
1983/4 in A	5	219.3	40	733	12	61.08
1983/4 v E	3	185	42	451	19	23.73
1984/5 v I	1	38	8	104	4	26.00
1984/5 v NZ	3	105.3	24	307	12	25.58
1984/5 in NZ	2	81	19	212	2	106.00
1985/6 v SL	3	102.3	26	278	9	30.88
1985/6 in SL	2	65.3	12	174	5	34.80
1986/7 v WI	3	132.2	19	361	18	20.05
1986/7 in I	3	68	8	242	4	60.50
1987 in E	4	175.4	46	450	11	40.90
1987/8 v E	3	234.4	68	437	30	14.56
1987/8 in WI	3	162.3	19	538	14	38.42
1988/9 v A	3	135	37	320	11	29.09
1988/9 in NZ	2	117.1	32	309	8	38.62

MALCOLM MARSHALL

Malcolm Denzil Marshall
(1958–   )
Barbados, Hampshire and
West Indies

It is tempting to think that modern fast bowling was consummated in Malcolm Marshall. He had the benefit of playing in county cricket with Hampshire for a decade; he had the benefit of the experience gathered by West Indian fast bowlers before him such as Andy Roberts; and in a world of ever more rapid communication (unlike the time when the googly took years to spread), he was able to keep up with what others like Lillee or Hadlee were doing, before putting it all into practice himself.

For ten years he ran to the crease like a long jumper, until the summer of 1988 when he cut down his run with no loss of lethalness. He is very light on his feet – a relaxed approach is an asset – and wears what can hardly be called boots on his slightly pigeon-toed feet. But his single greatest attribute is the whippiness of his shoulder. Nature decided that a boy born in Bridgetown in none too affluent circumstances in 1958 was to be given the ability to bowl quick when standing still, without any run-up.

To this Marshall added ambition. In England a fast bowler, like most other first-class cricketers, is all too ready to accept what is merely adequate: to bowl a few overs and take a wicket is often sufficient to satisfy the conscience and earn the salary. Marshall set himself the task of taking five wickets an innings for Hampshire, and would not stop trying and scheming until he had them. Maybe the motivation sprang from within; maybe the religious *milieu* of Barbados nourished the work ethic. In any event, Marshall has been almost as willing as his captains to bowl himself into the ground, summer and winter, for Hampshire and for West Indies.

At first he was a flat-out fast bowler, like Lillee before his back injury or Roberts and Holding before World Series Cricket. Marshall triumphed then through his speed, his outswinger and the stamina which kept him firing for long spells. He wasn't particularly successful initially, it may be surprising to recall: after 17 Test matches he had taken 55 wickets at 28 apiece. Three of those Tests had been in India in 1978/9, when he had to be selected for the tour after one game for Barbados as all the established bowlers had signed for WSC: at the end of that series he had three expensive wickets. Nonetheless it is true that Marshall, as a blaster, did not properly fit into the West Indian scheme until he was given the new ball and made leader of Clive Lloyd's attack.

In county cricket, meanwhile, Marshall was carrying out experiments on Hampshire's opponents. He reduced his run-up, developed an in-swinger and accumulated notes on every batsman for his mental file. He was still bowling all-out for West Indies, except when he was prevented from doing so in the Headingley Test of 1984 by a broken left hand. On that occasion he had perforce to give a preview of the

OPPOSITE: *The summer of*
1988: this victim is Gooch at
Headingley

medium bowler he was to be – and captured seven English wickets for 53.

Great bowlers are statistically ambitious. They want their names to be at the top of the all-time list however much they pretend otherwise; they all want to leave their mark on history, even if they are not quite so obsessive about it as Hadlee. In this respect Marshall is not exceptional. Where he was different was in reaching the threshold of history at such a young age. He has only to avoid injury and retirement to set a world record for Test wickets that will survive at least until the next century.

Marshall has almost everything that Lillee had, and a little more of his own. He may have lacked such a high degree of the predatory urge that drove Lillee on; but he learnt how to pitch the ball up at tail-enders, to uproot their stumps or trap them LBW with an inswinger, as Lillee never did. The West Indian is, to date, the equal of any fast bowler in history. And when someone in the twenty-first century gets around to redefining the hundred greatest bowlers, it may be that Marshall is then seen to have been supreme. Or perhaps a later member of the line will have become – arguably, of course! – even greater.

FIRST-CLASS CAREER (1977/8–   )

342 innings	42 not outs	6945 runs	average 23.15	4 hundreds
	1210 wickets	21655 runs	average 17.89	8–71 best

TEST RECORD (63 MATCHES)

80 innings	7 not outs	1354 runs	average 18.55	–
	307 wickets	6409 runs	average 20.87	7–22 best

Series	Tests	O	M	R	W	Av
1978/9 in I	3	78	11	265	3	88.33
1980 in E	4	172.3	42	436	15	29.06
1980/81 in P	4	98.3	12	319	13	24.53
1980/81 v E	1	21	2	64	3	21.33
1982/3 v I	5	174.1	39	495	21	23.57
1983/4 in I	6	221	59	621	33	18.81
1983.4 v A	4	158.5	24	480	21	22.85
1984 in E	4	157.4	50	437	24	18.20
1984/5 in A	5	215.2	45	554	28	19.78
1984/5 v NZ	4	170.1	30	486	27	18.00
1985/6 v E	5	169.3	36	482	27	17.85
1986/7 in P	3	114	27	266	16	16.62
1986/7 in NZ	3	119	21	289	9	32.11
1987/8 v P	2	91.4	14	284	15	18.93
1988 in E	5	203.1	49	443	35	12.66
1988/9 in A	5	192	42	488	17	28.71